IMAGINING THE

 Polynya Press An imprint of the University of Alberta Press

SUPERNATURAL NORTH

Eleanor Rosamund Barraclough, Danielle Marie Cudmore & Stefan Donecker, Editors

Published by

The University of Alberta Press
Ring House 2
Edmonton, Alberta, Canada T6G 2E1
www.uap.ualberta.ca

Copyright © 2016 The University of
Alberta Press

LIBRARY AND ARCHIVES CANADA
CATALOGUING IN PUBLICATION

Imagining the supernatural north / Eleanor
Rosamund Barraclough, Danielle Marie
Cudmore & Stefan Donecker, editors.

Includes bibliographical references and index.
Issued in print and electronic formats.
ISBN 978-1-77212-267-1 (paperback).—
ISBN 978-1-77212-295-4 (PDF).—
ISBN 978-1-77212-293-0 (EPUB).—
ISBN 978-1-77212-294-7 (mobi)

1. Supernatural. 2. Folklore. 3. Mythology.
4. Arctic regions. I. Barraclough, Eleanor
Rosamund, 1984–, editor II. Cudmore,
Danielle Marie, 1985–, editor III. Stefan,
Donecker, 1977–, editor

GR500.I43 2016   398'.4   C2016-903517-4

First edition, first printing, 2016.
First printed and bound in Canada by
    Houghton Boston Printers, Saskatoon,
    Saskatchewan.
Copyediting and proofreading by
    Brendan Wild.
Indexing by Judy Dunlop.

The University of Alberta Press is committed
to protecting our natural environment. As
part of our efforts, this book is printed on
Enviro Paper: it contains 100% post-consumer
recycled fibres and is acid- and chlorine-free.

The University of Alberta Press gratefully
acknowledges the support received for its
publishing program from the Government
of Canada, the Canada Council for the Arts,
and the Government of Alberta through the
Alberta Media Fund.

This work is published with the assistance
a grant from the Western Canadiana
Publications Project.

Canada

Canada Council   Conseil des Arts
for the Arts   du Canada

Alberta
Government

Contents

PART II | FROM THE MIDDLE AGES TO THE EARLY MODERN PERIOD

The Monstrous and the Demonic

PART III | THE NINETEENTH CENTURY   *The Scientific and the Spiritual*

Introduction

ELEANOR ROSAMUND BARRACLOUGH, DANIELLE MARIE CUDMORE,
and STEFAN DONECKER

*Into the North Window of my chamber glows the Pole Star with
uncanny light. All through the long hellish hours of blackness it shines
there. And in the autumn of the year, when the winds from the north
curse and whine, and the red-leaved trees of the swamp mutter things
to one another in the small hours of the morning under the horned
waning moon, I sit by the casement and watch that star. Down from
the heights reels the glittering Cassiopeia as the hours wear on, while
Charles' Wain lumbers up from behind the vapour-soaked swamp trees
that sway in the night wind. Just before dawn Arcturus winks ruddily
from above the cemetery on the low hillock, and Coma Berenices shim-
mers weirdly afar off in the mysterious east; but still the Pole Star leers
down from the same place in the black vault, winking hideously like
an insane watching eye which strives to convey some strange message,
yet recalls nothing save that it once had a message to convey.
(Lovecraft 33)*

IN H.P. LOVECRAFT'S 1920 short story "Polaris," among the earliest writings of the visionary pioneer of modern horror literature, the narrator finds himself driven to the verge of insanity by the baleful light of the Pole Star. The "insane watching eye" draws him into the mysteries of a long-lost Arctic civilization whose downfall and destruction he witnesses in his agitated dreams. As the visions of the imagined Arctic past overwhelm him, the narrator becomes convinced that the mundane life he once lived is merely a dream, and that he is truly part of a doomed Hyperborean civilization.

The spectral presence of the Pole Star in Lovecraft's tale is but one among many septentrional mysteries that have featured in various literary genres across the centuries.[1] "The further north and north we go / Grow soot and witches ervermo," wrote Johann Wolfgang von Goethe (292) in the Paralipomena to *Faust*.[2] H.C. Andersen's famous fairy tale followed innocent Gerda on her journey to the utmost North, trying to save her friend from the eponymous and enigmatic Snow Queen. In another Scandinavian classic, Selma Lagerlöf's *Nils Holgerssons underbara resa genom Sverige* ("The Wonderful Adventures of Nils"), the title character proceeds to a cave in the furthest North of Sweden, where, with the coming of winter, the summer sun is chased away by the three wolves of the Ice Witch. Representing the limits of human knowledge and experience, the frozen wastes of the Arctic frame the narrative of Mary Shelley's *Frankenstein* and provide the setting for the final showdown between monster and creator. Even Charlotte Brontë's *Jane Eyre* opens with the title character enthralled by descriptions of the remote North in a book on British birds:

> Nor could I pass unnoticed the suggestion of the bleak shores of
> Lapland, Siberia, Spitzbergen, Nova Zembla, Iceland, Greenland, with
> "the vast sweep of the Arctic Zone, and those forlorn regions of dreary
> space, —that reservoir of frost and snow, where firm fields of ice, the
> accumulation of centuries of winters, glazed in Alpine heights above
> heights, surround the pole, and concentre the multiplied rigours of

extreme cold." Of these death-white realms I formed an idea of my
own: shadowy, like all the half-comprehended notions that float dim
through children's brains, but strangely impressive.[3] *(Brontë 2–3)*

THE IMAGINATION OF NORTHERNNESS: SYMBOLIC GEOGRAPHIES AND MENTAL MAPS

Canadian novelist and poet Margaret Atwood alluded to these dream-
like, otherworldly qualities of the North in her 1987 essay "True North":
"Turning to face north, face the north, we enter our own unconscious.
Always, in retrospect, the journey north has the quality of dream"
(33). Drawing her readers' attention to the narrow limits of a purely
geographical understanding of this cardinal direction, she demonstrated
that the North defied any easy definition:

> *Where is the north, exactly? It's not only a place but also a direction,*
> *and as such its location is relative: to the Mexicans, the United States*
> *is the north, to Americans, Toronto is, even though it's on roughly the*
> *same latitude as Boston. Wherever it is for us, there's a lot of it.*
> *("True" 32)*

Atwood's reflections from the 1980s seem to forecast recent developments in the humanities, where there is growing interest in the semantics
of cardinal directions. North, South, East, and West are not simply abstract
determinants of spatial orientation. As "coordinates of a mental geography," to quote the German literary scholar Dieter Richter (9), cardinal
directions are the cultural artifacts that underpin our perception of the
world, imbued with symbolic, ideological, and political connotations.
Within this context, the North is much more than a random direction
on the compass rose.

On this "imagined" North in the literature of her home country,
Margaret Atwood writes that "popular lore, and popular literature, established early that the North was uncanny, awe-inspiring in an almost
religious way, hostile to white men, but alluring; that it would lead you on

and do you in; that it would drive you crazy, and, finally, would claim you for its own" (Atwood, *Strange* 22).

While Atwood refers specifically to Canada here, her comments can be legitimately applied to the North as a whole. For centuries, Europeans and Euro-Americans have perceived the North and its inhabitants as the quintessential Other. Ancient Greek texts envisioned Hyperborea, the fabled land beyond the northern wind, as a wondrous realm in close affinity to the gods. To the sixth-century Roman writer Jordanes, the island of Scandza, in the far North of the known world, was *officina gentium aut vagina nationum*—the womb that continuously gave birth to new barbarian tribes (Iord. Get. IV, 25). To Adam of Bremen, writing in Germany in the second half of the eleventh century, the North was *alter mundus*—an "other world" on the fringes of European Christianity (GHep IV, 21). To the eighteenth-century French political philosopher Montesquieu, it was *la source de la liberté de l'Europe*—"a repository of liberty" for the Age of Enlightenment (*De l'esprit des lois*, XVII, 5). Throughout the centuries, Europeans projected their fears and hopes upon the little-known lands of the North. Even as the "known world" gradually came to include more northerly lands, the underlying notion of otherness, the role of the North as foil to European conditions, remained essentially the same.

Particular motifs and assumptions, however, changed considerably. "North is multiple, shifting and elastic," the literary scholar Sherrill E. Grace (16) writes: "It is a process, not a condition." As Grace implies, the cultural meaning of Northernness is constantly being re-negotiated and re-imagined. For instance, the North was long regarded as a savage, backwards periphery. During antiquity and the Middle Ages, the embodiment of Northernness was the rampaging, aggressive barbarian: ferocious Scythians, uncivilized Goths, and marauding Vikings (Fraesdorff).[4] This stereotype slowly began to give way in the seventeenth and eighteenth centuries (see Barraclough et al. 31–6). During this period, European Protestants turned towards the Scandinavian kingdoms as defenders of their shared faith, and Enlightenment thinkers held the perceived liberties of the North in high esteem. By the mid-twentieth century, the old

negative images of the North had been mostly overturned. The modern
Scandinavian nations are often considered paragons of progress in terms
of welfare, education, gender equality, and work-life balance. Additionally,
increasing environmental awareness and the dangers of global warming
have turned the traditional topography of threat upside down. In current
media discourses, the icon of Northernness seems to be a noble yet vulnerable polar bear trapped on a shrinking ice floe. The North, once the
cardinal direction most clearly associated with being threatening, is now
perceived as threatened.[5]

THE SUPERNATURAL NORTH: A CONSTANT AMONG MUTABLE MOTIFS

In spite of all these shifting images of Northernness, one motif has
remained remarkably consistent: the notion of the North as a sphere of
the supernatural. As the contributions in this volume demonstrate, few
motifs in European cultural history show such longevity. The idea that the
North is associated with supernatural forces and endowed with metaphysical qualities has endured from antiquity to the present day (Barraclough
et al.). Throughout the centuries, authors have located all kinds of mysterious occurrences, otherworldly beings, and sorcerous inhabitants in the
North. Thus, the mysteries of Lovecraft's "Polaris" are by no means a
fringe case. From the Hyperboreans of ancient Greek mythology to the
baleful Scandinavian witches of early modern demonology, to the armored
polar bears and monstrous undead that feature in modern fantasy novels,
European imagination has envisioned a wide range of Northern mysteries.

This volume intends to cover this extraordinarily persistent motif
in a *longue durée* perspective. Such a complex topic is best addressed
through interdisciplinary cooperation, as this collection of papers seeks
to demonstrate. Previous research has addressed individual aspects of
the topic, but the full range of the Supernatural North—from the Old
Testament to the present day—has not yet been examined. By drawing
attention to the intrinsic variations of and different approaches to the
Supernatural North, we hope to provide additional stimulus for further

interdisciplinary research on the complex meanings of both Northernness and the supernatural.

CONCEPTUAL CONSIDERATIONS

Inevitably, such an encompassing approach poses certain challenges (Anderson). Different historical eras and different intellectual traditions have perceived the border between the natural and the supernatural in very different ways (e.g., de Lubac *Surnaturel*; de Lubac *Mystery*; Keitt; Watkins; Bartlett), if such a distinction made sense to them at all (Jindra; Deschrijver and Vanderheyden 526). Phenomena that modern Western observers might classify as "supernatural" in the colloquial sense of the word would have been judged differently in other historical contexts. Thomas Aquinas, for example, distinguished between supernatural and preternatural events (Daston 20; Bartlett 8). While the former were true miracles effected by God Himself, the latter were merely marvels caused by created beings—unusual and possibly wondrous, but certainly not miraculous phenomena. Thus, to a scholastic thinker following Aquinas, the hailstorms conjured by Scandinavian witches and their familiar spirits might have been extraordinary, but were by no means supernatural, since the perpetrators were created beings. A modern reader, on the other hand, would hardly hesitate to classify such reports of sorcery as tales of the supernatural.

Consequently, we have decided to interpret the term *supernatural* as broadly as possible. The individual chapters of this volume allow readers to trace motifs and themes throughout the centuries, and, for this purpose, a sharp distinction between supernatural, preternatural, miraculous, and other non-empirical phenomena is hardly useful (cf. Clarke). The catchword *supernatural* is intended as a simple, yet effective analytical tool that enables us to outline the trans-historical characteristics of certain recurring phenomena and motifs (Deschrijver and Vanderheyden 525).

In each historical era, authors re-envisioned and categorized the existing narratives of the wondrous North according to the conceptual paradigms of the day. Fairies might have been part of the natural world for pre-Christian Scandinavians; they were later assigned to a preternatural, demonic sphere in the Middle Ages and the early modern period. Presently, most people would see such entities as both supernatural and fictional, yet adherents of esoteric beliefs might perceive them as a manifestation of nature, or at least refuse to distinguish between the supernatural and the natural worlds. The motif is certainly the same, yet the classification varies depending on the historical and discursive context.

Our approach to the supernatural follows a definition suggested by the Polish philosopher Konrad Talmont-Kaminski in 2013. For him, the term *supernatural* encompasses "the concepts that human culture gives rise to when unconstrained by the need to accurately represent reality" (Talmont-Kaminski 458). This approach may seem imprecise, but in fact it is well suited to understanding the creative process of the historical *imaginatio borealis*, foregrounding the role of the human imagination in understanding and interpreting the world around us. Furthermore, such a perspective serves as a contrast to the overwhelming influence of natural sciences and its paradigms in depictions of the North. Throughout the centuries, the North was, to Europeans, a discursive Other, a space upon which expectations, fears, and hopes could be projected. Compared to well-known, civilized Europe, the North was a space unconstrained by the requirements of mundane realities. As such, it could be become a repository of the supernatural.

It is worth noting that the chapters of the book deal with images of Northernness within the European tradition. Of course, Europeans and North Americans do not have a monopoly over defining and imagining the North. The circumpolar region was inhabited by numerous indigenous communities long before the first explorers and colonizers from central Europe arrived, and each of these communities possesses its very own *imaginatio borealis*. However, the concept of the supernatural is an intrinsic part of the so-called "Western" intellectual tradition (Saler; Klass 25–7), rooted in the paradigms of classical antiquity and Christianity and re-shaped during the Enlightenment as an antithesis to rational, secular knowledge. Indigenous inhabitants of the North have developed different paradigms to perceive the fringes of empirical reality (Burch; Grønnow; E. Hill), and it would be hardly expedient to apply the European dichotomy of the natural and the supernatural to these indigenous traditions.

By focusing predominantly on European images of the North, we do not claim that indigenous views are by any means less significant. To foster a sense of coherence in addressing this vast topic, we decided to focus on European concepts and images.[6] The European discourses on the North were—and in many ways remain—discourses on otherness, demarcation, and power, and the supernatural was a means to express this otherness. By examining the history of the Supernatural North within the Western intellectual tradition, the book provides the starting point for a criticism of the discursive hegemony claimed by European-American observers over the North and its inhabitants.

A TIMELINE OF NORTHERN MYSTERIES

Some of mankind's earliest written sources from the ancient Near East show first traces of the enduring topos of supernatural Northernness (see Fass 465; Lutz 300–1). In their conceptions of the world, these authors assigned particular spiritual and metaphysical qualities to the North. It was both the sacred abode of the gods and a feared source of menacing invaders and otherworldly beings. This dichotomy becomes particularly evident in Jewish lore, which associates the North with God and the Messiah, but also with evil spirits and similar malevolent entities. The Old Testament repeatedly reiterated such beliefs, and, in doing so, it defined the ambivalence toward the North for centuries to come. The first part of the book, "Ancient Roots: The Menace and the Divine," investigates the origins of these long-lived topoi. Jewish accounts of the ambivalence toward the North have to be contrasted with the tales of Northernness in classical Greek literature: The manifold myths of the Hyperboreans, the wondrous people "beyond the North Wind," and the subtle, yet expressive references to the North and its qualities in proverbs and popular sayings all attest the complexity of ancient Greek attitudes towards the North. Together, biblical and classical descriptions set the stage for Christian Europe's enduring fascination with the sacred and uncanny North.

With the rise of Christianity in medieval Europe, this ambiguous image of the North became increasingly, though not exclusively, negative. In part two, "From the Middle Ages to the Early Modern Period: The Monstrous and the Demonic," the authors explain how the North came to be associated with the powers of evil. Medieval Scandinavian texts contain a bewildering variety of monstrous Northern beings—dog-headed and one-legged men, giants, and pygmies, as well as horned Finns, to name but a few—inspired by both classical Greco-Latin and local vernacular traditions. Areas on the fringes of the Old Norse world, such as Greenland, became particularly notorious for their monstrous inhabitants, as Scandinavian writers sought to re-locate the topos of the Supernatural North to the peripheries of their own worldview.

As Christianity became increasingly concerned with the devil's machinations in this world, the image of the North shifted from the monstrous to the diabolic. Medieval scholastic treatises associated the allegedly inferior and decrepit female physiognomy with coldness and, by extension, with the cold septentrional wind, thus laying the theoretical foundation for the popular image of the northern witch. During the early modern period, the era of the infamous European witch-hunts, the idea that the North was the preferred abode of witches and warlocks was already deeply rooted in the popular perception.

The Enlightenment dispelled assumptions of a literal diabolic presence in the North, but the underlying notions remained largely unchallenged. By the nineteenth and early twentieth centuries, an era that became known as the "heroic" age of polar exploration, perceptions of the North as a harsh testing ground for masculine endeavor and as a fatal beauty to be conquered only enhanced its supernatural connotations (Grace 174). Reports on deprivation, fatalities, and cases of anthropophagy among polar explorers circulated in the media and contributed to the image of the merciless, sublime North. In this period, spiritualism and mythic revival coexisted with increasing scientific understanding and practical experiences of the Arctic North. The case of mesmerist clairvoyants who contributed their extraordinary abilities to the search for the lost Franklin expedition, supported in part by the British Admiralty, showcases the close ties between polar exploration and fringe sciences in the Victorian Era. At the same time, with the growth of Romanticism and nationalism, the concept of Northernness became tied to processes of identity formation in northern Europe and North America. Part three, "The Nineteenth Century: The Scientific and the Spiritual" analyses the state of the Supernatural North at the onset of modernity. Case studies shed light on the perception of Northernness through the eyes of travellers and explorers, including early nineteenth-century travelogues from the peripheries of the British Isles that endeavor to determine the place of Gaels within the Supernatural North; the writings of Austrian travel writer Ida Pfeiffer who visited Iceland in the mid-nineteenth century and faced the island's reputation as a supernatural northern Arcadia; and, lastly, the publications of Knud Rasmussen and Hinrich Rink who disseminated Greenlandic legends and stories to European audiences.

In the modern era, images of the North have been shaped by the longing for the paranormal, for the distant and the unknowable, untouched and uncorrupted by civilization, in sharp contrast to the disillusioning realities of the twentieth and early twenty-first centuries. As environmental issues such as climate change and oil extraction dominate the headlines, the increasing precariousness of life for people in the far northern regions becomes more and more apparent. The authors in the fourth and final part, "Contemporary Perspectives: The Desire for a Supernatural North," explore the importance of the Supernatural North in a variety of different contemporary discourses, including literature, music, and academia, as well as different subcultures: Heavy metal music draws strongly upon well-established topoi of the Supernatural North in ways that could be described as idealizing. A less known example from popular culture is the "Otherkin" community, individuals who believe themselves to be not fully human, but ontologically consisting of different species.

Part of their being, in their self-perception, is an animal or a supernatural creature such as an elf or troll. Northern mythology, particularly Scandinavian, provides a narrative framework to this complex subculture.

Literary visions such as Vladimir Nabokov's elusive island of Zembla, characterized in the final sentence of *Pale Fire* as "a northern, distant land" (315), or Philip Pullman's subversion of the "Snow Queen" narrative in his fantasy novel *The Golden Compass* (1995), demonstrate how well-established historical topoi of Northernness are re-appropriated and reinterpreted to express the desire not only for an idealized place, but also an idealized past. The desire for a mysterious North has also influenced academia and has led to a biased perception of northern shamanism. In an oversimplification and misrepresentation of indigenous beliefs from Fennoscandia, Siberia, and the American Arctic, European and American scholars have exaggerated the importance of the shaman as a mediator between the mundane and the supernatural, and ignored the less spectacular daily ritual practices and beliefs of ordinary men and women in indigenous societies.

The idea of the Supernatural North has been with us for more than two millennia. Specific beliefs and ideas may have shifted, symbolic connotations may have changed, but the underlying notions remain fundamentally the same. The northern witch might find herself reinvented as a stock character in modern fantasy, yet she remains part of a tradition that stretches back to the Middle Ages. The mythical race of the Hyperboreans may have been dreamt up in past millennia by the ancient Greeks, but, today, Western esotericism still ascribes a particular spirituality to the inhabitants of the North. While the various trolls, giants, and dog-headed men that once roamed these far-flung lands have been replaced by lonely polar bears stranded on ice floes, their monstrous descendants continue to thrive in popular culture. However ancient its origins, the idea of the Supernatural North is every bit as meaningful and relevant today.

1. On the Arctic in the British and North American imagination see, in particular, Bloom; Spufford; and David.

2. "Wie man nach Norden weiterkommt, / Da nehmen Ruß und Hexen zu."

3. Jane also produces watercolor sketches of the Arctic. Jen Hill argues for the role of the Arctic in shaping the narrative of *Jane Eyre* and other literary works of the nineteenth century.

4. Even medieval images of the barbarous North were not devoid of subtleties. Despite its predominantly negative associations, the North could also be perceived as heroic (Rix) or, in very particular contexts, even as serene and paradisiacal (Molina Moreno).

5. The complexity of the various stereotypes, symbols, and ideological connotations that have been ascribed to the North in different historical periods, by different actors, and in different discourse genres has inspired numerous important scholarly inquiries during the last decades. Seminal contributions include Ryall et al.; Hormuth and Schmidt; Jakobsson; Chartier; Davidson; Arndt et al.; Möller and Pehkonen; Engel-Braunschmidt et al.; Henningsen; van Baak; Coates.

6. This is not to ignore, however, the cross-pollination of indigenous and European perspectives, particularly in North America. One example is the cannibalistic spirit known as the Wendigo among Algonquian-speaking peoples, which was also taken up by European American writers (see Atwood, *Strange* 75–103). Two of the contributors to this volume, Silvije Habulinec and Erica Hill, have examined European readings and interpretations of indigenous beliefs in their chapters, focusing, respectively, on Greenlandic legends and on the circumpolar phenomenon of shamanism.

WORKS CITED

Adam of Bremen. *Gesta Hammaburgensis ecclesiae pontificum*. Ed. B. Schmeidler. Hanover, 1917. MGH Scriptores rerum Germanicarum 2.

Anderson, R. "Defining the supernatural in Iceland." *Anthropological Forum* 13 (2003): 125–30.

Arndt, A., et al., eds. *Imagologie des Nordens: Kulturelle Konstruktionen von Nördlichkeit in interdisziplinärer Perspektive*. Frankfurt am Main: Lang, 2004. Imaginatio borealis 7.

Atwood, M. *Strange Things: The Malevolent North in Canadian Literature*. 1995. London: Virago P, 2004.

———. "True North." *Writing with Intent: Essays, Reviews, Personal Prose, 1983–2005*. 1987. New York: Carroll & Graf, 2005. 31–45.

Barraclough, E.R., D. Cudmore, and S. Donecker. "Der übernatürliche Norden. Konturen eines Forschungsfeldes." *Nordeuropaforum* (2013): 23–53.

Bartlett, R. *The Natural and the Supernatural in the Middle Ages*. Cambridge: Cambridge UP, 2008.

Bloom, L. *Gender on Ice: American Ideologies of Polar Expeditions*. Minneapolis: U of Minnesota P. 1993.

Brontë, C. *Jane Eyre*. 1847. New York: Knopf, 1991.

Burch, E.S. "The Nonempirical Environment of the Arctic Alaskan Eskimos." *Southwestern Journal of Anthropology* 27 (1971): 148–65.

Chartier, D., ed. *Le(s) Nord(s) imaginaire(s)*. Montréal: P de l'U du Québec, 2008.

Clarke, S. "The Supernatural and the Miraculous." *Sophia* 46 (2007): 277–85.

Coates, K. "The Discovery of the North: Towards a Conceptual Framework for the Study of Northern / Remote Regions." *The Northern Review* 12/13 (1993/94): 15–43.

Daston, L. "Preternatural Philosophy." *Biographies of Scientific Objects*. Ed. L. Daston. Chicago: U of Chicago P, 2000. 15–41.

David, R. *The Arctic in the British Imagination, 1818–1914*. Manchester: Manchester UP, 2000.

Davidson, P. *The Idea of North*. London: Reaktion, 2005.

Deschrijver, S., and V. Vanderheyden. "Experiencing the Supernatural in Sixteenth-Century Brabant: Construction and Reduction of the Exceptional in Everyday Life." *Journal of Social History* 46 (2012): 525–48.

de Lubac, H. *The Mystery of the Supernatural*. London: Chapman, 1967.

———. *Surnaturel: Études historiques*. Paris: Aubier, 1946.

Engel-Braunschmidt, A., et al., eds. *Ultima Thule: Bilder des Nordens von der Antike bis zur Gegenwart*. Frankfurt am Main: Lang, 2001. Imaginatio borealis 1.

Fass, D.E. "The Symbolic Uses of North." *Judaism* 37 (1988): 465–73.

Fraesdorff, D. *Der barbarische Norden: Vorstellungen und Fremdheitskategorien bei Rimbert, Thietmar von Merseburg, Adam von Bremen und Helmold von Bosau*. Berlin: Akademie-Verlag, 2005. Orbis mediaevalis 5.

Grace, S.E. *Canada and the Idea of North*. Montreal: McGill-Queen's UP, 2002.

Grønnow, B. "Blessings and Horrors of the Interior: Ethno-Historical Studies of Inuit Perceptions Concerning the Inland Region of West Greenland." *Arctic Anthropology* 46.1–2 (2009): 191–201.

Henningsen, B. *Der Norden: Eine Erfindung. Das europäische Projekt einer regionalen Identität*. Berlin: Nordeuropa-Institut der Humboldt-Universität. 1993.

Hill, E. "The Nonempirical Past: Enculturated Landscapes and Other-than-Human Persons in Southwest Alaska." *Arctic Anthropology* 49.2 (2012): 41–57.

Hill, J. *White Horizon: The Arctic in the Nineteenth-Century British Imagination*. Albany: State U of New York P, 2008.

Hormuth, D., and M. Schmidt, eds. *Norden und Nördlichkeit: Darstellungen vom Eigenen und Fremden*. Frankfurt am Main: Lang, 2010. Imaginatio borealis 21.

Jakobsson, S., ed. *Images of the North: Histories—Identities—Ideas*. Amsterdam: Rodopi, 2009. Studia Imagologica 14.

Jindra, M. "Natural/Supernatural Conceptions in Western Cultural Contexts." *Anthropological Forum* 13 (2003): 159–66.

Jordanes. *Romana et Getica*. Ed. T. Mommsen. Berlin: Weidmann, 1882. Hanover: Hahn, 1917. MGH Auctores antiquissimi 5.1.

Keitt, A.W. *Inventing the Sacred: Imposture, Inquisition, and the Boundaries of the Supernatural in Golden Age Spain*. Leiden: Brill, 2005.

Klass, M. *Ordered Universes: Approaches to the Anthropology of Religion*. Boulder: Westview, 1995.

Lagerlöf, S. *Nils Holgerssons underbara resa genom Sverige*. Stockholm: Albert Bonniers Förlag, 1907.

Lovecraft, H.P. "Polaris." 1920. *H.P. Lovecraft: The Complete Fiction*. Ed. S.T. Joshi. New York: Barnes & Noble, 2011. 33–6.

Lutz, H.L.F. "Plaga Septentrionalis in Sumero-Akkadian Mythology." *Semitic and Oriental Studies: A Volume Presented to William Popper, Professor of Semitic Languages, Emeritus, on the Occasion of his Seventy-Fifth Birthday, October 29, 1949*. Ed. W.J. Fischel. Berkeley: U of California P, 1951. 297–309.

Molina Moreno, F. "Bilder des heiligen Nordens in Antike, Patristik und Mittelalter." *Ultima Thule: Bilder des Nordens von der Antike bis zur Gegenwart*. Ed. A. Engel-Braunschmidt et al. Frankfurt am Main: Lang, 2001. 47–66. Imaginatio borealis 1.

Möller, F., and S. Pehkonen, eds. *Encountering the North: Cultural Geography, International Relations and Northern Landscapes*. Aldershot: Ashgate, 2003.

Montesquieu. *De l'esprit des lois*. 1758. Ed. L Versini. 2 vols. Paris: Éditions Gallimard, 1995.

Nabokov, V. *Pale Fire*. 1962. Berkley: Berkley Publishing, 1968.

Pullman, P. *The Golden Compass*. New York: Knopf, 1995.

Richter, D. *Der Süden: Geschichte einer Himmelsrichtung*. Berlin: Wagenbach, 2009.

Rix, R.W. *The Barbarian North in the Medieval Imagination: Ethnicity, Legend, and Literature.* New York: Routledge, 2015.

Ryall, A., J. Schimanski, and H.H. Wærp, eds. *Arctic Discourses.* Newcastle: Cambridge Scholars, 2010.

Saler, B. "Supernatural as a Western Category." *Ethos: Journal of the Society for Psychological Anthropology* 5 (1977): 31–53.

Spufford, F. *I May Be Some Time: Ice and the English Imagination.* New York: St. Martin's, 1977.

Talmont-Kaminski, K. "For God and Country, Not Necessarily for Truth: The Non-Alethic Function of Superempirical Beliefs." *The Monist* 96 (2013): 447–61.

van Baak, J. "'Northern Cultures.' What could this mean? About the North as a Cultural Concept." *Tijdschrift voor Skandinavistiek* 16 (1995): 11–29.

von Goethe, J.W. Faust (The so-called First Part, 1770–1808); *Together with the scene "Two Imps and Amor", the Variants of the Göchhausen Transcript; and the complete Paralipomena of the Weimar Edition of 1887.* Trans. R. McLintock. London: David Nutt, 1897.

Watkins, C.S. *History and the Supernatural in Medieval England.* Cambridge: Cambridge UP, 2007. Cambridge Studies in Medieval Life and Thought IV/66.

I   Ancient Roots

The Menace and the Divine

1 In Jewish Lore, Not Only Evil Descends From the North

YA'ACOV SARIG

THE NOTION OF the "North"—צָפוֹן (Ẓafon)—has attracted two apparently contradictory connotations in Jewish lore. One approach perceives the North as the source of wealth, blessing, and prosperity, while the other emphasizes the North as the location of Hell, evil and danger, and the dwelling place of demons.

The Hebrew verb צָפַן, deriving from the same root as the designation for the North, means "hidden" or "concealed," and underlies the mental-linguistic attitude toward this particular cardinal direction. The etymology of the word further stresses the notion of the North as uncanny. Through centuries of Jewish practice, such attitudes affected patterns of behavior and ways of thinking and found expression in Jewish religious worship, cult and folk belief, and customs.

ẒAFON: THE ANCIENT NORTH IN THE BIBLE

The Hebrew word Ẓafon designates not only the cardinal direction of the North, but also concrete toponyms, most notably the name of a mountain and a city. The city was situated east of the Jordan River, near Succoth and Beth Nimrah.[1] It was taken by the Israelites from the Ammonite King Sihon and subsequently granted to the tribe of Gad (Josh. 13:27). A later reference to Zafon is found in the book of Judges (12:1) as the place where the elders of Gilead gathered to meet with Jephthah.

More important to our discussion, though, is the fact that Zafon was also the name of a mountain to the north of the Land of Israel, located near the mouth of the Orontes River. It is identified as Mount Aqra` (Arabic: ğabal al-Aqra`) and was known as Mount Casius to the Greeks (Lane Fox 243–58). According to Ugaritic texts, the sacred mountain was a cult site, the abode of the storm god Baàl and of the war-goddess Anat, his sister and lover (244). It was known as an earthly place of assembly of the gods (243–58), a belief familiar also to Isaiah (14:13).

The word *Zafon* also appears in Genesis 13:14 and Deuteronomy 3:2, symbolically and philologically designating the cardinal direction of the North. Refuting the ascription of the North to the heathen deities, the Bible maintains that the North is the abode of the God of the Israelites, as stated in Psalm 48: "Great is the LORD, and highly to be praised, in the city of our God, His holy mountain. Fair in situation, the joy of the whole earth; even Mount Zion, the uttermost parts of the north, the city of the great King. God in her palaces hath made Himself known for a stronghold" (Ps. 48:2–4).[2] The prophet's description of Mount Zion as being located at the summit of Zafon (יַרְכְּתֵי צָפוֹן) seems to propagate the ideological victory of the God of Israel and His conquest of that sacred space. Hence also the blessing, "The LORD bless thee out of Zion; and see thou the good of Jerusalem all the days of thy life" (Ps. 128:5), which, in effect, relocates Zafon far away from its original geographic connection and places it in the holiest location in the Land of Israel.[3]

The prophets of the early Israelites constantly reiterated the North as God's abode, while, at the same time, warned against the nations of the North, which were depicted as a threat to Israel. The most explicit biblical verse dealing with these perils is found in God's words to Jeremiah upon his calling: "Then the LORD said unto me: 'Out of the north the evil shall break forth upon all the inhabitants of the land.'" ("מִצָּפוֹן תִּפָּתַח הָרָעָה")

(Jer. 1:14). In this prophecy, as well as other biblical texts,[4] the North is employed as a shorthand designation for the political danger that is predestined to emerge from that cardinal direction, underscoring the fear of actual enemies of the People of Israel that threaten their peace.

Addressing the people, prophets often referred to the North in their attempts to alarm their listeners. Both Jeremiah and Isaiah use extraordinarily startling wording in their prophecies related to the disastrous implications of the People's sinful behavior. Isaiah addressed mainly the people of Judah and Jerusalem, imploring the people to repent their sins before God. Alarming his people, he cried, "Howl, O gate; cry, O city; melt away, O Philistia, all of thee; for there cometh a smoke out of the north, and there is no straggler in his ranks. What then shall one answer the messengers of the nation? That the LORD hath founded Zion, and in her shall the afflicted of His people take refuge" (Isa. 14:31–32). Similar tones are sounded in another prophecy, once again pointing to the North as the dreadful source of the ultimate enemy: "I have roused up one from the north, and he is come, from the rising of the sun one that calleth upon My name; and he shall come upon rulers as upon mortar, and as the potter treadeth clay" (Isa. 41:25).

Jeremiah, more explicitly, strove to warn against the looming disaster that would befall his folk at the hands of the Babylonians: destruction of the land and deportation and exile of its inhabitants.[5] "Raise the signal to go to Zion! Flee for safety without delay! For I am bringing disaster from the north, even terrible destruction," he cried (Jer. 4:6). Jeremiah paints his prophecy in gloomy tones. His vision relates the castigations that God will inflict upon Israel and Judea for their sins: "The Lord Almighty, who planted you, has decreed disaster for you, because the house of Israel and the house of Judah have done evil and provoked me to anger by burning incense to Baal" (Jer. 11:17). The prophet portrays God's wrath over the sinners, and urges the people: "Flee for safety, people of Benjamin! Flee from Jerusalem! Sound the trumpet in Tekoa! Raise the signal over Beth Hakkerem! For disaster looms out of the north, even terrible destruction" (Jer. 6:1). Sounding a blast, using dramatic and vivid descriptions of utter disaster, he proclaims, "Listen! The report is coming—a great commotion from the land of the north! It will make the towns of Judah desolate, a haunt of jackals" (Jer. 10:22).[6]

In addition to political and religious catastrophes, Jeremiah delineates the varied natural disasters that will stem from the North as well: "See how the waters are rising in the north; they will become an overflowing torrent. They will overflow the land and everything in it, the towns and those who live in them. The people will cry out; all who dwell in the land will wail" (Jer. 47:2).

The North as the ultimate source of all evil found its way also to prophecies regarding the end of days and the events that precede messianic times. According to Jewish eschatology, Gog, king of Magog, will launch a war in the North that will usher in the beginning of the messianic era (see Vivian; Kaltner; Schwarzschild).

This myth of Gog and Magog is connected to the earliest history of humankind. Magog was the grandson of Noah (Gen. 10:2; see also 1 Chron. 1:5). His descendants, who are described as skilled warriors (Ezek. 38:15; 39:3–9; cf. Galambush), settled to the north of the Land of Israel (Ezek. 38:2). Yet, in biblical scripture, Gog and Magog are not only referred to as historical figures, but are also mentioned in the context of eschatological and apocalyptic prophesy.[7] Ezekiel foretells the final combat with the combined forces of the heathen nations, which will take place toward the "end of days." It is told that Gog will lead an overwhelming army of men, mainly from the North, and attack the Land of Israel (Ezek. 38:2–6; 15; 39:2).[8] Gog, however, will not be victorious, and will suffer defeat by God and a loss so great that it will take seven months to bury all the slain (Ezek. 39:11–12; see Ahroni). At the same time, the People of Israel will repent and return to their God and to their land from the ends of the diaspora:

And the nations shall know that the house of Israel went into captivity
for their iniquity, because they broke faith with Me, and I hid My face
from them; so I gave them into the hand of their adversaries, and they

fell all of them by the sword.... Therefore thus saith the Lord GOD: *Now*
will I bring back the captivity of Jacob, and have compassion upon the
whole house of Israel; and I will be jealous for My holy name...when
they shall dwell safely in their land, and none shall make them afraid.
(Ezek. 39:21–29)

Ezekiel's apocalyptic account of the battle of Gog and Magog is an
indispensable prelude to the messianic age. It resonates with Jeremiah's
prophecy in chapter 1:3–16, which reiterates the dreadful fear of the
people of the North (Blenkinsopp 178). In the end of days, maintains
Ezekiel, history will turn full circle and these oppressors will be defeated
(Van der Toorn, Becking, and Van der Horst 374).

Jewish tradition portrays the apocalyptic days before the ultimate
redemption in extraordinarily vivid colors. Eschatological beliefs are also
concerned with the afterlife and the revival of the dead, as well as with
cosmic changes that will occur prior to the end of days.

Indeed, some Biblical passages connect the hope for redemption with
the coming of the Messiah. The Jewish Messiah is described as a charismatic human leader, an offspring of the stock of King David (Jer. 23:5),
who is well versed in Jewish law and is observant of God's commandments
(Isa. 11:2–5; see Tate). He is also to be a great military leader who will win
battles for Israel and be a just and righteous judge (Jer. 33:15, see Joyce;
Talmon).[9] He is conceived of as both king and teacher. As king, his role is
to rectify and redeem Israel. Therein lies the secret of his first appearance
in the North.[10] Messiah ben Joseph, harbinger of the messianic age, will
appear in Galilee and will proceed to Jerusalem. The Jewish Messiah will
rebuild the Temple and resume the ritual there, but the peace that he will
bring about will last only forty years, until the final redemption through
Messiah ben David.[11] Once Israel has been redeemed physically, the
circumstances will be ripe for his teachings to spread to the four corners of
the earth.

Extraordinary events and dramatic symbolic changes will herald the
coming of the Messiah. The quintessential oeuvre on Kabbalah and Jewish

mysticism, the *Zohar*,[12] describes some of these cosmic revelations, while casting a special spotlight on the North:

> [O]ne awesome star will awaken in the middle of the firmament like Argaman,[13] flaming and sparking in the day in the eyes of the whole world. A flame of fire will arise on the North side in the midst of the firmament and these will stand one opposed to the other for 40 days and the star and the flame will make war in the eyes of all, and the flame will spread out with a burning of fire amidst the rakia[14] from the North side. Numerous rulers and kings and nations and peoples will be terrified of this. (Zohar, Shemot 8a)

The culmination and ultimate end of this turmoil is described in another passage: "A star on the East side will swallow seven stars on the North side, and a flame of black fire will be hanging in the firmament 60 days, and wars will be awakened in the world on the North side, and two kings will fall in these wars, and the entire world will come together against Bas" (*Zohar*, Vayera 119a).

THE NORTH IN THE TABERNACLE AND IN THE TEMPLE OF JERUSALEM

At the time of the Israelites' wandering in the desert and later, in the Temple of Jerusalem, the North played a significant role in the cult of sacrificial offerings performed by priests. Slaughtering took place on the northern side of the altar, as it is said: "And he shall kill it on the side of the altar northward before the LORD; and Aaron's sons, the priests, shall dash its blood against the altar round about" (Lev. 1:11). This stipulation is based on the notion that slaughtering is a negative act that violates the order of life. It should, therefore, be performed in a place that is associated with death and evil—the North. Thus, the Bible makes a clear association between death and the North, thereby affecting the strict procedure of ritual sacrifice carried out by the priests.

The *Mishnah* meticulously elaborates on the ordinance of the sacrificial deed at the Temple. In a tractate dedicated to ritual offerings, it is said:

> *The slaughtering of the bullock and the he-goat of the day of Atonement is [done] at the north, and the reception of their blood is [performed] with service vessels at the north, and their blood requires sprinkling between the staves [of the ark], on the veil, and on the golden altar; [the omission of] a single application of these invalidates [the ceremony]. The residue of the blood he [the priest] poured out on the western base of the outer altar, but if he did not pour it out, he did not invalidate [the sacrifice].* (Mishnah, *Zevahim 5:1*)

Among the daily rituals that took place at the Temple was the placement of twelve loaves of bread on the Showbread Table (Hartenstein). In fact, this tradition harks back to the time of the Tabernacle in the Desert.[15] The table was set with two rows of six loaves each, as an offering "from the children of Israel, an everlasting covenant" to "Aaron and his sons"—the priests (Exod. 24:6–9).

According to Exodus 26:35, the Showbread Table was to be placed on the northern side of the Tabernacle.[16] Describing the relative placement of the various implements that stood there, the injunction to Moses is this: "And thou shalt set the table without the veil, and the candlestick over against the table on the side of the tabernacle toward the south; and thou shalt put the table on the north side." This, precisely, is the part of the Tabernacle that was covered by the shadow of the Southern Wall during daytime, when the priests would consume their food.

Beyond this technical aspect, the insistence on setting the Table to the North is of great theological significance, emphasizing the unity of the Nation of Israel.[17] The offering of the showbreads, amounting to twelve, symbolized the twelve tribes of Israel and their covenant with God, and was therefore regarded as "most holy": "And thou shalt set them [the breads] in two rows, six in a row, upon the pure table before the LORD....

Every sabbath day he shall set it in order before the LORD continually; it is from the children of Israel, an everlasting covenant." The covenant between God and His people was given legal importance by placing the Showbread Table in the North, just as the seat of the supreme contemporary legal institution—the *Sanhedrin*—was set at the northern part of the Temple premises.

Each Sabbath, the loaves were removed from the table to be eaten by the outgoing serving squad of priests and simultaneously replaced by fresh loaves, so as to ensure their perpetual presence on the Table (Babylonian *Talmud*, Menaḥot 99b).[18] This tradition was carried over to the Solomonic Temple, where provision was made for the proper exhibition of the showbread, to carry over the propagation of national fraternity and unity.[19]

Later in Jewish history, when the Second Temple was built in Jerusalem under the leadership of the last three Jewish Prophets, Haggai, Zechariah, and Malachi, with the approval and financing of the Persian monarch, Cyrus the Great, a new approach to Jewish leadership evolved. During that period, spanning 516 BCE and 70 CE, when the Temple was destroyed by the Romans, rabbinic Judaism flourished. Yet, with the absence of authoritative prophets,[20] religious leadership was lacking, which gave rise to an alternative socio-religious system (Scott). This was the magistrate's court, the *Sanhedrin* (Greek: συνέδριον, synedrion, namely "sitting together" as a council). Beyond the local "Lesser Sanhedrin" that existed in every city, a "Great Sanhedrin" of seventy-one officials functioned as a supreme court and legislative body.[21]

In the Second Temple period, the Great Sanhedrin met in the "Hall of Hewn Stones" in the Temple premises. Both the *Talmud* and later scholarship maintain that this hall was built into the north wall of the Temple Mount (*Mishna* Peah 2:6; Eduyoth 7:4). Dealing with criminal law, among other issues, this location, inherently associated with evil, was most appropriate. Moreover, the hall in which the members of the Sanhedrin assembled was the only structure in the Temple complex that was built of hewn stones, which contrasted sharply with the directive regarding the Solomonic Temple. We are told of a strict prohibition against the use of any kind of metal appliance for cutting the stones, as it is said: "For the house, when it was in building, was built of stone made ready at the quarry; and there was neither hammer nor axe nor any tool of iron heard in the house, while it was in building" (1 Kings 6:7). The concept underlying this injunction is that any tool or implement that might be associated with evil or killing of any sort may not be employed for the construction of the House of God. Thus, the manner in which the stones were prepared for construction emphasizes the clear differentiation between hóly and profane. Whereas the duties of the priests were intimately associated with divine worship, the activity of the judges / legislators of the Sanhedrin was legal, yet inspired by religious law. It is for this reason that the chamber in which they assembled was made of hewn stones, visually distinguishing the area of holiness from that of profanity.

THE NORTH IN JEWISH FOLKLORE

Jewish legends that evolved from 530 BCE to 70 CE, between the construction of the Second Temple of Jerusalem and its destruction by the Romans, further developed the mythology of the North. The monolithic fear of the North was substituted with mellower notions. According to one approach, God's wrath was exegetically linked to the hardships that befell His People through devastation and exile, yet another view regarded the North as an embodiment of hope and redemption.

On the one hand, the Sages of the Second Temple period sought to trace the origin of the presence of evil in the North back to primordial days, to the first day of Creation. Laying the foundations of the Jewish doctrine of relative orientation, they stated that Paradise lies to the East, the ocean is situated to the West, whereas the South is the source of fire and smoke and the forge of blasts and hurricanes. As summarized by Louis Ginzberg in his monumental collection *Legends of the Jews*, "To the north are the supplies of hell-fire, of snow, hail, smoke, ice, darkness, and windstorms, and in that vicinity sojourn all sorts of devils, demons, and malign spirits. Their dwelling-place is a great stretch of land, it would take five hundred years to traverse it. Beyond lies hell" (7).

Conversely, later traditions describe the many merits of the North. An early legend, embedded in a non-canonical Babylonian *Talmud* tractate *Gan 'Eden we-Gehinnom, Seder Gan Eden,* deals with the righteous women who dwell in the Garden of Eden located at the northern side of Heaven. Seven halls (or, according to other traditions, six), each designated for a different righteous woman or group of women, are located in the Garden, as a reward for and a glorification of their good deeds. The inhabitants of these halls are Pharaoh's daughter Bityah; Yocheved, wife of Amram and mother of Moses; the prophetess Miriam; the prophetess Ḥulda; Abigail; and the four Matriarchs, Sarah, Rebecca, Rachel, and Leah, who dwell in the sixth hall (Jellinek, III).[22]

Wind coming from the North was regarded as a source of inspiration for David the musician. According to Rabbi Aha bar Bizna, based on a view expressed by R. Shim'on Ḥasida, a lyre used to hang above David's bed. At midnight, the North wind would blow on it and it played by itself. Thereupon, David set to study the *Torah* until dawn (Babylonian *Talmud,* Berakhot 3b).

Referring to the same legendary tradition, the *Zohar* maintains that when the North wind blows at midnight and The Holy One Blessed Be He enters the Garden of Eden, all aromatic species release their perfume and sing to Him, as it is written in Psalm 96:12: "Then all the trees in the woods sing in front of the Lord." Commenting on this teaching, Rabbi Shimon bar Yohai said:

> At this moment, the Holy One Blessed Be He leaves the worlds He so much loves, and comes to Gan Eden [i.e., the Garden of Eden] to enjoy with the Righteous; the herald says: "Wake up winds of the North and come winds of the South, refresh my garden to distill its fragrances, and come my loved to my garden and eat its delicious fruits" [Song of Songs 4:16]. (Zohar Haddash, Genesis, 532)

LATER FOLK BELIEFS AND CUSTOMS

The Ashkenazi Jews of Central and Eastern Europe, who were settled along the Rhine in the Roman period, developed a distinctive culture of their own, which expressed itself in many aspects of Jewish life. Exposed to foreign beliefs, the Jews adhered to several customs that were not inherently Jewish at all, including some traditions pertaining to marriage. One of their most intriguing wedding rites is the breaking of a glass by the bridegroom, which takes place at the end of the ceremony.

Apparently, breaking the glass at weddings was already practiced in the Talmudic period, most probably for apotropaic reasons, namely to overcome and deceive the evil spirits. In the Babylonian *Talmud* there are two parallel accounts recalling the wedding ceremonies of the respective sons of Mar, son of Ravina, and of Rav Ashi (Babylonian *Talmud*, Berakhot 30b–31a). In this short, intriguing passage it is told that in the midst of the banquets, when the fathers noted the excessive merriment of their invited guests, they smashed a glass and broke it in the presence of the entire company, thereby saddening their invitees.[23] Although in most communities the groom smashes a glass that is placed on the ground, other local practices exist as well.

At a certain point in the High Middle Ages or early modern period, the marriage ceremony among Ashkenazi in the Holy Roman Empire shifted from inside the synagogue to the adjacent courtyard. Perhaps the earliest visual testimony to this transition shows the bridal couple and the guests celebrating the nuptials near the northeastern buttress of the old synagogue of Fürth, Bavaria, consecrated in 1615–16 (reproduced in Eschwege 68). Standing slightly apart from the ingathered guests, the bridegroom is about to cast a flask or a glass at a decorated stone set into the buttress (see Wiesemann). This image reflects a unique custom that evolved among the medieval Jewish communities along the Rhine and Main valleys. In these regions, the bridegroom would throw the glass against the synagogue's exterior wall, near the place in which the ceremony was performed. Subsequently, a special stone was devised for this purpose.

In most cases it was embedded in the northern wall, and only in smaller edifices was it placed above the synagogue entrance, as a keystone.

Many marriage stones that have remained in situ and others that are otherwise visually documented are known to have been embedded in the northern wall of the synagogue (see Abrahams 177–210; Feuchtwanger; Wiesemann). This preference is founded on the folk belief that the evil spirits reside in the North (Lauterbach 369). It was probably further propagated by the newly established Christian custom of performing the civil part of the wedding by the northern transept of the church following the canon to that effect issued by the Fourth Lateran Council in 1215.[24]

Thus, the earlier accounts of the marriage banquets recorded in the *Talmud* become understandable. Mar, son of Ravina, and Rav Ashi broke the expensive glasses in order to frighten the demons and other supernatural entities. As Joshua Trachtenberg explains: "The demons were believed to come from the north, and therefore the detail that the glass was thrown against the north wall has special significance in this connection" (173). Moreover, according to folk belief, evil spirits are constantly on the watch for those unguarded moments in the life of a human being in which he is most vulnerable. They then attempt to seize and harm him. Excessive merriment was to be expected during rites of passage—joyous events that might arouse the envy of demons. Marriage is one of those events that are considered to be especially perilous, because it has implications for human propagation and thereby threatens to disrupt the balance between the human race and the supernatural beings.[25] Therefore, the loud noise caused by breaking the glass or smashing it on the northern wall was necessary to drive away the evil spirits on such occasions. The custom combined an attempt to frighten off the demons with noise and a direct physical attack. To further prevent their malice, it was advisable to disguise the merriment and thus confuse the spirits, and also, possibly, to appease them with a gift of wine.[26]

Similar tactics, intended to avert any malevolent act against mortals by supernatural creatures, are employed during another perilous time in male human life—the circumcision. Between his birth and circumcision, the Jewish male infant is considered to be especially vulnerable and demons, enraged by yet another occurrence of human procreation, attempt to harm him. Various measures are, therefore, taken to safeguard the child, among them a "wake" or a vigil (Steiman 56–7),[27] placing knives and amulets by his bedside,[28] and keeping a *Torah* scroll or other sacred texts in the vicinity of the parturient mother and the baby's crib (Holm and Bowker 121).

In many communities the placement of the circumcision chair(s) was of particular significance (see Gaimani). The Jews in the Holy Roman Empire, for example, employed two chairs for the ceremony. These were kept in the synagogue hall as a rule, but were transferred to a specific location in the prayer hall whenever a circumcision took place. A vivid description of the circumcision setting is offered in the seventeenth century by Yuzpa, the synagogue beadle from Worms. He relates that the chairs were turned to face the *Torah* Ark at the east, but were placed by the synagogue portal, which was at the northern wall of the prayer hall.

This custom may be founded on the notion that the rite of circumcision is something of a sacrifice. As sacrifices were offered in the northern part of the Temple, so too should the circumcision be performed in the northern part of the synagogue. This notion is stated explicitly in the *Zohar*, and may have influenced the custom in Germany (*Zohar* to Exodus, T'rumah, 169a).[29]

The surgical deed of circumcision enacted on the infant is not only reminiscent of a sacrifice. Due to the grave danger to the parturient mother in childbirth and the high mortality on such occasions, it was incumbent upon the new mother to bring offerings to the Tabarnacle, and later to the Temple in Jerusalem. Following a long period of confinement after giving birth, during which she was prohibited from participating in the rituals at the Temple, she was obligated to make two offerings at the Temple to be re-admitted to the holy premises and to public worship (Lev. 12:4). One type of offering, the *'Olah* (literally "ascending" in Hebrew), namely the burnt offering, was the oldest and most common sacrifice, and represented submission to God's will and gratitude for His salvation. It was to be totally consumed by fire. In addition to the *'Olah*, a sin offering called *Ḥaṭat* was made. It would only be offered for sins committed carelessly or unintentionally, in order to atone, and to achieve reconciliation with God.[30] In the postpartum period, the sacrifice performed by the mother was meant to indicate the resumption of unsullied contact between the woman and God.[31] After the destruction of the Temple and the annulment of any form of sacrificial activity, this custom, too, was discontinued and the substitute of a thanksgiving blessing was instituted in its place.[32]

The Bible prescribes the manner in which the *'Olah* should be performed: "If his offering be a burnt-offering of the herd,...he shall bring it to the door of the tent of meeting, that he may be accepted before the LORD.... And he shall kill it on the side of the altar northward before the LORD; and Aaron's sons, the priests, shall dash its blood against the altar round about" (Lev. 1:3–11).

In summary, both the birth and the circumcision deeds are connected to the order of sacrificial offerings in ancient Judaism. Once again, folk belief and, subsequently, folk custom draw a link between a biblical injunction and the fear of demons. Moreover, the Jewish notion of the North being the abode of supernatural beings has practical implications for folk beliefs and customs related to the crisis of birth. Of all the supernatural creatures, Lilith and her consort are particularly unscrupulous in their malevolent actions against humans, especially in moments of joy.[33] Performing an act that is reminiscent of sacrifice and that entails pain within their sphere of influence—the North—can mislead them. Contrary to the blissful event of welcoming the infant to the covenant of the Jewish community, the demons see the infant's anguish and leave it unharmed.

CONCLUSION

The images and symbolism of the North in Jewish lore has had an impact on various phases of the cycle of Jewish life. In fear of demonic beings, measures were taken to baffle them so that they would remain unaware of festive events. These malevolent creatures were combated with noise, shards of glass and mirrors, incantations, and amulets. Additionally, food and drink were offered in order to appease them. Thus, it became customary for the bridegroom to break a glass against the stone embedded in the northern wall in the synagogue at the peak of the wedding celebration, for both apotropaic and placating purposes.

Likewise, it was customary to place circumcision chairs at the north end of the synagogue's prayer hall. Although other rites exist with respect to the placement of the circumcision chair, preference was given to the North. According to the *Zohar*, the circumcision is, in a way, a substitute for a sacrifice.[34] For this reason, the preferred place to set the circumcision chair within the synagogue was in the North, in symbolic commemoration of the altar that stood in the north of the Temple courtyard. By performing the main covenant between the God of Israel and His people, a historical continuity is declared between the time in which the Temple stood erect and the present. At the same time, it links the public ritual and its national sanctity with the private celebration of the first Jewish rite of passage.

Perhaps in order to counter-balance the pagan overtones of the fear of the North, ancient Jewish cult worship was focused in the North. Thus, the placement of the Showbread Table in the north of the Tabernacle—and later the Temple—allotted this specific cardinal direction a pronounced positive notion. Offering the twelve loaves of bread and placing them on the Showbread Table symbolized the unity of the twelve tribes as parts of a unified people. Dedicating the loaves to the priests represented complete belief in God and allegiance to those who act in His service. In short, the Showbread Table, placed at the north of the sacred space, emphasized the bond of the people with their God and their faith in Him.

Two other significant functions that took place at the northern part of the Temple complex were not as explicitly positive, and were, in fact, tinged with some negative connotations. Performing the sacrificial procedures at the northern side involved the notion of death, even when the sacrifices were offered as atonement, purification, or thanksgiving. Justice, too, was carried out by the legislative institute of the Great Sanhedrin in the northern side of the Temple Mount, in the Hall of Hewn Stones, which could result in a death sentence. There is no doubt that the almost primordial fear of the North had a tremendous impact on the decision to choose the northern side for matters pertaining to justice and, therefore, to punishment.

Jewish lore presents various attitudes toward the notion of the North. Drawing on the examples cited above, it seems that negative associations are more prominent than positive ones. This impression is based on the psychological effect of the North on collective memory. Alongside what seems to be an inherent fear of the North and dread of its demonic inhabitants—common to many peoples of the ancient world—biblical history recounts factual, bitter crises originating in the North that befell the Israelite and Judean people. The most decisive catastrophes were the two encounters with Babylon and Assyria, which brought about the destruction of the two Temples and the subsequent exiles. Although set in the earliest days of Jewish history, these catastrophic moments had a tremendous impact on the Jewish people.

NOTES

1. It is identified with tell el-Qos, tell es-Saidiye, or tell el-Mazar. Further suggestions for its identification are offered as well: According to Adolf Neubauer (249), the city of Ẓafon should be identified with Amathus. Josephus, in *Antiquitates Iudaicae* XIV, v, 4, claims that this was the seat of one of the *Sanhedrin* ("Synedria") created by Gabinius.

2. All Biblical quotations follow the translation offered by Jewish Publication Society (JPS) 1917 edition (Mechon Mamre, 2016 [HTML version]).

3. Fass; Lauha.

4. See also Jeremiah 4:6–7, and 6–20.

5. According to the biblical account, Nebuchadnezzar deported the People of Judah three times. The first wave of exiled Judeans was deported around 605 BCE, the second around 597 BCE, and the third exile can be dated around 587 BCE. In the second siege, of 597 BCE, the Judean king Jehoiachin surrendered, and the Babylonian king led him to Babylon (2 Kings 24:10–17) after having stripped the

Temple of its remaining treasures (2 Kings 24:13), part of which had been carried away already in the first deportation (Dan. 1:2).

6. Compare Jeremiah 46:20: "Egypt is a beautiful heifer, but a gadfly is coming against her from the north."

7. The messianic overtones are described by Chaim Milikowsky.

8. On Ezekiel's view on Gog and Magog, see Ahroni; Block ("Gog and the Pouring"), and Block ("Gog in Prophetic"). Cf. also Gow.

9. The theological and historical aspects of Jewish messianism are delineated by Gerson David Cohen (183–212).

10. Per two biblical exegeses, founded on homiletic interpretation, the Messiah will appear from the Upper Galilee, which is located in the northern part of the Land of Israel. See *Midrash Vayiqra Rabba* 9:2, s.v. נתון בצפון, and *Midrash Bamidbar Rabba* (Vilna), Pericope *Nasso* §13. Compare also *Otzar Hamidrahim* (Eisenstein), 386, s.v. ומחץ פאתי מואב.

11. Jewish thought maintains that the messianic age will be dominated by two figures. The first, Messiah ben Joseph, is associated with warfare and bringing peace to the world, with the return of the People of Israel to their homeland, and the reconstruction of the Temple. The final redemption in the days to come will come through Messiah ben David, of Davidic lineage.

12. The *Zohar* is a group of books that include commentary on the mystical aspects of the *Torah* (the five books of Moses) and scriptural interpretations, as well as material on mysticism, mythical cosmogony, and mystical psychology. The *Zohar* contains a discussion of the nature of God, the origin and structure of the universe, the nature of souls, redemption, the relationship of Ego to Darkness and of "true self" to "The Light of God," and the relationship between the "universal energy" and man. Its scriptural exegesis can be considered an esoteric form of the Rabbinic literature known as *Midrash*, which elaborates on the *Torah*.

13. Hebrew: "dark red."

14. Hebrew: "sky."

15. See additional ordinances in Leviticus 24:5–9 and in Numbers 4:7; as well as Nehemiah 10:33; 1 Chronicles 9.

16. See also Babylonian *Talmud*, Baba Qama 25b, and Maimonides, *Mishneh Torah*, Rulings of the Temple, 1:7.

17. The differing interpretations of the Showbread Table motif in Jewish and Christian art of the Roman and Byzantine periods are discussed by Weiss.

18. The *Talmud* (literally "learning" or "study") is the main literal corpus of Jewish religious teachings and commentary. It is founded on the *Mishnah*—a compilation

of earlier discourses, originally oral, that were laid down around 200 CE. Further oral exegesis and disputations on the *Mishnah* took place in the two main centers of Judaism in the early centuries: Eretz Israel and Babylonia. These oral transmissions were eventually collected and redacted in the form of the Jerusalem *Talmud* (around 350 CE) and the Babylonian *Talmud* (compiled c. 500 CE), respectively.

19. This symbolism may well be the reason for the recurrence of the motif of the Showbread Table in Jewish coins, as a sign of longing for national and religious independence (Barag). An interesting interpretation of this iconography is offered by Zohar Amar.

20. As lamented, for example, in Psalm 74:9 and Ezra 2:63, as well as in the apocryphal 1 Maccabees 4:46; 14:41.

21. As described in *Mishnah* Sanhedrin 1:1. See also Babylonian *Talmud*, Sanhedrin 2a.

22. The text does not specify the inhabitant(s) of the seventh and final hall (Eisenstein).

23. According to Lauterbach (365), there is no reference to this custom at all until the twelfth century.

24. Among other rulings, it was decreed that the ceremony be carried out by a clergyman outside the church while the wedding mass was to be performed thereafter inside the church. Gradually, a special entrance was devised at the northern transept to accommodate the passage of the wedded couple, the priest, and the invitees into the church. Choosing the north presumably reflects the ancient belief in the North as the abode of the evil spirits and the attempt to deceive them during the merry event (Feuchtwanger 32–3).

25. On the rivalry between the offspring of Eve and Lilith, as portrayed in ancient and medieval rabbinic literature, see Mondriaan, Rousseau ("Lilith") and, more explicitly, Rousseau ("Eve").

26. There are other explanations for the custom of breaking a glass, including these: the breaking of the glass represents symbolically the breaking of the hymen and the consummation of the marriage, an expression of hope that one's happiness be as plentiful as the shards of glass or that one's children will be as plentiful as those shards (Lauterbach). The act of breaking the glass, first recorded as a means to ward off evil spirits, eventually gained a different significance—that of mourning over the destroyed Temple of Jerusalem.

27. The topic was elaborated by Elliott S. Horowitz, especially with regards to the Italian Jewry, and by Eric Karsenty.

28. See, for example, the customs of the Babylonian Jews described by Shalom Sabar.

29. In other places the custom is to place the chair(s) in the East.

30. The nature of these sins is discussed in the Babylonian *Talmud*, Niddah 31b.

31. The specific regulations for the offerings to be made by the new mother are delineated in Leviticus 12:1–8.

32. The general rule is stated in the Babylonian *Talmud*, Berakhot 54b.

33. For a comparative study on Lilith in folk culture, see Waldman. Lilith is a female apocryphal demon of the night who seeks to harm newborn children by either kidnapping or strangling them. The name first occurs in Isaiah 34:14 and is associated with the night—both words deriving from the same Hebrew root. The origin of Lilith and the myth connected with her are uncertain. According to one tradition, God created Adam and Lilith as twins joined together at the back. She demanded equality with Adam and, failing to achieve it, she left him in anger. Another version—following the interpretation in *Genesis Rabbah* 18.4—relating her origin regards her as Adam's first wife, before Eve. Following an argument between them on supremacy in their relationship, Lilith fled to the Red Sea, mated with demons, and gave birth to a hundred infants each day, who, later, served as her evil accomplices.

34. *Zohar* to Exodus, periscope T'rumah, 169a.

WORKS CITED

Abrahams, I. *Jewish Life in the Middle Ages*. New York: Atheneum, 1969.

Ahroni, R. "The Gog Prophecy and the Book of Ezekiel." *Hebrew Annual Review* 1 (1977): 1–27.

Amar, Z. "The Shewbread Table on the Coins of Mattathias Antigonus: A Reconsideration." *Israel Numismatic Journal* 17 (2009/10): 48–58.

Barag, D. "The Table of the Showbread and the Facade of the Temple on Coins of the Bar-Kokhba Revolt." *Ancient Jerusalem Revealed*. Ed. H. Geva. Jerusalem: Israel Exploration Society, 1994. 272–6.

Blenkinsopp, J. *A History of Prophecy in Israel*. Louisville: Westminster John Knox, 1996.

Block, D.I. "Gog and the Pouring Out of the Spirit. Reflections on Ezekiel XXXIX 21–9." *Vetus Testamentum* 37 (1987): 257–70.

———. "Gog in Prophetic Tradition: A New Look at Ezekiel XXXVIII 17." *Vetus Testamentum* 42 (1992): 154–72.

Cohen, G.D. *Jewish History and Jewish Destiny*. New York: Jewish Theological Seminary of America, 1997. The Moreshet series 15.

Eisenstein, J.D. *Otsar midrashim: Bet ʿeḳed le-matayim midrashim ḳ et anim ya-agadot u-maʿaśiyot be-seder alfa beta...* 1922. New York: Eisenstein, 1990.

Eschwege, H. *Die Synagoge in der deutschen Geschichte*. Dresden: Verlag der Kunst, 1980.

Fass, D.E. "The Symbolic Uses of North." *Judaism* 37 (1988): 465–73.

Feuchtwanger, N. "Interrelations Between the Jewish and Christian Wedding Customs in Medieval Ashkenaz." *Proceedings of the Ninth World Congress of Jewish Studies, Jerusalem, August 4–12, 1985. Division D, Volume II: Art, Folklore, Theatre, Music*. Ed. D. Assaf. Jerusalem: World Union of Jewish Studies, 1988. 31–7.

Gaimani, A. "The Chair of Eliyahu in the Circumcision Ceremony in Oriental Jewish Communities." *Aram Periodical* 20 (2008): 77–94.

Galambush, J. "Necessary Enemies: Nebuchadnezzar, Yhwh, and Gog in Ezekiel 38–39." *Israel's Prophets and Israel's Past; Essays on the Relationship of Prophetic Texts and Israelite History in Honor of John H. Hayes*. Eds. B.E. Kelle and M.B. Moore. New York: T & T Clark, 2006. 254–67. Library of Hebrew Bible / Old Testament Studies 446.

Ginzberg, L. *The Legends of the Jews, Vol. I. Bible Times and Characters from the Creation to Jacob*. Philadelphia: Jewish Publishing Society of America, 1966.

Gow, A. "Gog and Magog on mappaemundi and Early Printed World Maps: Orientalizing Ethnography in the Apocalyptic Tradition." *Journal of Early Modern History* 2 (1998): 61–88.

Hartenstein, F. (2003) "'Brote' und 'Tisch des Angesichts': Zur Logik symbolischer Kommunikation im Tempelritual." *"Einen Altar von Erde mache mir..." Festschrift für Diethelm Conrad zu seinem 70. Geburtstag*. Eds. J.F. Diehl, R. Heitzenröder, and M. Witte. Waltrop: Spenner, 2003. 107–27. Kleine Arbeiten zum Alten und Neuen Testament 4/5.

A Hebrew–English Bible: According to the Masoretic Text and the JPS 1917 Edition. Ed. Mechon Mamre. 2016 (HTML).

Holm, J., and J. Bowker, eds. *Rites of Passage*. London: Pinter, 1994.

Horowitz, E.S. "The Eve of the Circumcision: A Chapter in the History of Jewish Nightlife." *Journal of Social History* 23 (1989): 45–69.

Jellinek, A. *Bet haMidrash: Midrashim Ketanim Yeshanim uMa' amarim Shonim, Asafti ve`Arakhti' a. pi. Kitve Yad uDefusim*. 1853–57. Jerusalem: Bamberger, 1938.

Joyce, P.M. "King and Messiah in Ezekiel." *King and Messiah in Israel and the Ancient Near East: Proceedings of the Oxford Old Testament Seminar*. Ed. J. Day. Sheffield: Sheffield Academic P, 1998. 323–37. Journal for the Study of the Old Testament Supplement Series 270.

Kaltner, J. "The Gog-Magog Tradition in the Hebrew Bible and the Qur'an: Points of Similarity and Dissimilarity." *Union Seminary Quarterly Review* 49 (1995): 35–48.

Karsenty, E. "La Mishmarà degli ebrei romani: Fonti e usi analoghi in altre comunità ebraiche." *Rassegna mensile di Israel* 67 (2001): 419–30.

Lane Fox, R. *Travelling Heroes: In the Epic Age of Homer.* New York: Knopf, 2009.

Lauha, A. *Zaphon: Der Norden und die Nordvölker im Alten Testament.* Helsinki: Suomalainen Tiedeakatemia, 1943. Suomalainen Tiedeakatemia toimituksia B 49/2.

Lauterbach, J.Z. "The Ceremony of Breaking a Glass at Weddings." *Hebrew Union College Annual* 2 (1925): 351–80.

Milikowsky, C. "Trajectories of Return, Restoration and Redemption in Rabbinic Judaism: Elijah, the Messiah, the War of Gog and the World to Come." *Restoration: Old Testament, Jewish, and Christian Perspectives.* Ed. J.M. Scott. Leiden: Brill, 2001. 265–80. Supplements to the Journal for the Study of Judaism 72.

Mondriaan, M.E. "Lilith and Eve—Wives of Adam." *Old Testament Essays* 18 (2005): 752–62.

Neubauer, A. *La géographie du Talmud: Mémoire couronné par l'Académie des inscriptions et belles-lettres.* Paris: Michel Lévy frères, 1868.

Rousseau, V. "Lilith: une androgynie oubliée." *Archives de Sciences Sociales des Religions* 123 (2003): 61–75.

———. "Eve and Lilith: Two Female Types of Procreation." *Diogenes* 52.4 (2005): 94–8.

Sabar, S. "Childbirth and Magic: Jewish Folklore and Material Culture." *Cultures of the Jews: A New History.* Ed. D. Biale. New York: Schocken, 2002. 671–722.

Schwarzschild, S.S. "On Jewish Eschatology." *Der Geschichtsbegrif: Eine theologische Erfindung?* Ed. M. Bienenstock. Würzburg: Echter, 2007. 12–41. Religion in der Moderne 17.

Scott, J.J. "The Jewish Backgrounds of the New Testament: Second Commonwealth Judaism in Recent Study." *Archaeology of the Biblical World* 1 (1991): 40–9.

Steiman, S. *Custom and Survival: A Study of the Life and Work of Rabbi Jacob Molin (Moelln) known as the Maharil (c. 1360–1427) and his Influence in Establishing the Ashkenazic Minhag (Customs of German Jewry).* New York: Bloch, 1963.

Talmon, S. "The Concepts of Māšîaḥ and Messianism in Early Judaism." *The Messiah: Developments in Earliest Judaism and Christianity. The First Princeton Symposium on Judaism and Christian Origins.* Ed. J.H. Charlesworth. Minneapolis: Fortress, 1992. 79–115.

Tate, M.E. "King and Messiah in Isaiah of Jerusalem." *Review and Expositor* 65 (1968): 409–21.

Trachtenberg, J. *Jewish Magic and Superstition: A Study in Folk Religion.* New York: Atheneum, 1977.

Van der Toorn, K., B. Becking, and P.W. Van der Horst. *Dictionary of Deities and Demons in the Bible*. Leiden: Brill 1999.

Vivian, A. "Gog e Magog nella tradizione biblica, ebraica e cristiana." *Rivista Biblica* 25 (1977): 389–421.

Waldman, F. "Local and Universal Folklore: The story of Lilith." *Studia Hebraica* 8 (2008): 96–109.

Weiss, Z. "'Set the Showbread on the Table Before Me Always' (Exodus 25:30): Artistic Representations of the Showbread Table in Early Jewish and Christian Art." *The Archaeology of Difference: Gender, Ethnicity, Class and the "Other" in Antiquity. Studies in Honor of Eric M. Meyers*. Eds. D.R. Edwards and C.T. McCollough. Boston: American Schools of Oriental Research, 2007. 381–90. The Annual of the American Schools of Oriental Research 60/61.

Wiesemann, F. "'Masal tow' für Braut und Bräutigam: Der Davidstern auf Hochzeitssteinen." *Der Davidstern: Zeichen der Schmach—Symbol der Hoffnung. Ein Beitrag zur Geschichte der Juden*. Eds. W. Stegmann and S.J. Eichmann. Dorsten: Dokumentationszentrum für jüdische Geschichte und Religion, 1991. 86–91.

The Zohar by Shimon bar Yochai from the book of Avraham with the Sulam commentary by Yehuda Ashlag. Ed. and trans. M. Berg. 23 vols. New York: Kabbalah Centre International, 2003.

2 The Realm of the North in Ancient Greek Proverbs

MARIA KASYANOVA

A LARGE NUMBER of written sources reflect ancient Greek ideas about the North, its inhabitants, and natural features. In this analysis I will be focusing on one of these sources in particular, the *paroemiae* ("proverbs"; sing. *paroemia*). This is a term that usually refers to proverbs and other types of popular wisdom and sapiential expressions (Shapiro 92). The *paroemiae* are a tricky body of material to work with. For one thing, they are for the most part fragmentary reconstructions of once-oral sayings and popular opinions. For another, there were many different terms for such expressions in the ancient Greek language.[1] Nevertheless, the aim of this chapter is to study all phenomena that reflect cases of popular conceptions of the North, such as proverbs, sayings, proverbial comparisons, weather lore, and even popular short fables. The terminological differences among these phenomena are not the focus of this discussion. Rather, they can all be subsumed under the category of *paroemia*.

The following analysis draws on texts from as early as the Homeric period and all the way up to late antiquity. In addition, Byzantine lexicons and scholia have been used if they contain important commentaries on ancient passages.[2] Some Latin sources have been also taken into account if they appear to reproduce or allude to Greek tradition. It should be mentioned here that the texts in which *paroemiae* are found include, on the one hand, philosophical and scientific works, such as the writings of Aristotle and Theophrastus, and, on the other hand, mythological epic, poetry, drama, and narrative writing. As might be expected from such diverse material, the *paroemiae* are employed in very different ways in different texts. For instance, authors of special meteorological works explain the origin of the proverbs and make *paroemiae* the object of their investigation. In contrast, poets and narrative writers (such as Hesiod, Aristophanes, Callimachus, Plutarch, and Flavius Philostratus) use them as a tool to make their ideas more exact and their language more elegant.

NORTHERN TERMINOLOGY AND GEOGRAPHY

Any study of *paroemiae* pertaining to the North must be preceded by remarks on the terminology and geographical understanding of "North" in ancient Greece. The Greek language had a wide range of words meaning "North." The two main ways to indicate the North were the use of the names of stars and winds. Among the stars, the constellations Ursa Major and Ursa Minor (the Great and Little Bear) designated the northern part of the world. The most common word for these constellations was the word "bear" (ἄρκτος, pl. ἄρκτοι). Thus, the North was the direction of the Bear or Bears, and northern countries were described as countries lying under the Bears. This word was used in the following way: toward the bear (bears) (i.e., toward the north)—πρὸς ἄρκτον (ἄρκτους); under the bear (bears) (i.e., in the north)—ὑπὸ τὴν ἄρκτον (τὰς ἄρκτους); under the very bears (i.e., in the very north)—ὑπ' αὐτὰς τὰς ἄρκτους. There is also a paronymous adjective "northern"—ἀρκτικός—which derives from the same root. Sometimes, separate names were applied to the two northern constellations. The Great Bear was also known as "wagon" (ἅμαξα) or "Helike" (Ἑλίκη, a girl's name, which also means "turning," as in when the star turns around the Pole).[3] The Little Bear, sometimes referred to as the Pole Star, was called "Cynosure" (Κυνόσουρα, "dog's tail").[4]

From a geographical point of view, the earliest texts from ancient Greece regard Thrace as the most northern region of the known world. The Greeks referred to Thrace as the territory lying to the north of Thessaly, with no definite boundaries (Robson 1176). A fable reported by Andron of Halicarnassus, a historiographer from the fourth century BCE (Tzetz. ad Lycoph. 894), states that Oceanus had four daughters: Asia, Lybia, Europa, and Thracia. The names of the daughters corresponded to four quarters of the world, and Thracia was the northern quarter. However, as the Greeks extended their geographical knowledge, the designation Thrace became more restricted in its application (Robson 1176).[5] In mythology, Thrace was considered to be the realm of the North wind Boreas. Somewhere beyond Thrace lay the fabled Hyperborea, the very distant and fabulous North inhabited by the mythical Hyperboreans.[6]

Thus, the idea of "North" in the Greek language covered an enormous range of both natural and supernatural qualities, geographical features and inhabitants. In the collective Greek consciousness, therefore, geographical and meteorological features of the North interacted with supernatural ideas also linked to that part of the world. This intersection between the natural and the supernatural can be seen, for example, in the figure of Boreas, the Greek god of the North wind.

NORTHERN STARS IN ANCIENT GREEK *PAROEMIAE*

Strictly speaking, there are no *paroemiae* that address northern stars. However, there are some references to northern stars in metaphors written by Greek and Roman poets. These often take the form of literary clichés and were intended for educated readers who could well understand their mythological allusions. Most of these allusions are connected to Greek myths about Callisto, the daughter of the Arkadian king Lykaon. Callisto, so the story goes, was transformed into a bear by Zeus and placed among the stars. She was especially revered by the citizens of the Arcadian town Tegea. Thus, in Ovid's *Ars amatoria*, the Great Bear is literally called "a Tegean girl" (*virgo Tegeaea*), a reference explicitly connected to the

North (Ars am. II 55). Again, in his *Tristia*, Ovid writes that Scythia is the land that lies under the Lycaonian pole (*Lycaonio terra sub axe iacet*, Tr. III 2, 2). Likewise, Nonnos of Panopols, a Greek epic poet from the fifth century CE, calls the Great Bear "the Lycaonian Wagon" (Λυκαονίης ἐλατὴρ Ἀμάξης, Dion. I 462).

Paroemiae Concerning The Northern Winds

The most representative group of *paroemiae* uses the names of the northern winds. In his *Meteorologica*, Aristotle describes six north winds (Mete. 363a–365a). In the North are Aparktias (ἀπαρκτίας) and Boreas (βορέας); in the North-East are Meses (Μέσης) and Kaikias (Καικίας); and in the North-West are Thraskias (Θρασκίας) and Argestes (Αργέστης). The most common way to designate the North was to use the name of Boreas, so that "northward" was expressed as "towards Boreas" (πρὸς βορέαν, εἰς βορέαν), and to be "in the North" was to be "under Boreas" (κατὰ βορέαν). The name Aparktias was occasionally used as well ("towards Aparktias" or "under Aparktias"—πρὸς ἀπαρκτίαν, κατὰ ἀπαρκτίαν).

Among the north winds mentioned above, Boreas is evidently the most important, as he is also a famous mythological figure who played an important role in Greek religion and had sanctuaries throughout Greece.[7] As a mythological figure, Boreas was thought to have been a king of Thrace and lord of the winds, and he abducted and brought to Thrace an Athenian girl named Oreithyia. Among their children was Chione ("snow").

Boreas and Coldness

The first group of proper *paroemiae* to be discussed is connected with winter, coldness, and snow. Perhaps unsurprisingly, these natural phenomena were associated with the North, and, according to the Greeks, the North Wind was the bearer of winter. Since the time of Homer (Od. XIV, 475–7, Il., XV, 170–1) and until that of Roman authors (Ov., Tr. III 10) Boreas was the harbinger of winter, so it is no wonder that this idea was also reflected in weather lore and proverbs. A proverb cited by both Aristotle and Plutarch states: "If the South Wind summons the North Wind, winter is upon us" (Εἰ δ' ὁ νότος βορέαν προκαλέσσεται, αὐτίκα χειμών) (Arist., Pr. 945a; Plut., Mor. 949 B). According to Aristotle, the cause of this phenomenon is that it is the nature of the South Wind to collect clouds and heavy rain. When the North Wind blows as well, it carries all this moist matter with it, freezes it, and produces winter. Hence another proverb: "When Boreas finds mud, soon comes the season of winter" (Εἰ βορρᾶς πηλὸν καταλήψεται, αὐτίκα χειμών) (Arist., Pr. 945b; Theophr., Fm. 5, 46). The connection between the North Wind and frosts seems to have been an obvious one to the Greeks, since this was one of the most popular conceptions concerning Boreas. The popularity of such associations can be illustrated by a number of poetic phrases in both Greek and Latin (although they are not designated as specifically proverbial): "The frosts... are cruel when Boreas blows over the earth" (...πηγάδας, αἵ τ' ἐπὶ γαῖαν πνεύσαντος Βορέαο δυσηλεγέες τελέθουσιν) (Hes., Op. 504); "The hurricane of Boreas brings evil breath of frost to cloakless men" (βορέαο κατάιξ ἔρχεται ἀχλαίνοισι δυσαέα κρυμὸν ἄγουσα) (Callim., Hymn III, 114–5). A similar sentiment is found in Latin, in Virgil's *Georgics*: "When Boreas blows, then winter grips the land with frost" (...*Borea...spirante...rura gelu tum claudit hiems*) (II 316–7).

Two other remarkable examples discuss the aforementioned coldness and snow that characterize northern weather. Once again, these examples are not technically classed as proverbs, but they have a clear paroemiological sense. The first example comes from the Roman poet Martial. During the winter, the hero of the poem is visiting his friend. He complains about his host, who lives in a warm house but assigns his guest Martial to a garret with an ill-fitting window, in which even Boreas himself would not care to live (*At mihi cella datur, non tota clusa fenestra, in qua nec Boreas ipse manere velit*) (Mart. VIII, 14). In this instance, Boreas is obviously a personification of coldness.

Another—somewhat more unusual—example concerns the snow, which was considered by the Greeks to be a typical feature of northern weather. As mentioned above, the personification of snow, Chione, was a daughter of Boreas. In Aristophanes' play *The Acharnians*, a hero named Diceopolis complains that some time ago he was greatly disappointed: He went to the theater to see a tragedy written by Aeschylus, but the play was unexpectedly swapped for another one. Instead of Aeschylus, Diceopolis had to watch a play by the poet Theognis. Happily, there are extant *scholia* to *The Acharnians* that survive today, wherein the scholiast explains why Diceopolis was so disappointed by the play he unexpectedly saw. According to the scholiast, "this Theognis was a very cold tragic poet, one of the Thirty Tyrants,[8] and was even nicknamed 'the Snow'" ("Θέογνις δὲ οὗτος τραγῳδίας ποιητὴς πάνυ ψυχρός, εἷς τῶν Τριάκοντα, ὃς καὶ χιὼν ἐλέγετο") (Scholia. in Ar., Ach. 11.1). In his commentary to Aristophanes, B.B. Rogers notes that "cold" in these contexts means "dull, without a vivifying spark of life or genius" (Rogers, *Comedies* 22). Furthermore, in his play *The Thesmophoriazusae*, Aristophanes himself characterizes the same Theognis as a cold poet: "the works of a poet are copied from himself.—Ah! so it is for this reason that Philocles, who is so hideous, writes hideous pieces; Xenocles, who is malicious, malicious ones, and Theognis, who is cold, such cold ones?" (Ὅμοια γὰρ ποεῖν ἀνάγκη τῇ φύσει.—Ταῦτ' ἄρ' ὁ Φιλοκλέης αἰσχρὸς ὢν αἰσχρῶς ποεῖ, ὁ δὲ Ξενοκλέης ὢν κακὸς κακῶς ποεῖ, ὁ δ' αὖ Θέογνις ψυχρὸς ὢν ψυχρῶς ποεῖ) (Thesm. 167–70). Again, in the same comedy, Aristophanes calls the tragedy *The Palamedes*, by Euripides, "cold": "No doubt he is ashamed of his cold Palamedes" (Οὐκ ἔσθ' ὅπως οὐ τὸν Παλαμήδη ψυχρὸν ὄντ' αἰσχύνεται) (Thesm. 847–8). Thus, these *scholia* exemplify how common it was to characterize a poor poet's talent and literary qualities as "cold."

Using the concept of "coldness" to describe an author's creative weakness was not unique to ancient Greek literature; similar sentiments occur in Roman texts as well. Thus in Cicero's *Brutus* the author names an orator's peculiarity of speaking "almost cold" (*in dicendo...paene frigidus*) (Brut. 178). In his speech *In defense of Caecina*, Cicero speaks about "feeble or lame calumny" (*frigida calumnia*) (Caecin. 61). Cicero also uses the term "cold letter" to describe some correspondence (*frigidas...litteras*; Fam., X, 16, 1).

Virility and Weakness Of Boreas

The next feature of Boreas reflected in *paroemiae* is the abruptness of his appearance and his initial virility, in contrast to his eventual weakness. Theophrastus describes this quality in the following way: "The North Wind...bursts all of a sudden as squalls do, and sudden winds quickly cease, according to the proverb: 'From a weak beginning no great end can come'" (Ἀπ' ἀσθενοῦς γὰρ ἀρχῆς οὐδὲν μέγεθος) (Theophr., Fr. 5, 50). Although this proverb does not directly concern the North, it is an interesting illustration of the nature of Boreas, whose action can be described with the help of the proverb.

The weakness of Boreas mentioned in the example above is strongly connected with the following feature of this wind: If the North Wind arises at night, he is weak by nature. Both Aristotle and Theophrastus, who describe this quality of the North Wind, cite the proverb: "A northwind rising in the night never sees the third day's light" (Οὔποτε νυκτερινὸς βορέας τρίτον ἵκετο φέγγος; Arist., Pr. 941a, 20; Theophr., Fm. 5, 49). Both philosophers explain this characteristic by noting that the North Wind blows at night—a time when there is little heat—so a small amount of heat moves a small quantity of air and ceases quickly.

A similar image of the North Wind can be found in Aesop's well-known fable concerning a competition between Boreas and the Sun that aimed to decide which of the two was stronger. The challenge was to make a passing traveller remove his cloak. Boreas tried by force to rob the man of his cloak, and blew briskly against him, but the man only drew his garment closer to him and held it more tightly. When the heat of the sun succeeded the wind, the man began to get warm and, later, very hot, and he finally stripped off his shirt as well as his cloak (Aesop 46). There is an interesting allusion to this fable in Plutarch's *Moralia*. The author gives advice to married couples on family life, saying that most women act like the traveller from the fable: When their husbands try forcibly, as Boreas, to remove their luxury and extravagance, they continue to fight and are very cross; but if the women are convinced by the help of reason, they peaceably put aside these things and practice moderation (Plut. Mor. 138 e-d).

Another interesting example that combines the natural qualities of the North Wind with its mythological personification can be found in a famous story, first told by Herodotus (VII 189). When the Persian King Xerxes intended to attack Greece, the Delphic oracle informed the Greeks that they should pray to the winds, for the winds would provide aid. The Athenians had called upon Boreas to help them, for Boreas had married Oreithyia, a woman of Attica. The Athenians believed that this marriage made Boreas their son-in-law, so he would come and destroy the Persian ships. When the storm did indeed come about, the Athenians declared that it was Boreas who was responsible for the storm that destroyed the Persian fleet.

Another version of this story can be found in *The Life of Apollonius of Tyana*, written by Philostratus, a Greek author from the third century CE. The main hero of this book, Apollonius, put the Athenians to shame when he said that they had become too effeminate and corrupt. He claimed that on the festival of Dionysus they had imitated the winds by waving their skirts, pretending that they were ships with their bellowing sails aloft. "You"—said Apollonius—"might at least have some respect for the winds that were your allies, instead of turning Boreas who was your patron, and who of all the winds is the most masculine, into a woman" (IV 21). Citing this example, it seems that it was common to regard Boreas as a symbol of courage and masculinity.

North Winds and Quality of the Sky

Although Boreas brings snow and winter weather, the sky remains clear after his disappearance. According to Aristotle, this is a feature of all northern winds. He asserts that northern winds blow from places that are very close to Greece, and this is why these winds are greater and stronger than others. Due to their proximity to Greece, they overpower other winds and blow away the clouds. The idea that Boreas makes the sky cloudless is apparent in the adjective αἰθρηγενής ("born in clear sky"), applied to Boreas even by Homer (Il. XV 171) and then, with some variations, by Orphics

(Hymn. LXXX 2). A similar idea is found in Latin poetry: *clarus aquilo* means "clear North wind" (Verg. G. I 1).

Kaikias, one of the Northeast Winds mentioned above, was said to combine the qualities of the North and South Winds. Consequently, Kaikias does not make the sky clear like other northern winds, but blows on a curved trajectory and attracts clouds to himself, hence the oft-cited proverb: "Bringing it on himself as Caecias does clouds" (ἕλκων ἐφ᾽ αὑτὸν ὥστε καικίας νέφος/νέφη) (Arist., Mete. 364b; Pr. 940a; Theophr., Fm. 5, 37). This proverb was, it seems, one of Plutarch's favorites, for he uses it several times. To paraphrase Plutarch, when one is calumniated, the best way to defend oneself is turn the lie back on the slanderer himself. This is a just thing to do, Plutarch argues, for as Kaikias, the Northeast Wind, gathers clouds, so a bad life brings revulsion upon itself (Plut., Mor. 88e). Elsewhere, Plutarch says that a good civil servant must spend all his hours in office and help people, rather than seeking money and drawing it to himself as the Northeast Wind draws clouds from every quarter (Plut., Mor. 823c).

It should be mentioned here that Kaikias was considered to be a bad wind, so that Aristophanes in his famous comedy *The Knights* invents the name of a new wind, using Kaikias as a model.[9] The new wind is called Sycophantias, the sycophant-wind, the wind of calumnies: "Look out and slack the sheet away, I hear a loud Nor'-Easter[10] there or Sycophanter blow" (Ἄθρει καὶ τοῦ ποδὸς παρίει· ὡς οὗτος ἤδη καικίας καὶ συκοφαντίας πνεῖ) (Ar., Eq. 437).

Hyperborea in Proverbial Expressions

Finally, some proverbial phrases address the fabulous images of the Far North, namely, Hyperborea.[11] Hyperborea (literally "beyond Boreas") was a legendary land in the Far North, where a race of Apollo-worshippers was said to live. According to Delphic legend, Apollo spent the winter months with the Hyperboreans, as there was no snow in Hyperborea during the wintertime. In his tenth *Pythian Ode*, Pindar gives one of the most detailed accounts of the blessed existence of Hyperboreans, who live unaware of diseases, old age, labor, or battle.[12] In spite of the popularity of this myth amongst Greek authors, there are only a few examples of Hyperborean images employed in a proverbial sense. The first example is a "Hyperborean fate" (τύχης...ὑπερβορέου) used in *The Libation Bearers* by Aeschylus (Supp. 373). This term refers to a blessed or happy fate. The chorus tells Electra that what she is saying is better than gold and surpasses great fortune, even that of the Hypeboreans.

Two other such cases come from Latin literature. Here authors speak about Hyperborean snows, but, according to all other accounts of this Greek myth, there is no snow in Hyperborea. In the first case, the Roman poet Statius depicts Jupiter lashing the green fields with Hyperborean snow (*Hyperborea...nive*; Theb., V 390). In the second, the Hyperborean snow, together with lakes and rivers of Scythia, pities Medea as she is carried away by Jason (*Hyperboreas...pruinas*; Val. Fl., Argon. VIII 210). Thus it seems, here, that the adjective "Hyperborean" is used as a synonym for the adjective "northern" in an emphatic sense, meaning "very strong snow" or even a "snowstorm."

CONCLUSION

What conclusions can be drawn from the present study of Greek *paroemiae*? First of all, it can be pointed out that—regardless of the type of proverbial expressions and regardless of the text's genre—where *paroemiae* occur, most of them agree with each other and express similar ideas. This means that natural phenomena that the Greeks connected with the northern part of the world often corresponded with its supernatural personifications. Nevertheless, it should also be noted that there is much variation in how *paroemiae* are employed in texts of different genres. While Aristotle and Theophrastus explain the origins of their proverbs scientifically, other authors such as Plutarch and Philostratus use the same material as didactic examples, framing them in a moral or ethical sense.

At the same time, it is clear that *paroemiae* form very versatile and sometimes discrepant images of the North. Consequently, it is impossible to describe these northern images as wholly positive or negative. It is well known that proverbs first existed in oral form; consequently, the examples we have at our disposal are a small fraction of what must have once existed. Nevertheless, as this analysis has sought to demonstrate, the very existence of these proverbs and sayings that refer to the North in Greek and Roman texts proves that they were an intrinsic part of how the world was conceived and imagined in the classical world.

NOTES

1. The Greeks used the following words for sapiential expressions: παροιμία ("proverb," "maxim"), ὑποθήκη ("suggestion," "counsel"), ἀπόφθεγμα ("terse pointed saying"), and γνώμη ("judgement," "opinion"), of which γνώμη seems to be the most comprehensive (Lardinois 214). At the same time, proverb-like expressions could be marked by words such as ἔπος, λόγος, and αἶνος ("word," "saying"), which are used for a variety of speech genres (214), or simply by the verb "λέγεται" ("it is said"), which lacks any specific terminological sense.

2. *Scholia* are grammatical notes or explanatory comments inserted in the margins of manuscripts.

3. The story of Helike in Greek mythology is rather complicated. According to Cretan myth, there were two nymphs, Helike and Kynosoura, who nurtured Zeus as he hid from his father Cronus. Later, Zeus placed them in the sky, so that Helike became the constellation of Ursa Major and Kynosoura became Ursa Minor. The Achaean version refers to the second nymph as Aiga, not Kynosoura. The most popular tale among Greek and Roman authors was an Arcadian story that referred to Helike (or Callisto in some versions, see below) as a daughter of Lycaon, king of Arcadia, and as a nymph of Artemis. Zeus fell in love with her, and Hera (or Artemis) turned the girl into a bear. Then Zeus put the bear in the sky as Ursa Major (for details and a list of sources see Stoll 1884–90; 1985–86).

4. The origin of the name was unclear even in ancient times. In *Scholia to Ilias* (Sch. vet. XVIII 487) it is said that the name belongs to a dog that has a tail that bends backward (See also Gundel 36–41 for various versions of the Cynosure myth).

5. On boundaries in different periods of Greek and Roman history, see Oberhummer 394–471 and Hammond and Scullard, s.v. "Thrace."

6. On Hyperborea and its inhabitants, see Mayer 2805–41.

7. On the cult of Boreas, see Rapp 813–4.

8. The Thirty Tyrants were a pro-Spartan oligarchy, which governed Athens from 404–403 BCE.

9. The suffix that forms the word "συκοφαντίας," is common for masculine words of technical and popular vocabulary (Chantraine 96). For example, ἀπαρκτίας is a name of the North Wind and ὀρνιθίας, a "bird-wind," a name of the annual wind in spring that brings with it the birds of passage (the latter used by Aristophanes as well: Ach. 877). In old scholia to Aristophanes, the author comments in the following way: "The name of the wind is Kaikias. When it blows, it brings clouds on himself. That is why it is said 'slack the sheet away.'" Aristophanes forms the word both from "sycophancy" and "evil" ("kakia"), brought by the wind (ὄνομα ἀνέμου ὁ καικίας·.... οὗτος δὲ ὅτ' ἐμπνεῖ τὰ νέφη εἰς ἑαυτὸν ἕλκει. ἀκολούθως δὲ εἶπε διὰ τὸ προειρηκέναι <"τοῦ ποδός">, ἅμα δὲ πρὸς τὴν συκοφαντίαν καὶ κακίαν αὐτοῦ τὰ ὀνόματα πλάττει) (Sch. vet. Eq. 437a.5). There is a fragment of anonymous comedy in which the proverb about Kaikias and clouds, mentioned above, is used in relation to evils: "drawing evils to himself as the North-East wind clouds" (κακὰ ἕλκων ἐφ' αὐτὸν ὥστε καικίας νέφος") (Kock fr. 1229). The very name of Kaikias may be considered to be a pun with word κακία ("evil") or αἰκία ("cruel treatment"; "misfortune") (as probably Plutarch did, as commentators to Aristophanes note [Knights of Aristophanes, ed. Neil 66]). That is why the author of the old scholia assumes the wordplay here: as Kaikias brings evils, so the Sycophant-wind brings sycophancy, which is evil as well.

10. That is, Kaikias.

11. See the contribution by Athanasios Votsis in this volume.

12. On Hyperborea, see Hammond and Scullard, s.v. Hyperboreans; and Mayer 2805–41.

WORKS CITED

Aeschylus. *Oresteia: Agamemnon. Libation-Bearers. Eumenides.* Ed. and trans. A.H. Sommerstein. Cambridge: Harvard UP, 2009.

Aesopica: A Series of Texts Relating to Aesop or Ascribed to Him or Closely Connected with the Literary Tradition that Bears his Name. Ed. B.E. Perry. Vol. 1. Urbana: U of Illinois P, 1952.

Aristophanes. *The Knights of Aristophanes.* Ed. R.A. Neil. Cambridge: Cambridge UP, 1901.

———. *The Knights of Aristophanes.* Trans. B.B. Rogers. London: Bell, 1930.

———. "Women at the Thesmophoria." Trans. E. O'Neill. *The Complete Greek Drama: All the Extant Tragedies of Aeschylus, Sophocles and Euripides, and the Comedies of Aristophanes and Menander, in a Variety of Translations.* Eds. W.J. Oates and E. O'Neill. Vol. 2. New York: Random, 1938.

Aristotle. "Meteorologica." Trans. E. W. Webster. *The Works of Aristotle.* Ed. W.D. Ross. Vol. 3. Oxford: Clarendon, 1931.

———. *Minor Works. On Colours. On Things Heard. Physiognomics. On Plants. On Marvellous Things Heard. Mechanical Problems. Of Indivisible Lines. Situations and Names of Winds. On Melissus, Xenophanes, and Gorgias.* Trans. W.S. Hett. Cambridge: Harvard UP, 1936.

———. "Problemata." Trans. E.S. Forster. *The Works of Aristotle.* Ed. W.D. Ross. Vol. 7. Oxford: Clarendon, 1927.

Callimachus. *Hymns and Epigrams.* "Lycophron." "Aratus." Trans. A.W. Mair and G.R. Mair. Cambridge: Harvard UP, 1995.

Chantraine, P. *La Formation des noms en grec ancien.* Paris: Peeters, 1979.

Cicero. *Brutus. Orator.* Trans. G.L. Hendrickson and H.M. Hubbell. Cambridge: Harvard UP, 1939.

———. *Letters to Friends.* 3 vols. Ed. and trans. D.R. Shackleton Bailey. Cambridge: Harvard UP, 2001.

———. *Pro Lege Manilia. Pro Caecina. Pro Cluentio. Pro Rabirio Perduellionis Reo.* Trans. H. Grose Hodge. Cambridge: Harvard UP, 1927.

Gundel, H. "Kynosura." *Paulys Realencyclopädie der classischen Altertumswissenschaft* 23. Eds. G. Wissowa and W. Kroll. Stuttgart: Metzlersche Verlagsbuchhandlung, 1924. 36–41.

Hammond, N.G.L., and H.H. Scullard, eds. *The Oxford Classical Dictionary.* Oxford: Clarendon, 1977.

Herodotus. *The Persian Wars.* Trans. A.D. Godley. Vol. 3. Cambridge: Harvard UP, 1922.

Hesiod. *The Homeric Hymns, and Homerica.* Trans. H.G. Evelyn-White. London: Heinemann, 1914.

Homer. *Ilias.* Ed. T.W. Allen. 3 vols. Oxford: Clarendon, 1931.

———. *Odyssea.* Ed. P. Von der Mühll. Basel: Helbing, 1946.

Kock, T., ed. *Comicorum Atticorum Fragmenta.* Vol. 3. Leipzig: Teubner, 1888.

Lardinois, A. "Modern Paroemiology and the Use of Gnomai in Homer's *Iliad.*" *Classical Philology* 92.3 (1997): 213–34.

Martial. *Epigrams.* Trans. W.C.A. Ker. London: Heinemann, 1919.

Mayer, M. "Hyperboreer." Roscher 2805–41.

Nonnos. *Dionysiaca.* 3 vols. Trans. W.H.D. Rouse. Vol. 1. Cambridge: Harvard UP, 1940.

Oberhummer, E. "Thrake." *Paulys Realencyclopädie der classischen Altertumswissenschaft* 11. Eds. G. Wissowa and W. Kroll. Stuttgart: Metzlersche Verlagsbuchhandlung, 1936. 392–552.

Orphei Hymni. Ed. W. Quandt. Berlin: Weidmann, 1962.

Ovid. *The Art of Love, and other Poems.* Trans. J. H. Mozley. London: William Heinemann, 1929.

———. *Tristia. Ex Ponto.* Trans. A.L. Wheeler. Cambridge: Harvard UP, 1924.

Philostratus. *The Life of Apollonius of Tyana.* Trans. F.C. Conybeare. London: Heinemann, 1912.

Pindar. *Olympian Odes. Pythian Odes.* Ed. and trans. W.H. Race. Cambridge: Harvard UP, 1997.

Plutarch. *Moralia.* 15 vols. Cambridge: Harvard UP, 1959–76.

Rapp, A. "Boreas." Roscher 804–14.

Robson, J. "Thracia." *Dictionary of Greek and Roman Geography* 2. Ed. W. Smith. London: Walton, 1872. 1176–90.

Roscher, W.H., ed. *Ausführliches Lexikon der Griechischen and Römischen Mythologie* I. Leipzig: Teubner, 1884–90.

Scholia Graeca in Homeri Iliadem (Scholia vetera). Ed. H. Erbse. 7 vols. Berlin-New York: de Gruyter, 1969–88.

Scholia in Aristophanem. Prolegomena de Comoedia. Scholia in Acharnenses, Equites, Nubes. Eds. D. Holwerda, D. Mervyn Jones, W. J. W. Koster, N. G. Wilson. Groningen: Forsten, Groningen, Forsten and Bouma, 1969–77.

Shapiro, S. "Proverbial Wisdom in Herodotus." *Transactions of the American Philological Association* 130 (2000): 89–118.

Statius. *Thebaid.* Ed. and trans. D.R. Shackleton Bailey. 2 vols. Cambridge: Harvard UP, 2004.

Stoll, H.W. "Helike." Roscher 1985–86.

Theophrastus of Eresus. *On Winds and on Weather Signs.* Trans. J.G. Wood. Ed. G.J. Symons. London: Stanford, 1894.

———. "Fragmenta." *Theophrasti Eresii opera quae supersunt omnia.* Ed. F. Wimmer. Vol. 3. Leipzig: Teubner, 1862.

Valerius Flaccus. *Argonautica.* Trans. J.H. Mozley. Cambridge: Harvard UP, 1934.

Virgil. *Eclogues. Georgics. Aeneid.* Trans. H.R. Fairclough. Cambridge: Harvard UP, 1916.

3 The Ancient Greek Myth of Hyperborea

Its Supernatural Aspects and Frameworks of Meaning

ATHANASIOS VOTSIS

INTRODUCTION

According to ancient Greek sources, the Hyperboreans were a race that lived in a remarkable land somewhere in the Far North and possessed supernatural qualities. Intriguing stories about them have been transmitted to us by ancient Greek writers, in mythological, historical, and geographical texts. Major mythological characters such as Apollo, Artemis, and Hercules were said to have dealings with them, and Hyperborean ghosts supposedly defended the Delphic oracle when it was threatened by invading Gauls in the third century BCE.

The etymology of the word *Hyperborea* derives from *hyper-* ("beyond") and *-borea* (deriving from *Boreas*, the god of the northern wind).[1] Thus, the name suggests a place beyond the North Wind, or a place in the extreme North. Who the Hyperboreans were and where they lived has been the subject of much scholarly speculation. In the mid-nineteenth century, Dawson W. Turner (211) commented that the name Hyperboreans was used indiscriminately by ancient authors to refer to anyone living in the Far North and suggested that there might be a connection to Russians and Siberians. In the early twentieth century, Casson debated whether or not Hyperborea should be placed inside or beyond the Greek peninsula, noting the distinction between actual pre-Hellenic Hyperboreans and the later, mythical ones. More recently, Timothy P. Bridgman has discussed the connection of Hyperboreans to, and possible identification with, the Celts.

This chapter will examine the supernatural aspects of Hyperborea from a semiotic perspective. Semiotics is the study of how meaning is signified, communicated, and received, usually in the context of material (e.g., art and architecture) and non-material (e.g., literature, mythology) culture. The text discusses key frameworks within which the supernatural characteristics of the Hyperboreans appear to have been perceived in ancient Greece. The analysis is based on primary literary sources from the Archaic, Classical, and Hellenistic periods. Methodologically, the study draws on semiotic studies of the European cultural and mythological systems, and predominantly on Algirdas Greimas's work on structural semantics. The chapter does not seek to present a comprehensive analysis of the Hyperborean myth. Rather, its aim is to illuminate interesting aspects of the inner structure of the myth, as well as to demonstrate the relevance of semiotic methodology to the field of classical studies.

The Greek sources provide stimulating and culturally rich references to the Hyperborean people and their supernatural qualities. They include *Bibliotheca* by Apollodorus (or pseudo-Apollodorus; he lived in the BC era, although a more precise date is not commonly agreed), the *Argonautica* by Apollonius Rhodius (a Hellenistic writer from the third century BCE), *Bibliotheca Historica* by Diodorus Siculus (a late Hellenistic historian from the first century BCE), the *Histories* of Herodotus (a classical Greek historian of the fifth century BCE), the *Description of Greece* by Pausanias (a Hellenistic geographer and travel writer from the second century BCE), *Hymn IV (to Delos)* by Callimachus (a Hellenistic scholar of the third century BCE), and the *Olympian* and *Pythian* odes by Pindar (a late Archaic Greek lyric poet from the fifth century BCE). These references revolve around three main areas: sacred architecture and smaller artefacts, discourses, and a number of binary oppositions upon which the myth relies. In this chapter I will refer to these three areas as frameworks of meaning that determined the Hyperboreans' position and role in the mythological, cultural, and value systems of the ancient Greek world.

The question of the geographical location—the *topos*—of the Hyperboreans deserves special attention. The literary sources provide geographical and climatological evidence, but these cannot be treated as map directions and, unfortunately, following them would not enable us to discover Hyperborea. Rather, the Hyperborean *topos* is a structural feature of the myth with a function close to that of the notion of semiotic space (Lotman): a loose network of spatial, cultural, and historical relations between places, people, and events. Such a topology functions as a basic structure upon which the various frameworks of meaning are constructed. Thus, the Hyperborean *topos*, which is discussed briefly in the following section, cannot be treated as a framework of meaning in itself, but as a sort of logical or semiotic precondition for the generation of meaningful frameworks.

THE HYPERBOREAN *TOPOS*

The ancient Greeks' interest in the Hyperboreans was almost entirely related to their supposed supernatural characteristics and their prox- imity to the affairs of the gods. Consequently, the sources do not address the mundane physical aspects of the Hyperboreans in much detail. Nevertheless, a general and abstract Hyperborean *topos* receives some attention. Collectively, they tell us of a city sacred to Apollo (Diod. Sic. 2.47.1–6), who enjoyed spending time there (Pind., Pyth. 10.27). Hyperborea must have had a climate capable of sustaining wheat or corn, fruits and olive trees—produce that had religious and historical impor- tance in relation to the Hyperborean myth, as detailed below.

However, the general location of Hyperborea is in the Far North of the Greek world. Pindar writes that "neither ship nor marching feet may find the wondrous way to the gatherings of the Hyperborean people" (Pind., Pyth. 10.27). The exact location of Hyperborea is ambiguous, but northern or central Europe appears to be the favoured deduction. Pindar places the Hyperboreans along the river Ister or Istros, which is the modern-day Danube (Pind., Pyth. 10.27). Apollonius Rhodius writes that the Argonauts, returning from Colchis via the Black Sea, passed through a system of rivers mythically connected to Hyperborea, which are located in central Europe. These include Eridanos (an unidentified river flowing into the Rhone) and Rhodanos (the Rhone) (Apoll. Rhod. 4.594). On the other hand, Diodorus Siculus reports that Hyperborea is an island no smaller than Sicily, in the ocean beyond the land of the Celts (Diod. Sic. 2.47.1–6).

Opinions on the Hyperboreans' neighbours were likewise mixed: Pausanias suggests they were located close to the Gauls—i.e., the Celts, in the terminology of classical Greek ethnography—since both they and the Hyperboreans lived in the immediate vicinity of the northern European river Eridanos: "These Gauls inhabit the most remote portion of Europe, near a great sea that is not navigable to its extremities, and possesses ebb and flow and creatures quite unlike those of other seas" (Paus. 1.4). Herodotus, on the other hand, identifies the Scythians as neighbours of the Hyperboreans (4.32–6), thus situating the latter in the north-east of the Greek world.

SACRED ARCHITECTURE AND ARTEFACTS

The first framework of meaning that I want to discuss relates the super-natural dimension of the Hyperboreans to sacred artefacts and structures. These two elements seem to have been particularly important in the original sources of the fifth, fourth, and third centuries BCE, and remained so up until their reiterations by Hellenistic historians and geographers of the first centuries CE.

First, it must be noted that there are two main types of references to sacred architecture linked to the Hyperboreans and their supernatural attributes. The first category is related to Apollo's temple at Delphi, and the second revolves around the tomb of two Hyperborean maidens at Delos. Pausanias talks about the second temple (chronologically) of Apollo at Delphi, which was constructed by Hyperborean sages from beeswax and feathers (10.5.7–9). Regarding the Delian tomb, Herodotus informs us that it was located near the temple of Artemis and that it contained the remains of the Hyperborean maidens Hyperokhe and Laodike. They had been the first Hyperboreans to bring offerings of their people to Greece, but their arduous journey through Europe brought about their deaths, and they were buried at Delos (Hdt. 4.34). No information is given about the architectural details of the Delphic temple or the Delian tomb. Moreover, Herodotus provides little spatial information about the tomb, only mentioning that it was located to the left of the entrance of Artemis' temple, at the foot of an olive tree (4.34). This sacred structure went on to become part of a tradition observed by young Delian girls and boys, who would leave a lock of their hair on the tomb as an offering in honour of the maidens (Hdt. 4.32–6). The symbolic correlation with both the olive tree and the goddess is an important one; I will discuss it in more detail in the chapter's final section.

Second, references to smaller artefacts concern objects that are mentioned in the context of mythological or religious events. Pindar (Ol. 3.10–20) notes that the olive tree was brought by Hercules from Hyperborea to be the prize at the Olympic Games, which he had established. This link between the Hyperboreans and olive trees correlates with the location of the aforementioned Delian tomb at the foot of such a tree. Connected to Hercules, a later Hellenistic source identifies Hyperborea as the home of Atlas and the location of a garden containing the golden apples belonging to the nymphs called the Hesperides (Apoll. Rhod. 2.114).

Another important reference to divine objects is given by Herodotus (4.32–6) regarding the offerings sent by the Hyperboreans to the gods. They were wrapped in straw and transported from Hyperborea through eastern and southeastern Europe to Greece, and then across Greek religious centres until they reached Delos. Callimachus reports that these offerings were "three cornstalks and holy sheaves of corn-ears" (Callim. Hymn IV), whereas Pausanias tells us that they were "first-fruits" wrapped in wheat straw (Paus. 1.31.2). These divine objects are complemented by a few more artefacts. Herodotus mentions a Hyperborean hero named Abaris, who travelled across the world with the help of a golden arrow given to him by Apollo (4.32–6). Lastly, Diodorus Siculus notes that the Hyperboreans are players of the *kithara*, which is a stringed musical instrument related to the lyre (2.47.1–6). This reference must be placed in the overall context of Hyperborea as a place associated with Apollo, who was a god of music and often associated with the lyre.

DISCOURSES

The second framework of meaning involves a "culture" or "world" broader and more comprehensive than individual artefacts and architecture. In this case, the supernatural dimension of Hyperborea was perceived by the Greeks through a number of discourses, some of which were widespread, while others were constructed specifically for individual cases. The previously discussed references to material culture often contribute to the core of these discourses, but their scope extends beyond the objects themselves and focuses on aspects of non-material culture.

The overarching "discourse" that must be addressed is the relationship between the affairs of the ancient Greeks and the affairs of their gods. Here, the supernatural quality of Hyperborea is moulded into a mediator between divine and mortal affairs. This was indeed an implicit force behind the references to material culture, but here it becomes explicit, extensively incorporating Hyperborea into divine (gods, titans, nymphs, etc.) and mythological structures (heroes, demi-gods, genealogy, etc.). Moreover, it is evident that in this overarching discourse Hyperborea is never of the present, but is usually invoked together with past divine incidents in relation to more recent (but not necessarily current) Greek affairs. Stemming from the overarching, generic discourse, it is possible to identify a number of concrete cases in the sources.

The first such case is Pindar's tenth *Pythian Ode*, which was commissioned to praise a young victor of the Pythian Games. Pindar extols the young athlete, yet reminds us that his achievement cannot be bettered by mortals, because Hyperboreans have performed even greater feats, far beyond human abilities. Pindar states that this is why it takes more than mortal power and knowledge to find the Hyperboreans (Pind., Pyth. 10.27). He goes on to explain attributes of Hyperborea that make Apollo delighted to spend time there, and mentions that Perseus, a hero with supernatural qualities, has visited the place too.

Second, the aforementioned passage from Pindar's third *Olympian Ode* is in fact part of a broader narrative that incorporates Hyperborea into the affairs of Zeus, Artemis, and Hercules. According to Pindar's narrative, Zeus assigned to Hercules the task of finding a tree to shade all people and a crown to honour the victors of the Olympic Games. This led Hercules to Hyperborea, where he was welcomed by the goddess Artemis. It was there that he found the olive tree and persuaded the Hyperboreans to take it to Greece.

Third, Pausanias links the sacred space of Delphi to Hyperborea. In particular, the Delphic sanctuary was established for Apollo by Hyperborean sages, and one of those sages, Olen, served as its first oracle (Paus. 10.5.7–9). Centuries later, when the sanctuary faced a Gallic assault, the spirits of two Hyperboreans—Hyperochos and Amadokos—appeared as phantasms to protect it (Paus. 1.4).

THE UNDERLYING BINARY OPPOSITIONS AND THEIR FUNCTION

What is said about the supernatural aspect of Hyperborea, and how this is communicated in the sources, indicates the following pattern:

a. *A relatively stable set of actors or objects, their properties, and their fundamental relationships is repeated;*
b. *These actors, objects, and properties assume the function of elementary concepts, which, via the identified relationships, are joined together in order to produce binary oppositions.*[2]

The pattern described in (a) and (b) produces narratives about the Hyperboreans that revolve around sacred artefacts, architecture, and discourses. In turn, those narratives establish a particular understanding of Hyperborea in ancient Greek culture. Ever-present in this structure is the supernatural aspect, which is sometimes expressed directly through singular ideas, but most of the time emerges from the overall relation of Hyperborea to ancient Greece and its religious and mythological world. The following table summarizes the constructive elements of this structure, as demonstrated by the literary sources discussed.

TABLE 3.1 *Actors, Objects, and Properties as Constructive Elements of Binary Oppositions*

ACTORS	PROPERTIES
Apollo, Artemis, Zeus	*divine, immortal, ruling, fate-setting*
Hercules	*Greek, demi-god, hero, executor of the divine will*
Abaris	*Hyperborean, hero, supernatural achievement*
Delian maidens	*Hyperborean, honoured, grantors of good fate*
Sages	*Hyperborean, protector, spirit, architect, founder, oracle/priest*
Greek athlete	*great achiever, mortal, Greek, celebrated*
Hyperborean people	*fortunate, longevity, divine servants, divine company*
Greek people	*mortal, protected, honour-giving*

ARCHITECTURE, ARTEFACTS AND NATURAL FEATURES	
Temple of Artemis	*divine, Hyperborean*
Tomb of Maidens	*Hyperborean, honoured, good fate*
Sanctuary of Delphi	*protected, Hyperborean foundations*
Olive tree	*Hyperborean origin, prize, life-quality*
Wheat straw	*Hyperborean origin, offering to the gods, good luck*
North wind	*geographic denotative limit with qualitative connotations*
Water	*geographic denotative limit with qualitative connotations*
Lyre/*kithara*	*divine, Hyperborean*

Looking at the qualities attributed to the Hyperboreans, Greeks, and gods in Table 3.1 reveals that there is a firm set of properties associated with Hyperborea. These properties are part of a system of attributes that assigns particular characteristics to Olympians, Greeks, and Hyperboreans:

TABLE 3.2 *Attribution of Properties to the Olympians, Hyperboreans, and Greeks*

	OLYMPUS	HYPERBOREA	GREECE
Immortal	+	−	−
Remarkable longevity	+	+	−
Remarkably good fortune	+	+	−
Remarkable abilities	+	+	−
Honouring	−	+	+
Honoured	+	+	−
Protectors	+	+	−
Beyond the reach of mortals	+	+	−
Origin of material goods	−	+	−
Origin of spiritual goods	+	+	−
Fine art	+	+	−

As can be seen from Table 3.2, Hyperborea is assigned a mixture of divine and mortal characteristics. The Hyperboreans share with the gods a considerable number of properties, yet certain defining characteristics—mortality and serving the gods—constantly pull them toward the sphere of the mortals. However, their status is always higher than that of mortals. The following summary can be constructed from Table 3.2:

a. *Hyperboreans are mortal, with remarkable longevity, good fortune, and great abilities. They pay due honour to the gods and are honoured by mortals. They cannot be reached by mortals, they protect the Greeks, and they are the originators of material and spiritual goods. They are also masters of fine art.*

b. *Greeks are mortal. They pay due honour to gods and Hyperboreans, and they benefit from the remarkable qualities assigned to both gods and Hyperboreans.*

c. *The Olympian gods are immortal, with good fortune, and great abil-*
ities. They are honoured by the Hyperboreans and Greeks. They
cannot be reached by mortals, they protect the Greeks and are the
originators of material and spiritual goods. Like the Hyperboreans,
they are masters of fine art.

Based on this set of interrelationships, a semantic assumption can be
made concerning Hyperborea. Hyperborea is placed between the divine
world of Olympus and the mortal world of Greece. In the literary sources,
this is conveyed in two ways: through the comparison of the supernatural abilities (or lack thereof) of the Hyperboreans, Greeks, and gods,
and through the overall understanding of Hyperborea in relation to
Greece and Olympus. These two related ways of placing Hyperborea in
the conceptual map of Greek culture are invariably present whether the
sources speak of artefacts and architecture, or of mythical narratives and
divine affairs.

Following the work of Greimas on structural semantics, the aforementioned relationships can be represented through the semantic square, also
known as the square of oppositions. The semantic square outlines four
elements of a binary opposition A–B. While A and B might be direct oppo-
sites, not-A and not-B can also be used to express the same opposition,
albeit with slightly different connotations. Cultural production relies on
the full spectrum of such semantic alternatives, with indirect oppositions
(e.g., non-god vs. god) having a position as important as direct oppositions
(e.g., mortal vs. god) (cf. Schleifer's interpretation in Greimas, xxxii–
xxxiii). Mapping the aforementioned relationship between Hyperboreans,
the Greeks, and their gods results in the two semantic squares in Figures
3.1 and 3.2.[3] The Hyperborean actors and objects, as well as their properties, are located at the negation part of the semantic square. As it can
be seen in the literary sources, the Hyperboreans are mortals, but, at the
same time, they live extremely long lives with supernatural and divine
characteristics. When such qualities are compared to gods and mortals,
the semantic content of Hyperborea shifts to that of neither mortals nor

FIGURE 3.1 *The grand placement of Hyperborea in the ancient Greek mythical system.*

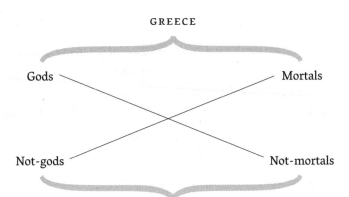

FIGURE 3.2 *Understanding Hyperborea through the supernatural aspect.*

gods (Figure 3.1). The situation is similar concerning the supernatural quality of Hyperborea: Hyperborean people or objects, although without divine origin, do have divine characteristics and magical properties, as can be seen from their appearance as ghosts during the troubles of the Delphic sanctuary (Figure 3.2).

All in all, there is a pronounced dual quality in the way the Greeks present the Hyperboreans as simultaneously divine and mortal. An exclusive focus on this duality, however, would explain neither the role of Greece and Olympus as fundamental elements in the Hyperborean myth, nor would it show that the three-way relationship between Hyperboreans, Greeks, and gods was perhaps the most important element of the myth. Especially concerning the latter, by appreciating the broad use of semantic negation (e.g., non-mortals) in place of the simpler direct opposite (e.g., god), one is allowed to account for the relatively harmonious placement of the Greeks and their gods in one unified schema, with Hyperboreans as an interesting mediator. Greeks and gods indeed exist in the Hyperborean myth and play a crucial role in the construction of the meaning of Hyperborea itself. A further important benefit exists in such an analysis. It enables us to understand how the several concepts surrounding the myth help achieve the goal of the cultural self-reflection of the Greek people, that is, the particular position that the Greeks thought they held in their rich hierarchy of myths, religions, heroes, and divinities.

CONCLUSION

The present analysis of the ancient Greek myth of Hyperborea supplies strong semiotic evidence that the meaning of the myth itself was far less important than the use of the various elements of the myth for the understandinging the Greek cultural order. This implies that Hyperborea, as a land and its people, was placed in a broader system of narratives surrounding real or legendary actors, objects, and their characteristics. This system of narratives had as its primary goal the establishment of a particular understanding of ancient Greece in relation to its divinities and mythological figures and their affairs. The understanding of Hyperborea emerged from this context. Hyperborea was a mediator that connected Greeks to the gods, and mortals to divine qualities. The presented semiotic analysis of literary sources cannot maintain that a once-real Hyperborea is the source of the ancient Greek myth. What can be maintained with confidence, however, is that the topology of relationships established by the Hyperborean myth was a strong reality for the Greeks. In other words, truth did not come before the myth as its source, but it was established by the myth in a distinctly semiotic fashion.

This conclusion does not deny the objective existence of Hyperborea, since the geographical information in the sources have rather strong correlations to real locations and historical ethnic groups in the European continent. Yet, the Hyperborea of ancient Greece is a symbolic cultural establishment, and its location—though elusive—was certainly a reality for the Greeks.

NOTES

1. See the contribution by Maria Kasyanova in this volume.
2. A binary opposition is a logical construction that brings two concepts together and against each other, for example, white and black, mortal and god. This juxtaposition is most often of an opposing nature, with the two concepts assuming two extreme poles (i.e., a "binary") with opposing connotations (i.e., an "opposition"). Binary oppositions are not found only in verbal and textual materials, but are also widespread in music, visual art, and architecture.
3. In the context of both figures, "Greece" refers to the self-image of the Greek people as we find it in the texts describing Hyperborea; it includes the Greek pantheon (Olympus) as an important element of this self-image.

WORKS CITED

Apollonius Rhodius. *The Argonautica.* Trans. R.C. Seaton. Cambridge: Harvard UP, 1967.
Bridgman, T.P. *Hyperboreans: Myth and History in Celtic-Hellenic Contacts.* New York: Routledge, 2005.

Callimachus. *Hymns and Epigrams.* 2nd ed., rev. Trans. A.W. Mair and G.R. Mair.
Cambridge: Harvard UP, 1960. Loeb Classical Library No. 129.

Casson, S. "The Hyperboreans." *The Classical Review* 34.1–2 (1920): 1–3.

Diodorus of Sicily. Trans. G.H. Oldfather. Cambridge: Harvard UP, 1968.

Greimas, A.J. *Structural Semantics: An Attempt at a Method.* Lincoln: U of Nebraska P, 1983.

Herodotus. Trans. A.D. Godley. Cambridge: Harvard UP, 1960.

The Library of Apollodorus. Trans. R. Hard. Oxford: Oxford UP, 2008.

Lotman, Y. *Universe of the Mind: A Semiotic Theory of Culture.* Bloomington: Indiana UP, 1990.

Pausanias. *Description of Greece.* Trans. W.H.S. Jones. Cambridge: Harvard UP, 1965.

Pindar. *Olympian Odes. Pythian Odes.* Trans. W.H. Race. Cambridge: Harvard UP, 1997.

Turner, D.W. *Notes on Herodotus: Original and Selected from the Best Commentators.* London: Bohn, 1857.

II

From the Middle Ages to the Early Modern Period

The Monstrous and the Demonic

4   Monstra septentrionalia

Supernatural Monsters of the Far North in Medieval Lore

RUDOLF SIMEK

BOTH LATIN AND VERNACULAR TEXTS from the medieval Nordic
world refer to many monstrous humanoid creatures that are said to
inhabit the far corners of the earth. The enumerations of such beings in
vernacular texts are mainly translations or adaptations from similar lists
of monstrous races to be found in medieval Latin encyclopedic literature.
Other monstrous humanoids have found their way into narrative texts,
where they pop up in unlikely places, such as the one-legged *Einfœting*
that appears in chapter 12 of *Eiríks saga rauða* ("The Saga of Eiríkr the
Red") as a native of Vínland.[1] In the following chapter, I will investigate
the ways in which local lore about the legendary inhabitants of the remote
parts of the Nordic world combined with learned medieval etymology of
indigenous names and classical, encyclopedic learning as a way of interpreting vaguely known ethnonyms of far-flung peoples. I will also explore
the depictions of such peoples on maps in order to create an understanding
not only of how the supposed denizens of the monstrous North were
perceived, but also their precise geographic locations.

The following remarks are not intended to detail all appearances of fabulous creatures in the Nordic Middle Ages, but I shall attempt to give a survey of the diversity of monsters and of the various literary genres in which they appear, concentrating on humanoid monsters rather than zoomorphic ones.[2]

The terato-ethnographical lists in both Latin and vernacular manuscripts from northern Europe follow earlier European traditions, which originally situated such monsters at the southern- and easternmost edges of the earth. By contrast, these creatures rarely inhabited the Far North. However, from the end of the first millennium onwards, the "marginal beings" of these monster-catalogues tended to escape their traditional literary (and, on world maps, iconographic) habitats. They began to appear in the Far North, which in classical and medieval geography consisted of northwestern Asia; Scandinavia; the border area between these territories, marked by the River Tanais (the Don), the Riphaean Mountains, and the Meotidean swamps; as well as, slightly further to the south, in Scythia. North-eastern Scandinavia, then considered one of the most remote areas of the world, proved an excellent place for (re)settling monstrous races— nearly as good as easternmost India or the sun-scorched, almost deserted south of Africa.

THE NORTHERN TERATOLOGY OF ADAM OF BREMEN

Apart from Old English texts such as *The Wonders of the East* and *Alexander's Letter to Aristotle*, which preferred detailed descriptions of the monsters over their exact whereabouts, there is little evidence of monsters in the literature of northwestern Europe before 1100.[3] The only exception is Adam of Bremen's *Gesta Hammaburgensis ecclesiae pontificum* ("Deeds of the Bishops of the Hamburg Church," c. 1070), in which Adam describes at length the monsters and fabulous races that live somewhere between the Gulf of Bothnia and furthest northeastern Europe. Despite the author's undoubted first-hand knowledge of much of his subject matter, and his high-ranking informant, King Sven Estridsson of Denmark (died 1074), who had been brought up at the Swedish court in Uppsala, it seems that Adam's work is not only the oldest detailed description of Scandinavia, but also one of the most fabulous.

In the fourth book of Adam's text, the entire last chapter of his famous description of *Scandinavia* is devoted to the areas beyond the Baltic countries inhabited by the Samlanders and the *Pruzzi*. Here, Adam discusses in detail these wondrous islands and countries more or less inaccessible to travellers:

IV. 19: Sunt et aliae in hoc ponto insulae plures, ferocibus barbaris omnes plenae, ideoque fugiuntur a navigantibus. Item circa haec littora Baltici maris ferunt esse Amazonas, quod nunc terra feminarum dicitur. Eas aquae gustu dicunt aliqui concipere. Sunt etiam qui referant eas fieri praegnantes ab hiis qui praetereunt negociatoribus, vel ab hiis quos inter se habent captivos, sive ab aliis monstris, quae ibi non rara habentur. Et hoc credimus etiam fide dignius cumque pervenerint ad partum, si quid masculini generis est, fiunt cynocephali; si quid feminini, speciosissimae mulieres. Hae simul viventes, spernunt consortia virorum; quos etiam, si advenerint, a se repellunt viriliter. Cynocephali sunt, qui in pectore caput habent in Ruzzia videntur sepe captivi, et cum verbis latrant in voce. Ibi sunt etiam qui dicuntur Alani vel Albani, qui lingua eorum wizzi dicuntur, crudelissimi ambrones; cum canicie nascuntur; de quibus auctor Solinus meminit. Eorum patriam canes defendunt. Si quando pugnandum est, canibus aciem struunt. Ibi sunt homines pallidi, virides et Macrobii, id est longi, quos appellant Husos; postremo illi, qui dicuntur antropofagi, et humanis vescuntur carnibus. Ibi sunt alia monstra plurima, quae recitantur a navigantibus sepe inspecta quamvis hoc nostris vix credibile putetur.

IV. 20: Haec habui, quae de sinu illo Baltico dicerem, cuius nullam mentionem audivi quempiam fecisse doctorum nisi solum, de quo supra diximus, Einhardum. Et fortasse mutatis nominibus arbitror illud fretum ab antiquis vocari paludes Scithicas vel Meoticas, sive

deserta Getharum, aut litus Scithicum, quod Martianus ait confertum
esse multiplici diversitate barbarorum. Illic, inquit, Gethae, Daci,
Sarmatae, Alani, Geloni, Antropofagi, Trogloditae.

IV. 25: *Ab oriente autem Ripheos montes attingit, ubi deserta ingentia,*
nives altissimae, ubi monstruosi hominum greges ultra prohibent
accessum. Ibi sunt Amazones, ibi Cynocephali, ibi Ciclopes, qui unum
in fronte habent oculum; ibi sunt hii, quos Solinus dicit Ymantopodes,
uno pede salientes, et illi, qui humanis carnibus delectantur pro cibo,
ideoque sicut fugiuntur, ita etiam iure tacentur.

IV. 19: In this sea there are several other islands, all full of wild barbarians, and are thus avoided by sailors. Similarly, the shores of the Baltic
Sea are said to be inhabited by Amazons, which is now called the Land
of Women; some say that they conceive by drinking water, others
report that they become pregnant from those occasionally trading
there, or from men whom they hold captive, or from monsters, of which
there are plenty there. This we think is more worthy of credibility, and
when it comes to birth, those of male gender are dogheads, and those
of female the most beautiful of women. These live together and shun
the company of men, whom they drive off in manly fashion if they
approach. Dogheads are those with heads on their chests; in Russia
they are frequently seen as captives, and they speak by barking. There
are also those which are called Albani or Alani, or in their language are
called Wizzi, the most cruel Ambrones. They are born with grey hair,
as the author Solinus reminds us. Dogs defend their country, and when
they have them fight, they form battle ranks from dogs. There are
also pale, green people, and the Macrobii, which are called Husi;[4] and
finally those that are said to be Anthropophagi and eat human flesh.
There are also many other monsters, which the sailors report to have
seen often, even though it appears hardly credible to us.

IV. 20: This I have to say of the Baltic Sea, which I have not found
mentioned by any author, except the aforementioned Einhard.

Perhaps, I assume, the ancients called that sea by different names, like
the Scythian or Meotidan swamps, or the desert of the Goths, or the
shores of the Scythians, of which Martianus says that they are inhab-
ited by a manifold diversity of barbarians: Here, he says, are Goths,
Dacians, Sarmatians, Alani, Geloni, Anthropophagi and Troglodytes.

IV. 25: In the East [Sweden] touches the Riphean mountains, where
huge wastes, the deepest snows and hoards of monstrous peoples
prohibit access. There are Amazons, there are Dogheads, there are
Cyclopses, who only have one eye on their forehead. There are those,
whom Solinus calls Ymantopodes, who hop on one foot, and those
who delight in human flesh for their food and are therefore as much
avoided as rightly passed over in silence.[5]

These passages have frequently been misinterpreted or even mistrans-
lated because scholars have ignored the fact that Adam is quoting mainly
from classical literature. Adam's main authority for the description of
monstrous races in the three chapters of Book 4 (quoted above) is Gaius
Solinus, whom he names twice, whereas he refers to Martianus Capella a
single time. His descriptions are an effort to correlate the stories about odd
people in the northeast of Scandinavia with classical information about
monstrous races; certainly there is no attempt to create an ethnography of
Karelia and northern Scythia from eyewitness accounts.

We shall, in due course, analyze the races mentioned, but first we
must consider Adam's enumerating style. He employs the same method
prevalent from antiquity to the Middle Ages for listing people about whose
countries the author has no verifiable or experiential information: He simply
states the fact that "there are" people: *Ibi sunt etiam qui dicuntur....; Ibi*
sunt homines...; Ibi sunt alia monstra plurima.... This method is also used by
later encyclopedists such as the thirteenth-century Thomas of Cantimpré
in his *Liber de natura rerum*, especially when listing the monstrous races
in Book III, where he has little to say concerning where such races
actually live.[6]

At first glance, it might appear that Adam is constantly misquoting Solinus, as his descriptions do not fully correspond to those in Solinus' *Collectanea rerum memorabilium*: Solinus, despite several references to the *Amazones* (17.2, 38.12, 40.2), does not elaborate on the way in which they conceive their offspring. According to him, the *Blemmyae*, rather than Adam's *Cynocephali* ("Dogheads") have their faces on their chests (31.5), and the *Ambrones* and *Macrobii* (30.9f) are separate races rather than alternative epithets for other creatures named by Adam. Also, the *Himantopodes* (31.6) are actually men with thin extremities, unable to walk upright, while Adam clearly thinks of them as the *Sciopodes* hopping along on their one big foot. In the case of the *Albani*, on the other hand, Adam provides a description that remains close to his source (Solin. 15.5), whom he here expressly mentions, albeit with more concise phrasing and with the added Germanic pseudo-ethnonym *Wizzi*, "the White Ones." Quite obviously, Adam is not referring directly to a manuscript of Solinus. Rather, he may have had second-hand access to Solinus through another source or could have been quoting from memory. This begs the question of why he thought he could get away with such a free adaptation of his source material in such a learned environment as the bishop's see in Bremen. The answer may well lie in his intention to relate only snippets of classical information, attaching them travellers' hearsay (to whom he refers a couple of times in the above quoted text), trying to establish new monstrous races for eastern Scandinavia rather than directly transferring ancient ones to the North.

An example of this method may be found in the descriptions of the *Amazones*, whom Adam mentions twice as inhabitants of the North. This is the earliest example of a Scandinavian tradition lasting through the Middle Ages: namely, that a *terra feminarum* is situated somewhere between the Baltic and the White Sea. It is a well-known fact that *Kvenland* actually took its name from a Karelian tribe called the *Kvenir* (or *Quenir*: Krabbo 49; Wiklund; Vilkuna), but its misleading-sounding name meant that it was interpreted as *Kvennaland*, "Land of Women," throughout the late Middle Ages. Adam provides the earliest extant written evidence of this etymology, though it may predate him in the learned tradition. The misunderstanding was still prevalent in the thirteenth and fourteenth centuries: in both the semi-mythical Norwegian prehistory *Fundinn Noregr* ("The Founding of Norway"; Ásmundarson 19) and the late Icelandic *Bárðar saga Snæfellsáss* ("The Saga of Bárðr, God of Snæfellsnes"; Vilmundarson and Vilhjálmsson ch. 1), *Kvenland* or *Kvænland* is the home of giantesses. Even continental *mappae mundi* show the *Amazones* in the northern part of Asia that borders Europe.[7]

Therefore Adam may be either the originator of this information or our earliest preserved source for a learned tradition both within and beyond northern Europe. Whether or not Adam is the originator of this etymology, he certainly makes the most of this knowledge by repeatedly referring to the *Amazones*. He merges the local tradition of the *Kvenir* with his obvious knowledge of Scandinavian languages (or else internal traditions) to introduce the *Kvenir* into Latin literature as *Amazones*. As for their location in Scythia, he found support in the works of Solinus and Martianus, who both mention *Amazones* living between the Black Sea and the Caspian Sea.[8] In the passage quoted above, Adam cites Martianus as an authority for the great diversity of strange peoples in the northeast and follows his list of ethnonyms to a certain degree.

According to Adam, Martianus lists *Getae, Daci, Sarmatae, Alani, Geloni, Anthropophagi,* and *Troglodytae,* and this is indeed a partial version of the list given in the Martianus manuscripts. In these, the *Getae,* Dacians, Sarmatians, Amaxobians, *Troglodytes, Alani,* and *Germani* are named in the one sentence following the reference to northeastern Scandinavia as being densely populated by barbarian races. However, later in the paragraph, with reference to the river *Borysthenes* (Dnieper), Martianus adds the *Geloni,* the *Agathyrsi,* the *Anthropophagi,* and the *Arimaspi.* Adam combines and limits himself to seven out of the eleven races mentioned in his source, but it is telling that none of the races he speaks of comes from any other source. Thus, Adam's ethnography of northeastern Scandinavia is revealed to derive from a late classical source rather than the eyewitness accounts he relies on for the descriptions of Denmark and Sweden, among others.

In addition to Martianus and Solinus, Adam also used the description of Scythia in Isidore of Seville's *Etymologiae*. Isidore (9: 2, 66) mentions the *Hugnos antea Hunnos vocatos* ("the Hugni, previously called the Huns") directly after the *Amazones* and the *Albani* (9: 2, 64f). As no other solution has been suggested to explain Adam's *Husi*, who do not correspond to any known Scandinavian or northern Asian tribe, it seems likely that here he has misquoted Isidore.

Adam's remarkable attempt at localizing monsters in the North in accordance with late classical authors such as Solinus and Martianus may thus mark the first step in a development that later gained much greater importance for the geography and ethnography of the North, namely the harmonization of local lore, learned etymology of indigenous names (as in the name of the *Kvenir*), and classical encyclopedic learning.

NORWEGIAN AND ICELANDIC MONSTER CATALOGUES

That this development became popular in both Latin and vernacular literature, and in both scholarly and literary texts, is evident from the anonymous Latin *Historia Norvegiae* ("History of Norway"), written in Norway around 1220, about 150 years after Adam (Storm 75). In his first chapter, the author gives a wide-ranging geographical survey of the Nordic world before concentrating on Norway itself. This includes a short tract on the half-known or unknown areas to the northeast of Norway:

> *Versus vero septemtrionem gentes perplures paganismo (proh dolor)*
> *inservientes trans Norwegiam ob oriente extenduntur, scilicet Kiriali et*
> *Kwœni, cornuti Finni ac utrique Biarmones. Sed quœ gentes post istos*
> *habitent, nihil certum habemus. Quidam tamen nautœ cum de Glaciali*
> *insula ad Norwegiam remeare studuissent et a contrariis ventorum*
> *turbinibus in brumalem plagam propulsi essent, inter Viridenses et*
> *Biarmones tandem applicuerunt, ubi homines mirœ magnitudinis et*
> *virginum terram (quœ gustu aquœ concipere dicuntur) se reperisse*
> *protestati sunt. Ab istis vero Viridis terra congelatis scopulis dirimitur;*

quæ patria a Telensibus reperta et inhabitata oc fide catholica roborata
terminus est ad occasum Europœ, fere contingens Africans insulas, ubi
inundant oceani refluenta. Trans Viridenses ad aquilonem quidam
homunciones a venatoribus reperiuntur, quos Scrœlinga appellant.

But northward and spreading from the east across Norway there are
many peoples devoted to paganism: Kirjalians, Kvenir, Horn-Lapps and
the people of the two Bjarmalands. Of what peoples live beyond these
we have no certain knowledge. However, when certain shipmen were
trying to return to Norway from Iceland, they were driven by contrary
tempests into the wintry region and at last made land between the
Greenlanders and the Bjarmians where, so they claimed, they found
men of prodigious size and a country of maidens (these are said to
conceive children by a drink of water). Greenland is cut off from these
by icy crags. This country, which was discovered, settled and confirmed
in the universal faith by Icelanders, is the western boundary of Europe,
almost touching the African islands where the waters of ocean flood in.
Beyond the Greenlanders some manikins have been found by hunters,
who call them Skraelings.[9]

Here, the author refers to the *cornuti Finni* ("Horn-Lapps"),[10] the
homines mirœ magnitudinis ("the men of prodigious size," i.e., the giant
men of Bjarmaland), and the *terra virginum* ("land of maidens," presumably the land inhabited by *Amazones*) in the northeast. That the author
of the *Historia Norvegiae* has also incorporated indigenous traditions is
apparent from his inclusion of the fabulous, half-mythical land of the
Giants (Bjarmaland) between Norway and Greenland, which he presents
in Latin as the home of *homines mirœ magnitudinis* and that goes back,
no doubt, to old Scandinavian concepts of *Jötunheim*, or *Rísaland*.[11]

Although the knowledge of Adam's work is vouched for in medieval
Icelandic sources,[12] it is not necessary to assume that it was first and fore-
most the *Gesta Hammaburgensis ecclesiae pontificum* that was exploited for
Icelandic lists of monstrous races in vernacular Old Icelandic writing. In

fact, the two key manuscripts, AM 544, 4to (*Hauksbók*; Simek, *Altnordische* 466–7) and AM 194, 4to (470–1), seem at first glance to owe little to Adam. Rather, they appear to go back directly to Isidore and other encyclopaedic sources, but add a good deal of additional material to Isidore's list. The two Old Norse manuscripts differ not so much in content as in the order of the monsters in the list. Between them, the texts in these two manuscripts enumerate an extraordinary number of monstrous races, exceeding most Latin continental sources. They name *Rísar* (*Gigantes*), *Albani i Sithio, Ciclopi, Lamnies* (recte: *Blemmyae*), *Cenocefali* (recte: *Cynocephali*), flat-faced *Arhines*, large-lipped *Amycteres*, small-mouthed *Astomi*, large-eared *Panadios* (recte: *Panoti*), the Tongueless, *Ardabadite* (recte: *Artibatirae*), *Satiri*, one-footed *Skiopodes, Antipedes, Ippopodes* (recte: *Hippopedes*), *Acrobi* (recte: *Macrobii*), *Pygmei*, short-lived women, *Ermafrodites* (recte: *Hermaphrodites*), *Pagasi* (recte: *Panphagi*), *Trogodite, Antiofagi* (recte: *Ichthyophagi*), *Anthrofagi* (recte: *Anthropophagi*), *Magog, Patrophagi*, poison-immune *Getuli, Macrobii* born with white/grey hair, *Pilosi, Ichthyophagi*, white-haired *Albani, Kvennir* (= *Amazones*), *Hornfinnar* (= *Satiri*), and *Hundingiar* (= *Cynocephali*). As can be seen from the many garbled names, the Icelandic authors' grasp of the Greek language was not quite equal to their enthusiasm for monstrous races. Yet their encyclopedic efforts are remarkable, compiled from different Latin sources and indigenous material. The latter includes *Einfœtingar, Hornfinnar, Hundingjar, Kvennir* and *Rísar*. The lists also mention monsters that rarely make it into Latin encyclopedic literature at all, namely *Magog*, the *Patrophagi*, the *Getuli*, and the *Albani*.

The interdependence of Latin and vernacular texts in Iceland, the site of the most prolific manuscript production in the medieval Nordic world, is hardly surprising, as both must have originated in the same cultural and intellectual milieu within Icelandic society. This is demonstrated by a detail even so small and odd as the reference to Africa in the above quotation from the *Historia Norvegiae*, which describes Greenland as being the furthest extent of Europe, nearly reaching those islands lying off the coast of Africa. The author voices a concept that can also be found in a short Icelandic cosmography preserved as part of ms AM 736 I, 4to, 1r:

fra biarmalandi ganga lavnd til obygda ab nordr ett allt til þes er gren-
land tekr vid. fra grenaland i sudr ligr hellu land þa markland þadan
er eigi langt til vinla<n>d er sumir menn etla at gangi af affrica.
Enngland oc scotland ei ein ero. oc er þo sitt huart konungs riki Irland
er ey mikil. Island er oc ey mikil i nordr fra irlandi. þessi lavnd aull ero
i þeim luta heims er eoropa er kalladr. (Simek, Altnordische *428–35)*

From Bjarmaland there is uninhabited land from the north all the
way to Greenland. South of Greenland is Helluland, then Markland,
and then it is not far to Vínland, which, some people believe, reaches
out from Africa. England and Scotland are one island, but each is a
kingdom; Ireland is a large island. Iceland is also a large island north
of Ireland, and all these lands are in that part of the world that is
called Europe.[13]

Despite differences in the precise wording of the descriptions in the
Historia Norvegiae and AM 736, the underlying concept is the same:
Greenland is connected to Europe in the North, all the lands in the west
are as such part of Europe, and in the South these western regions may
reach all the way to Africa (cf. Simek, "Elusive" with reconstructed maps
of this concept).[14]

THE LASTING INFLUENCE OF CLASSICAL LORE

Both the Latin and Icelandic texts discussed here present a worldview
of the North that is solidly based on classical learning, with occasional
attempts (as by Adam) made to combine this learning with indigenous
lore to create one image of the monstrous North. The local knowledge
contained in the above descriptions encompasses the Land of Giants in
the North, an acquaintance with the tribe of the *Kvenir*, the land bridge
between Norway and Greenland as well as knowledge of Greenland and
other countries in the North Atlantic and their inhabitants.

However, the weight of classical education in these texts is more
important, and thus more prominent, than all the information gleaned

from eyewitnesses, hearsay, or local traditions, especially regarding those areas where all such information was scarce. What classical authors had invented or extrapolated about the territories north of Scythia—which occupied the northernmost parts of both Asia and Europe—was copied, appropriated, and applied to Scandinavia.

Two methods can be detected by which this material was expanded and augmented. Firstly, information from several classical or early medieval authors could be compiled to fill in the possible gaps. This is how Adam used Solinus, Martianus, and Isidore in his description of fabulous races of the North. Secondly, an attempt could be made to conflate classical learning with local lore, through either a geographical or etymological connection. The etymological method was used by Adam in the case of the *Kvenir*, whose (supposed) derivation from *kvinna/kvenn-* ("woman, female") gave him the chance to identify them with the Amazons, and possibly in the case of the *homines palides et virides*, "pale and green people." The Latin term for the Greenlanders, *Virides*, allowed him to associate them with this particular monstrous race. The geographical method is used to fill in gaps left by classical authors in the geography of the North, and thus the author of *Historia Norvegiae* is able to place both the giants and the *Amazones* on the land bridge between Norway and Greenland.

CARTOGRAPHIC DEPICTIONS OF NORTHERN MONSTERS

Even apart from the vernacular texts of the High Middle Ages, these methods and the Latin texts on Scandinavian peoples that resulted from them had a lasting influence throughout the Middle Ages and well into modern times. Interestingly enough, this type of information, exactly because it was available in Latin as well as the vernacular, made its impact felt even outside Scandinavia. This can be seen from its insertion on the two largest medieval world maps known to date, the Hereford and the Ebstorf *mappae mundi*.[15]

The English Hereford *mappa mundi* is the largest extant medieval world map. It has a diameter of 1.3 m, and was probably constructed in the last decade of the thirteenth century.[16] In the periphery of the map, an illustrated description of northern Europe and Scythia is provided.[17] The map maker has included not only the *Cynocephali* (illustrated by two little dog-headed people and the caption *In hoc tracto sunt cinocephales*, ("in this area there are Cynocephali"), the night-sighted *Albani*, the *Essedones* who eat their own parents (otherwise called *Patrophagi*), the *Anthropophagi*, "the damned sons of Cain" who eat human flesh and drink blood, the *Yperborei*, and finally even *simiae* (monkeys). Whether these are filling the space normally reserved for the *Pygmei* (Pygmies) in the depiction of Scandinavia[18]—perhaps the most likely explanation in view of the fact that the *Pygmei* were often considered to be only one step closer to humanity than the apes—or whether they were moved here from Asia for another reason is impossible to say. It is, however, apparent that in his depiction of Scandinavia the Hereford mapmaker is following the tradition of Adam of Bremen. Via Adam, he came upon material that originates with Solinus, but he was also able to use Solinus directly (as the *Essedones* from Solin. 15.13 show) as well as the geography of Aethicus Ister.

The Ebstorf map, dated to about 1235–41 (Hahn-Woernle, *Ebstorfer*, 87–8), was even larger than its Hereford counterpart. Although it was lost in the bombing of Hanover in 1944, the map is well documented by earlier photographs. Despite the fact that this map, like the Hereford map, boasts its own "monster gallery" in the far south, there are also several monsters placed in the extreme north of Scandinavia and bordering on Asia. These include the *Amazones* (conspicuously absent from the Hereford map), the *Anthropofagi* (depicted here with horse hooves), the *Albani*, and the *Trogodites* (*Trogloditae*). Yet despite the considerable extra space and the extra legends that the Ebstorf map could accommodate within its diameter of 3.5 m, the number of monsters shown for Scandinavia is no higher than on the Hereford map, probably due to the fact that there was only a limited stock of such monsters in literature available for the North.

To sum up the medieval traditions on Scandinavia and Scythia—the latter of which was considered by learned Scandinavians as an extension of Scandinavia to the east[19]—those monstrous races that occur most frequently in texts and/or pictures are the *Amazones*, the *Albani*, the *Cynocephali*, and the *Anthropophagi*. In addition to these, some authors and mapmakers add the *Cornuti Finni*, the *Pygmei*, and occasionally the *Sciopodes*, whether they are called *Unipedes*, *Einfœtingar*, or (wrongly) *Himantopodes*. Surprisingly, what the medieval monsters of the North have in common is that they all can be traced back to Solinus. It seems that his disparate notes on Scythia and its strange races were ultimately the basis for further descriptions of this area, and, despite occasional additions, remained the standard catalogue, albeit limited, of fabulous humanoid creatures associated with the North.

In the later Middle Ages, this rather limited inventory of monsters of the Far North was even further reduced, as demonstrated by later medieval cartography. In the fifteenth-century, Claudius Clavus Swart from Salling on the Danish island of Fyn, was the first Scandinavian cartographer to use the Ptolemean principle in practical mapping. He left extensive tables of coordinates for European towns and places (mainly promontories), although his original map of Scandinavia from the early 1420s is lost and only survives in a copy by Cardinal William Fillastres from 1427 (Gamborg Briså and Lavold 76). Most maps of Scandinavia created over the next 200 years were influenced by his maps, their keys, and their tables of coordinates. They depict the land bridge between Bjarmaland and Greenland, and the cartographer filled this space with, among other legendary peoples and regions, the *Unipedes Maritimi* ("coastal Unipeds"), *Pigmei Maritimi* ("coastal Pygmies"), *Griffonum regio uastissima* ("the expansive region of Griffons"), and *Wildhlappelandi* ("land of the Wild Lapps"). Thus even Claudius Clavus, a serious cartographer who portrays Norway, Denmark, and Sweden with relative accuracy, refers back to classical traditions when confronted with the regions of the Far North. His *Unipedes* answer to Adam's *Himantopodes* (and, of course, to the Vínland *Einfœtingr* of *Eiríks saga rauða* ch. 12) and refer to the *Sciopodes*; his *Pygmei* are also specified by the epithet *maritimi*, thus distinguishing them from the African *Pygmei*; and the griffons are yet again taken from the description of Scythia in Solinus' *Collectanea* (15.22).

The German cartographer Henricus Martellus took up Claudius' coordinates to produce his own maps, printed in Venice before 1490. In all his maps, whether those of Europe as a whole or only of Scandinavia, he depicts Greenland connected to Europe by a land bridge. However, he refrains from peopling the northern lands with fabulous beings, and only has *Pillapelant* (likely Claudius' *Wildhlappelandi*) to the East of the Baltic Sea. Only on the furthest western coast of Greenland does he add a few legends of his own, but these only refer to promontories and rivers and seem to be the author's own invention.

Despite the reticence of Henricus Martellus, by the late Middle Ages the monsters seem to belong to the concept of the "furthest North" to such an extent that they even make an appearance in Central European geography. A globe-cup produced in Switzerland in 1552 still shows the monstrous races to the northeast of Scandinavia, although the artist places *Risenland* ("Giantland") on the southern tip of South America, and *Lütfresser* ("Man-eaters") on the island of *Iava maior*. The artist was able to use contemporary maps for this gilded silver globe, in particular a world map produced by Johannes Honter in his *Rudimenta cosmographica*, published in Zürich in 1546 and again in 1558 (Seidner; Nagel 135 and fig. 36ff.). An even more traditional map was published by the Bavarian professor Jacob Ziegler (c. 1470–1549) at Vienna University, who included a map of the North Atlantic and Iceland in his 1532 book on the Holy Land. The map shows the land bridge between Norway and Greenland, but Ziegler, surprisingly enough, refrains from depicting or mentioning any monsters whatsoever (Dreyer-Eimbcke 50–1).

The tradition of cartographic monsters in the Far North survived not only in central Europe as part of late medieval map-making, but also continued in Iceland and Sweden. In some works from the sixteenth century the tradition is already much reduced to some semi-mythological depictions of Lapps and Finns,[20] for which the works of the last Catholic bishop of Uppsala, Olaus Magnus, may serve as an example. His *Carta Gothica*, printed posthumously in 1567, shows only the *Skridfinnar* on the northernmost tip of mainland Scandinavia (as does his *Carta*

Marina of Scandinavia in 1539), but no other monstrous races in the
northeast (Knauer). He also refers to these *Skridfinnar* in his *Historia
de gentibus septentrionalibus* ("History of the Northern Peoples") of 1555
(Magnus: I, 3ʳ–3ᵛ), but they are described in ethnological terms and not
as monsters. Giants are mentioned in the *Historia* (Magnus: V, 52ᵛff.), but
here as elsewhere Magnus uses the term *giant* in the same sense as Saxo
Grammaticus—one of his main sources—namely as an euhemeristic
explanation for the heroes of old.

In Iceland during this time, only the reformed bishops had access to a
printing press. Yet despite their official Protestant skepticism toward the
more fabulous and superstitious elements of Icelandic culture, they were
surprisingly uncritical of the old traditions of monsters in the North. Two
maps, produced at the see in Skálholt, are both similarly indebted to the
medieval worldview. The first of these was Sigurdur Stefánsson's map of
the North Atlantic. He was the grandson of the radical reformer bishop
Gísli Jónsson (c. 1515–87) and for a brief period (before his death at the age
of 25 in 1594) head of the school in Skálholt. His map, which must have
represented the state of learning of the Icelandic intellectual elite, encompasses not only Norway in the East and Vínland in the southwest, but
also Greenland and the land bridge to Bjarmaland in the North. This land
bridge bears the legends *Riseland* (*Rísaland*) in the west, and the obviously
synonymous *Jötunheimar* further east. His original map is no longer extant,
but was reprinted in 1670 by Thordur Thorlaksson, who mistakenly dated
it to 1579 (*Sigurdi Stephanii terrarum hyperborearum delineatio Anno 1579*,
"The Depiction of the Hyperborean Lands of Sigurdur Stefánsson in the
Year 1579"), although it must have been produced between 1592 and 1594
(Dreyer-Eimbcke 81). A second, very similar map was made by Thordur
Thorlaksson himself and published in 1668. It has fewer entries, but retains
the same legends for the Far North as Sigurdur's map. It is therefore obvious
that reformed churchmen in sixteenth- to eighteenth-century Iceland
were willing to accept the image of the Far North as the home of giants,
even though that may have been a denotation that referred more to the
distant past than actual remote lands.

However, it is not the giants that seem to have had the longest life of all the fabulous races of the North, but the *Pygmei*. Independently of the lists of monstrous races found in Adam's *Gesta*, the *Historia Norvegiae* and the Old Norse lists of monsters in Icelandic manuscripts, a tradition seems to have developed that identified the *Skrælingar* (mentioned both in sagas and in scholarly medieval literature as inhabitants of Greenland and the countries to the west of it) with the *Pygmei* of classical tradition, mentioned by Claudius Clavus in the 1420s.[21] This identification seems to have been only latent during the Middle Ages, but from Claudius Clavus' maps onwards it becomes a dominant trait in the depiction of Greenland and the lands north of it (either on the fictitious land bridge, or else an even more fictitious Arctic continent) on early modern maps. On the *Septentrionalium regionum descriptio* of Abraham Ortelius, for example, printed in Antwerp between 1592 and 1601 as part of Ortelius' *Theatrum orbis terrarum*, the Arctic continent bears the legends *Pigmei hic habitant* ("Pygmei live here"). A similar legend, but now at the southern tip of Greenland, is to be found in the *Carta Marina* of Scandinavia by Olaus Magnus of 1539, which has a legend that not only mentions the *Skrælingar*, but also the *Pygmei*, despite the fact that his map is otherwise free of monstrous races on land (as mentioned above), though Olaus Magnus does fill the sea with aquatic monsters.

All these maps serve to show that even in the sixteenth to eighteenth centuries, medieval traditions about the Far North still flourished, even if they had been somewhat rationalized. The mythic *Hornfinnar/Satiri* became exotic, while the certainly existent Lapps and Finns, and the *Pygmei* had merged with the *Skrælingar*/Inuit as inhabitants of Greenland and the fictitious Arctic landmass. Elsewhere, the races of giants left their trace only in the place names of *Riseland* (*Rísaland*) and *Jötunheimar* in the Far North. The *Amazones*, *Unipedes*, and *Anthropophagi*, however, had disappeared entirely, and even the monkeys had left northern Scandinavia, finally resulting in the modern maps of the Nordic world that were far more realistic, but perhaps also far less interesting.

NOTES

1. Elsewhere I discuss the two main Old Norse-Icelandic manuscripts that record such fabulous races, namely AM 544, 4to (*Hauksbók*) and AM 194, 4to, where I dealt with the textual traditions behind these two differing lists of monstrous beings (Simek, "Wunder").

2. Monstrous creatures of both classical mythology and/or indigenous Germanic mythology that did not find their way into other texts outside mythography fall outside the scope of the present chapter. For these, see Simek, *Lexikon;* Heizmann "Fenriswolf"; Heizmann, "Midgardschlange."

3. Early medieval Celtic literature, which contains numerous references to monstrous beings, is beyond the scope of this chapter.

4. *Husos* = ? The German translation in the bilingual edition connects the pale and green people (*homines pallidi, virides*) with the *Macrobii*, in my opinion wrongly, as the former, alone, are a frequently named people of very large stature, cf. Solinus 9–10, with an etymology from the Greek *macron* "large, tall," which suggests that Adam used Solinus via a medieval source.

5. Author's translation.

6. Boese 168–70: *Sunt et homines alii ...; Homines etiam magni sunt ...; Sunt alii homines ...; Sunt alie...; Sunt ibi homines ...;* etc.

7. For example, on the *mappamundi* by Heinrich of Mainz from the twelfth century (cf. Miller vol. 2, table 13).

8. VI, 665 (Stahl, Johnson, & Burge 2: 248).

9. Translation from Kunin and Phelpstead 2–3.

10. These beings are possibly inspired by the *Satyri* of the Latin tradition, who are always imagined as being horned.

11. Elsewhere I have examined these indigenous traditions and their influence even on authors writing in Latin, such as Saxo Grammaticus (Simek, "Elusive" 247–75).

12. There is a translation of Adam's work in the manuscript AM 415, 4to, 12^r–12^v.

13. Author's translation.

14. This conceptualization is based on the medieval *mappae mundi*, particularly T-O maps, to be discussed below.

15. On medieval cartography, in particular the T-O maps, see Simek, "Skandinavische"; Simek, "Europa"; Simek, *Heaven;* Simek, "Shape."

16. Cf. the various articles in Harvey.

17. The edition by Miller 1895–98, Vol. 4, gives a distorted picture of this area as he separates the treatment of northeastern Europe (16–8) and northwestern Asia (24–8) into two different chapters.

18. On the location of the *Pygmei* in the Far North, see Seaver.

19. *Scythia major* answers to *Sviðþjóð in micla*, "Greater Sweden," in Snorri; see Simek, *Altnordische* 426.

20. Medieval and early modern terminology tends to be rather imprecise in this respect. The term *finnar* was used as an umbrella term for people that we, using modern ethnonyms, would designate as either Finns or Sámi.

21. See Seaver, esp. 69–74 for information on the *Skrælingar*, and 84–5 for information on Claudius Clavus.

WORKS CITED

Adam of Bremen. *Gesta Hammaburgensis ecclesiae pontificum.* Ed. B. Schmeidler. Hanover: Hahn, 1917. MGH Scriptores rerum Germanicarum 2.

Ásmundarson, V., ed. "Fundinn Noregr." *Fornaldarsögur Norðrlanda.* Vol. 2. Reykjavík, 1886. 16–20.

"Bárðar saga." *Harðar saga.* Eds. Þ. Vilmundarson and B. Vilhjálmsson. Reykjavík: Hið íslenzka fornritafélag, 1991. 99–172. Íslenzk fornrit 13.

Dreyer-Eimbcke, O. *Island, Grönland und das nördliche Eismeer im Bild der Kartographie seit dem 10. Jahrhundert.* Hamburg: Geograph. Ges, 1987. Mitteilungen der Geographischen Gesellschaft in Hamburg 77.

Gamborg Briså, B., and B. Lavold. *Kompassrosen: Orientering mot Nord.* Oslo: Nasjonalbiblioteket, 2009.

Hahn-Woernle, B. *Die Ebstorfer Weltkarte.* Ebstorf: Kloster Ebstorf, 1987.

Harvey, P.D.A., ed. *The Hereford World Map: Medieval World Maps and their Context.* London: British Library, 2006.

Heizmann, W. "Fenriswolf." Müller and Wunderlich 229–55.

———. "Midgardschlange. " Müller and Wunderlich 413–38.

Isidore of Seville. *Etymologiarum sive Originum Libri xx.* 2 vols. Ed. W.M. Lindsay. Oxford: Oxford UP, 1985.

Knauer, E.R. *Die Carta Marina des Olaus Magnus von 1539: Ein kartographisches Meisterwerk und seine Wirkung.* Göttingen: Gratia, 1981. Gratia 10.

Krabbo, H. "Nordeuropa in der Vorstellung Adams von Bremen." *Hansische Geschichtsblätter* 15 (1909): 37–51.

Kunin, D., trans. Phelpstead, C., ed. *A History of Norway and Passions and Miracles of the Blessed Óláfr.* London: Viking Society for Northern Research, 2001. Viking Society for Northern Research Text Series 13.

Magnus, O. *Historia de gentibus septentrionalibus.* Antwerpen: Johannes Bellerus, 1672.

Martianus Capella. *De nuptiis Philologiae et Mercurii*. Ed. F. Eyssenhardt. Leipzig: Teubner, 1866. Bibliotheca Scriptorum Graecorum et Romanorum Teubneriana.

Miller, K., ed. *Mappaemundi. Die ältesten Weltkarten*. 6 vols. Stuttgart: Roth, 1895–98.

Müller, U., and W. Wunderlich, eds. *Dämonen, Monster, Fabelwesen*. St. Gallen: UVK, 1999. Mittelalter Mythen 2.

Nagel, F. "Wissenschaft und neues Weltbild im Spiegel des Basler Globuspokals von Jakob Stampfer: Mit einem Ausblick auf den Tractatus de quadrante des Johannes von Gmunden." *Johannes von Gmunden—zwischen Astronomie und Astrologie*. Eds. R. Simek and M. Klein. Wien: Fassbaender, 2012. 131–49. Studia medievalia Septentrionalia 22.

Seaver, K.A. "Pygmies of the Far North." *Journal of World History* 19.1 (2008): 63–87.

Seidner, M. "Der Globuspokal des Züricher Goldschmieds Jakob Stampfer und die Karten Honters." *Zeitschrift für Siebenbürgische Landeskunde* 29 (2006): 227–9.

Simek, R. *Altnordische Kosmographie: Studien und Quellen zu Weltbild und Weltbeschreibung in Norwegen und Island vom 12. bis zum 14. Jahrhundert*. Berlin: de Gruyter, 1990. Ergänzungsbände zum Reallexikon der Germanischen Altertumskunde 4.

———. "Elusive Elysia, or: Which Way to Glæsisvellir? On the Geography of the North in Icelandic Legendary Fiction." *Sagnaskemmtun: Studies in Honour of Hermann Pálsson on his 65th Birthday, 26th May 1986*. Eds. R. Simek, J. Kristjánsson, and H. Bekker-Nielsen. Wien: Böhlau, 1986. 247–75. Philologica Germanica 8.

———. "Europa in der Vorstellung des mittelalterlichen Nordens." *Das Danewerk in der Kartographiegeschichte Nordeuropas*. Eds. D. Unverhau and K. Schietzel. Neumünster: Wachholtz, 1993. 63–77.

———. *Heaven and Earth in the Middle Ages*. Cambridge: Boydell, 1996.

———. *Lexikon der germanischen Mytholgie*. 3rd ed.. Stuttgart: Kröner, 2006. Kröners Taschenausgabe 368.

———. *Monster im Mittelalter: Die phantastische Welt der Wundervölker und Fabelwesen*. Köln: Böhlau, 2015.

———. "The Shape of the Earth in the Middle Ages and Medieval Mappaemundi." Harvey 293–303.

———. "Skandinavische Mappae Mundi in der europäischen Tradition." *Ein Weltbild vor Columbus: Die Ebstorfer Weltkarte. Interdisziplinäres Colloquium 1988*. Eds. H. Kugler and E. Michael. Weinheim: VCH, 1991. 167–84.

———. "Wunder des Nordens: Einfoetingar, Hornfinnar, Hundingjar und Verwandte." *triuwe. Studien zur Sprachgeschichte und Literaturwissenschaft: Gedächtnisbuch für*

Elfriede Stutz. Eds. K.-F. Kraft, E.-M. Lill, and U. Schwab. Heidelberg: Heidelberger Verl.-Anst., 1992. 69–90. Heidelberger Bibliotheksschriften 47.

Stahl, W.H., R. Johnson, and E.L. Burge, trans. *Martianus Capella and the Seven Liberal Arts.* 2 vols. New York: Columbia UP, 1971–77.

Storm, G., ed. *Monumenta Historica Norvegiæ: Latinske kildeskrifter til Norges historie i middelalderen.* Kristiania: Brøgger, 1880.

Thomas of Cantimpré. *Liber de Natura Rerum: Teil I, Text.* Ed. H. Boese. Berlin: de Gruyter, 1973.

Vilkuna, K. *Kainuu—Kvänlan: Ett finsk-norsk-svenskt problem.* Uppsala: Lundequist, 1969. Acta Academiae Regiae Gustavi Adolphi 46.

Wiklund K.B. "Om kvänerna och deras nationalitet." *Arkiv för nordisk filologi* 12 (1896): 103–17.

5 From Eiríkr the Red to Trolls in the Wilderness

The Development of Supernatural Greenland in the Old Norse Sagas

ELEANOR ROSAMUND BARRACLOUGH

INTRODUCTION

In the summer of 1341, a Norwegian priest left his home in Bergen, bound for the far west. His name was Ívarr Bárðarson and his destination was Greenland. Once safely on the other side of the ocean, Ívarr's job would be to run the bishop's estate at Garðar, in the region known as the Eastern Settlement. Situated on the green, grassy slopes between the deep fjord waters and the steep mountainsides, the bishop's residence boasted some of the most fertile land and finest cattle byres in the country. Irrigation channels brought water down from the hillsides to the farmed fields below. There was beef and wild caribou on the dinner table (unlike the blubbery seal that the region's poorer inhabitants had to put up with). Every summer, visiting merchants arrived from the east, anchoring their ships in the sheltered fjord waters. By the time the priest arrived in Greenland, there had been Norse settlers in the country for over 300 years. Perhaps for the residents of Garðar, it was unthinkable that their way of life would ever come to an end. But further north, the wind of change was already blowing.

Ívarr's description of Greenland, apparently composed when he returned to Norway after two decades, only survives in later manuscripts in which omissions and additions seem to have been made. Even so, the account indicates that changes were already afoot. Sailors making the long and dangerous journey to Greenland already had to find new routes because of the ice that now clogged the seas:

> From Snæfellsnes in Iceland, which is the closest point to Greenland,
> it is two days and two nights sailing due west to Gunnbjorn's skerries,
> which lie exactly between Greenland and Iceland. That was the old
> sailing route, but now ice comes down from the north of the ocean, so
> near to the aforementioned skerries that no one can sail the old route
> without putting their life in danger.[1]

Worse, during Ívarr's time in Greenland, he had been part of an expedition sent to investigate rumours of trouble further up the coast, in what was called the Western Settlement. According to the account, when they arrived they found "only horses, goats, cows and sheep there, all running wild, and no people, neither Christian nor heathen."[2] The *Skrælingar* (sing. *Skræling*), the Norse term for the nomadic hunter-gatherers who lived in the north of the country (the ancestors of modern Greenlanders), were blamed for having destroyed everything.

During the initial period of Norse occupation in Greenland (from c. 985 CE), conditions had been relatively favourable in the Norse settlements, known somewhat idiosyncratically as the Eastern Settlement (despite its location close to Greenland's southernmost tip) and the Western Settlement (despite being situated 300 miles further north, in the fjords inland from Greenland's modern capital, Nuuk). Judith Jesch amongst others has pointed out that "the summer pastures of Greenland would have seemed particularly lush and green to those raised in the rockier, volcanic island of Iceland" (Jesch 120; see also Seaver 21).

However, as average temperatures in the region began to decline over the twelfth to fifteenth centuries, the viability of Norse-Greenlandic society was placed increasingly under threat.[3] Within the country itself, subsistence failure was an ever-present danger in this marginal, seasonally vulnerable landscape—vulnerable, at least, in terms of the Norse-Greenlandic economic model, which relied on both hunting and farming—and by the fourteenth and fifteenth centuries, it seems a tipping point had been reached. At the same time, as Ívarr Bárðarson's account suggests, large volumes of sea ice had started to clog the traditional sailing routes to and from Greenland. This made it increasingly difficult for merchants and travellers to reach the country and trade Greenlandic resources such as walrus ivory and furs for essential supplies such as metal, wood, and grain. This difficulty was exacerbated by socio-political developments back east, such as plague epidemics (which reached Norway in the mid-fourteenth century and Iceland at the start of the fifteenth century), the growing trade and taxation monopoly of the Norwegian crown in the North Atlantic, and a change in European economic conditions that meant that ivory and furs could be acquired from regions more accessible than Greenland (see Arneborg, "Greenland" 308–10). Such reduced cultural contact and climate change seem to have been key to the decline of Norse Greenland, combined with other possible factors such as increasing hostilities with the Inuit population and settler impacts on the environment (for an overview of such factors see McGovern). Archaeological and written evidence suggests that the Western Settlement was abandoned around the mid-fourteenth century, particularly affected by deteriorating climatic conditions that made it difficult to cultivate the land and keep livestock (see Barlow et al.). What role, if any, the *Skrælingar* played—as Ívarr's account suggests—is unclear. In any case, approximately a century later, it seems that the Eastern Settlement had gone the same way. Soon, Norse Greenland would be little more than a distant memory.

Scientific studies and archaeological research give us some idea of the mechanisms for this decline, although the actual end of the settlement and fate of any remaining Norse Greenlanders is still a matter of speculation. There is little written evidence to ascertain how these changes

affected Norse-Greenlandic society and its interaction with the wider
world; certainly nothing survives from Greenland itself. What we do
have are the Norse-Icelandic sagas, some of which are set in Greenland
or include episodes that take place there. First and foremost, these are
literary texts rather than historical records, written in Iceland between
the thirteenth and fifteenth centuries but describing life in Iceland and
the wider Norse diaspora in the preceding centuries. Their unique blend
of fiction and history, oral narratives and literary shaping, makes them
an interesting—albeit complex—corpus to work with. While their
descriptions of Norse Greenland certainly cannot be taken as factually
rigorous accounts of life and society in the country, they provide us with
glimpses of this western outpost of the Norse cultural diaspora, as well
as insights into the interactions that took place between Greenland and
the wider world, and the oral tales that travelled from Greenland with
voyagers and traders sailing east to Iceland and Norway.

A broad chronological pattern emerges from these texts, for in those
thought to be earliest, a realistic Norse-Greenlandic society is described,
detailing the country's settlement by Eiríkr *inn rauði* ("Eiríkr the Red")
and his company, life in the settlements, explorations further west, and
the various legal and ecclesiastical machinations that take place in the
country. In later texts, however, this realism is gradually replaced with
a supernaturally tinged world of wildernesses, shipwrecks, and uncanny
happenings.[4] Eventually, the human community disappears altogether,
and visitors to Greenland's shores are confronted by an eerie world inhabited by trolls and ogres. The following discussion explores this shift from
relative social realism to wild, supernatural instability, examining possible
reasons for this development and what it reveals about the changing
perception of Greenland from the point of view of the wider Norse (and
specifically Icelandic) diaspora over the centuries.

Establishing a chronology for the sagas is no easy task, partly due to the
fact that many of the tales may have had long periods of oral development
before being recorded, partly due to the fact that they often continued to
develop and evolve as they were copied from manuscript to manuscript,

and partly due to the fact that relatively few of these manuscripts are still extant today. However, there is broad agreement that amongst the oldest texts can be counted *Grænlendinga þáttr* (late twelfth century), *Fóstbrœðra saga* (thirteenth century, but possibly set down before 1200; see Schach 1993), *Auðunar þáttr Vestfirzka* (early thirteenth century), and the two Vínland sagas *Grænlendinga saga* (early thirteenth century) and *Eiríks saga rauða* (early to mid-thirteenth century). Later texts include *Flóamanna saga* (late thirteenth/early fourteenth century), *Króka-Refs saga* (fourteenth century), *Bárðar saga* (late fourteenth century) and *Jökuls þáttr* and *Gunnars saga* (both late fourteenth/fifteenth century).[5]

A REALISTIC NORSE-GREENLAND

The earliest sagas set in Greenland describe the country's landscape and Norse society in detail. This is particularly true of *Grænlendinga þáttr* ("The Tale of the Greenlanders," also known as *Einars þáttr Sokkasonar* after its chief protagonist Einarr Sokkason), where many farmsteads, place names, and personal names are mentioned specifically. Acts are carried out "according to Greenlandic law,"[6] while the chief protagonist Einarr explicitly links the country's distinctive legal processes to its separate cultural identity, stating, "we wish to follow those laws that operate here."[7] The tale's references to a separate Greenlandic identity and the need for Greenlandic law to be upheld invite the possibility that the narrative was shaped with the interests of the Greenlandic community in mind, perhaps originating in an oral form in Norse Greenland itself before travelling with voyagers east to Iceland to be written down and developed within an Icelandic context. It has been suggested by Else Ebel (1999) that thirteenth-century Icelandic salvage laws are incorporated into the sole surviving version of the tale, preserved in the late fourteenth-century manuscript *Flateyjarbók*. If this is the case, then the tale underwent further development within an Icelandic context, even if its origins lay in Greenland. Nevertheless, it seems likely that whoever composed the tale had access to oral sources from Greenland or had been there personally;

it has even been suggested that some of the people who had been involved in the events narrated were still alive when the *þáttr* was recorded (Halldórsson 160).

Norwegian merchants play a prominent part in *Grœnlendinga þáttr*, highlighting the importance of the trade links between Greenland and the world back east. Elsewhere, in *Auðunar þáttr Vestfirzka* ("The Tale of Auðunn of the Westfjords") from the early thirteenth century, Greenland is set within a historically realistic context, despite reading like a "historified folktale," as Marlene Ciklamini has described it (72). Charting the travels of the impoverished Icelander Auðunn, the *þáttr* includes descriptions of Greenland's unique trading goods such as walrus ivory, walrus-hide rope, and a far-travelling polar bear, taken to the Danish court as a present for the king. The historical importance of such Greenlandic trade goods is also attested in sources such as the Norwegian text *Konungs skuggsjá* ("The King's Mirror") from c. 1250 and the Icelandic manuscript *Hauksbók* from c. 1300, which also contains descriptions of the Greenlanders' northern hunting grounds beyond present-day Disko Bay, where they went in the summer to obtain walrus ivory and skins (for details see Arneborg, "Greenland").

Briefly fast-forwarding to the fourteenth-century, *Króka-Refs saga* ("The Saga of Refr the Sly") also includes references to such Greenlandic trading goods, including a polar bear and chess pieces (presumably of walrus ivory) that are presented to the Norwegian king. When Refr himself arrives in Norway in disguise, his walrus-hide belt, dark hood, and spear set him apart, marking him out as an uncanny and mysterious figure. As the enigmatic man who has named himself "Narfi" disappears from the assembly, the king asks "who was that man, unknown to us, who stood before us for a while in a blue-black hooded cloak and belted with a big walrus-hide rope and with a spear in his hand, and where did he come from?"[8] It is indeed Refr, whose walrus-hide belt signals where he has come from, while his *blá* (blue-black) hood and spear hint at his bloody intentions (see Woolf 71, where she discusses how those who the sagas describe as being dressed in dark or *blá* clothing are often bent on vengeance). Later, at the Danish court, the king grants him estates in exchange for the valuable Greenlandic goods he has brought, including walrus-hide ropes for their ships, walrus ivory, furs, five polar bears, and fifty falcons (chapter 18). A reader might suspect that this is a rather exaggerated tally of finery, a suspicion that may support Elizabeth Ashman Rowe's (369) assertion that the inspiration for the overblown events described in this particular text seems to have come from earlier sagas rather than authentic historical traditions (this point will be returned to later in the discussion).

Spooling back to the thirteenth-century *Fóstbrœðra saga* ("The Saga of the Sworn Brothers"), we find the same representation of a realistic Norse Greenlandic society. In his survey of the representation of Greenland in the saga corpus, Jonathan Grove describes *Fóstbrœðra saga* as the saga "with the most realistic Greenlandic setting" amongst the "atavistic works that exploit their audiences' interest in the real or imagined accomplishments of their forebears" (33). The saga tracks Þormóðr Bersason, one of the two eponymous anti-heroes of the saga title, as he travels to Greenland to avenge his sworn brother Þorgeirr Hávarsson. He travels to the Eastern Settlement where he takes bloody vengeance on Þorgeirr's murderer Þorgímr *trölli* (troll), killing him and several members of his family. The Eastern Settlement is very much populated, and there is little sense of any overtly supernatural dimension in its portrayal.

Finally, the sagas most famously associated with Greenland and the Norse expeditions to the North American continent are the thirteenth-century Vínland sagas, *Grœnlendinga saga* ("The Saga of the Greenlanders") and *Eiríks saga rauða* ("The Saga of Eiríkr the Red"). There is a close relationship between the two in terms of their subject matter, parallel episodes and protagonists, but the general scholarly consensus is that this is a result of common oral traditions rather than a direct literary relationship. Like *Grœnlendinga þáttr*, *Grœnlendinga saga* seems to have been shaped by those with close connections to Greenlandic society—either through direct experience of the country or through knowledge of oral tales travelling from west to east—for descriptions of the country are relatively familiar and detailed, with the different characteristics of the Eastern and Western Settlements highlighted. Helge Ingstad has posited Greenlandic origins for *Grœnlendinga saga* precisely for this reason, since in comparison to *Eiríks saga*, Greenlanders dominate the saga. He suggests that the term "Greenland family saga" would describe the text admirably, since "it seems hardly likely that Icelandic sources would devote so much attention to four Greenlanders who were either unknown in Iceland, or at least of little interest to the people of that country" (Ingstad 153).

In both Vínland sagas, the Eastern Settlement is depicted as the more homely and welcoming of the two, perhaps partly because of its more easterly, southerly location, which would have made it a natural first port of call for ships arriving from the east. Thus, in *Eiríks saga* when Þorbjǫrn reaches Brattahlíð, "Eiríkr welcomed him joyfully and said it was good that he had come."[9] Yet in both settlements there is a sense of instability and marginality both geographically and culturally speaking, and in terms of the country's ability to support its Norse population, for famines, sicknesses, and unnerving pagan activities feature frequently. Such characteristics define the Western Settlement in particular, where they are conveyed with dramatic literary patterning that helps to shape the key events that take place there. For example, in both sagas we are introduced to the pagan farmer Þorsteinn *inn svartr* ("the black"), who shelters Þorsteinn Eiríksson and his wife, Guðríðr, when they are prevented from sailing west to Vínland (on the North American continent) by fierce storms that blow them back to Greenland. When he greets them in *Grœnlendinga saga*, he dampens the mood still further by linking the remoteness of their location to his pagan religious beliefs, stating lugubriously that "you will be very lonely staying with me...because I am very solitary; also I have another faith to you."[10] Things only get worse once winter sets in, for in both texts a deadly plague ravages the farmstead, followed by ghostly hauntings.

It is an intriguing possibility that part of the reason for this more negative, quasi-supernatural depiction of the Western Settlement—which is also present to a greater or lesser extent in *Grœnlendinga þáttr*, *Flóamanna saga*, and *Króka-Refs saga*—is the actual geographical and cultural conditions of the region. Situated 300 miles further north than its eastern counterpart, the Western Settlement was more geographically marginal despite its initially optimal climate, requiring a longer and more arduous voyage as meteorological conditions began to deteriorate at sea as on land. By 1350 the settlement seems to have collapsed, and it is possible that this geographical and cultural marginality is what is reflected in the more negative depiction of this more northerly site in the sagas (for details see Barlow et al.; McGovern). Nevertheless, the key point is that there *is* still a populated Western Settlement in these two texts, which is not the case for many of the later sagas, to which we now turn.

THE DEVELOPMENT OF SUPERNATURAL GREENLAND

In the fourteenth- and fifteenth-century sagas describing Greenland, the realistic saga society with its Eastern and Western Settlements is gradually replaced by a small human population under threat from the natural world and supernatural elements beyond. Eventually, the country is transformed into an icy wilderness populated by vulnerable humans and aggressive supernatural creatures. In the strange, troll-populated world of *Bárðar saga Snæfellsáss* ("The Saga of Bárðr, God of Snæfellsnes"), Helga Bárðardóttir drifts to Greenland from Iceland in seven days on an ice floe, where she is taken in by Eiríkr the Red and the community at Brattahlíð, in the Eastern Settlement. Yet this is not the full-bodied, wholly populated Eastern Settlement described in earlier texts such as *Grænlendinga þáttr*, *Fóstbræðra saga*, and the Vínland sagas. Rather, it is a small, threatened group open to attack, for "over the winter, trolls and monsters came down into Eiríksfjörðr and caused the greatest harm to men."[11] Perched on the edge of the Greenlandic landscape, Eiríkr's small community is faced with a coalition of forces that include the cold and dark of winter combined with malevolent supernatural creatures. Moreover, it is Helga who protects the group, for the manner of her arrival and her quasi-supernatural heritage (as the daughter of Bárðr Dumbsson, the half-giant half-troll hero of this strange saga) mark her out as "other" from the start: "the way in which she arrived was thought strange, and so by some she was called a troll."[12] Consequently, she is able to meet these creatures on equal terms, defending the human community from these eerie intruders.[13]

In *Flóamanna saga* ("The Saga of the People of Flói") and *Jökuls þáttr Búasonar* ("The Tale of Jökull, the son of Búi"), Greenland is presented most explicitly as an eerie, unstable world of trolls and magic. The same is true of *Gunnars saga Keldugnúpsfífls* ("The Saga of Gunnarr, the Fool of Keldugnúpr"), although Greenland is not explicitly mentioned, and may not represent an independent textual tradition. Indeed, Margrét Eggertsdóttir (250) has suggested that the text was pieced together from a number of other sagas, with the description of the shipwreck in the northern wilderness closely resembling that of *Jökuls þáttr*. Consequently, the following discussion will focus on *Flóamanna saga* and *Jökuls þáttr* rather than *Gunnars saga*.

Beginning with *Flóamanna saga*, the pagan god Þórr appears to the hero Þorgils on the voyage to Greenland and threatens to bring about a shipwreck if Þorgils refuses to believe in him, showing him a cliff "where ocean waves dashed against the rocks,— 'in such waves you will be and never escape.'"[14] Thus, the land ahead becomes associated with supernatural agency and menacing paganism, but worse is to come in Greenland itself, where sickness, madness, and death await the company in the wilderness. The mood is wintry and dark, the dead return to trouble the living, and there are fights with troll women over a beached whale. Both the human and supernatural populations of Greenland are in competition for the natural resources of the land, and the fact that the land is not bountiful enough to support everyone creates deadly tensions. Trapped in the wilds of the country during the winter, the company's livestock die, and even when spring comes "they couldn't get away because of the ice."[15]

The supernatural theme is most pronounced in *Jökuls þáttr*. The young hero Jökull is caught up in a ferocious shipwreck off the coast of Greenland, and is washed up in the wilderness where he finds a violent society of trolls and giants. There is no sense of a more realistic community elsewhere in the country; the only humans he encounters are Hvítserkr and Marsibilla, son and daughter of the Saracen king, who have been brought to Greenland and held captive through the witchcraft of the giant king Skrámr. As with Helga Bárðardóttir, Jökull is a quasi-supernatural figure himself, which seems to allow him access to Greenland's grisly society of trolls and ogres, located deep within the fjord. Devoid of human habitation, the Greenland that Jökull has entered is characterized by uncanny creatures with "frowning faces, long noses, and lips hanging down onto their chests."[16]

THE *ÓBYGGÐ*

In these later saga accounts of Greenland, this *óbyggð* ("wilderness" or, more literally, "uninhabited place") becomes an increasingly central location for episodes set in the country, ultimately supplanting the settlements entirely. By its very definition it should be "uninhabited," at least by humans, and so it is perhaps unsurprising that the experiences of unfortunate voyagers are largely negative. In *Flóamanna saga*, the topography of the *óbyggð* is threatening and claustrophobic, and the company cannot escape for many months because of the ice that traps their ship. When Þorgils' wife Þorey asks her husband if they might "seek a way out of the wilderness,"[17] his hopeless response is that he "could not see a way."[18] The phraseology is significant; literally, Þorgils cannot see "over" (*yfir*) the wilderness, for it is all encompassing and presses in around them. In *Jökuls þáttr*, the *óbyggð* is also the key setting, and the word is used despite the fact that this "uninhabited place" is home to a large community of non-human creatures. Jökull's initial contact with them is through two troll daughters whom he meets in the "wilderness in Greenland."[19] Later, one of them—by this time he has killed the other—takes him to the Yule Feast of Skrámr, who is, "king of all the uninhabited wilderness in Greenland, and all giants fear him."[20]

As might be expected, there are exceptions to any trend, and this is partly the case in the fourteenth-century text *Króka-Refs saga* ("The Saga of Refr the Sly"). In many ways the picture of Greenland that emerges is consistent with that presented in other later sagas; indeed, the very fact that the wilderness features so prominently in the narrative is significant. Nevertheless, unlike other later sagas, a realistic Norse-Greenlandic society is still in evidence, and Refr initially enters into the spirit of things, marrying a local girl, taking over a farm, and living peacefully there for eight years. Eventually, clashes with the community lead him to become a socially disruptive element within it, and he is forced to disappear into the natural world beyond the settlements. In contrast with the miserable months in the wild endured by the company of *Flóamanna saga*, Refr is able to build a fine home in his wilderness: "a fortification stood near the edge of the shore. They went up to it, walked around it and considered it carefully, and thought that they had never seen a building so beautiful."[21] Significantly, Elizabeth Ashman Rowe (369) has noted that although *Króka-Refs saga* "has very little connection with historical traditions," archaeological excavations of a Norse site at Narssaq in Greenland seem to corroborate some of the details of Refr's fortification as described in the text. In particular, there is some correlation with the unusual waterworks system that Refr uses to extinguish the fires lit to smoke him out.[22] This is a reminder of just how little is known about life in Norse Greenland, the timeframe for the decline of the settlements and their eventual collapse, and the complex relationship between these historical events and the saga literature describing the region.

WHY THE SHIFT?

From the earliest times, Norse Greenland seems to have occupied a unique geographical and cultural place in the collective imagination of the wider Norse diaspora; as Vésteinn Ólason has observed in terms of the country's depiction in saga literature, "outside Iceland it is particularly the remote northern regions, Finnmark and Greenland, which seem to be the refuge for forces beyond the framework of conventional nature" (*Dialogues* 82). Even so, in the first centuries of the settlement it seems likely that, as Niels Lynnerup has suggested, Greenland was seen as "an extension of habitable lands and fjords stretching over the Shetlands, Orkneys, Faeroes, and Iceland all the way to Labrador and Newfoundland" (294). Therefore, although the early sagas' descriptions of Greenland might be tinged with a sense of uncanny "otherness" as befits the country's location on the north-western edge of the Norse world, it is only in later texts that this uncanny tinge becomes the dominant hue.

When considering reasons for this shift from social realism to supernatural instability in the depiction of Greenland in the Old Norse-Icelandic sagas, a number of literary, geographical, historical, and cultural factors must be taken into account. Starting with the literary corpus itself, it is true that over the centuries there was a broad movement away from the realistic narrative themes of the genre known as the *Íslendingasögur* ("sagas of Icelanders") and a growing penchant for more fantastical stories generally classified as *fornaldarsögur* ("sagas of ancient times") and *riddarasögur* ("chivalric sagas"). The interplay between these changing literary fashions and the adverse social, political, and geographical conditions that overtook Norse Greenland is crucial to understanding the changing picture of the country that emerges from the sagas. Such a relationship has been noted by Jonathan Grove, who states that

> [t]he tendency towards the adoption of a narrative mode concerned
> with superhuman feats in outlandish settings complies with the
> changing generic parameters of post-classical saga literature in the
> 14th century. It is nevertheless striking that the remaking of Greenland
> as a rendezvous for fabulous adventures...becomes most apparent at a
> time when regular communications with Greenland were diminishing,
> but, strangely perhaps, not necessarily before they had ceased
> altogether. (37)

While I agree almost entirely with Grove's comments, it is in fact this intervening period before contact was lost altogether that may be most significant rather than strange, for during this time it is likely that reports of Greenland returning east with the sailors would have been increasingly negative.[23] In time, reports of blocked sea routes, storms, and failing resources, meagre trading goods, and perhaps even incomers from the north would have entered into the broad cultural consciousness of Norse-Icelandic society to be reimagined and stylized in the saga narratives (which were developing a taste for the fantastic and outlandish in any case). In the collective saga imagination, the outermost colony of the Norse diaspora became a brave new world fit not for mankind, but rather for trolls, giants, and other ungodly creatures.

AUTHOR'S NOTE

This chapter was written when the author held a Leverhulme Early Career Fellowship at the University of Oxford. In conducting this research, the author wishes to acknowledge the generous support of the Leverhulme Trust and The Queen's College, University of Oxford. Since then, this research topic has been developed further in the author's monograph, *Beyond the Northlands: Viking Voyages and the Old Norse Sagas* (Oxford University Press, 2016).

NOTES

1. "Item fraa Snefelsnes aff Island, som er stackist till Grönnland, 2 Dage och thou Netters Seyling, rett i Vester att zeylle, och der liger Gunbjernerschier rett paa Mittveyen emellum Grönland och Island. Thette vaar gammell Saylling; en nu er kommen Is udaff landnorden Botnen saa ner forschreffne Scher, att ingen kan uden Liffs Fare denn gamble Leed seyle" (Magnusen and Rafn 250).

2. "...noch Heste, Geder, Nød, Faar, alt villdt och ingen Follch, christenn eller hedenn" (Magnusen and Rafn 259).

3. See Kuijpers et al., which shows how the Western Settlement and northern hunting grounds (beyond the Arctic Circle, in the area now known as Disko Bay) had already experienced major climatic deterioration in the early 1200s. The Eastern Settlement was not so badly affected until c. 1400, when the fjords began to block with ice during the summer, thus limiting sailing and farming in coastal areas.

4. This has also been noted and discussed by Jonathan Grove in his article on the literary patterns associated with Greenland (33). I am extremely grateful to Dr. Grove for providing me with a draft of his article prior to its publication.

5. For more on the dating of these sagas and their earliest manuscripts see Grove (33) and Ólason ("Family" 114–6).

6. "at grænlenzkum lǫgum" ("Grœnlendinga þáttr" 279).

7. "viljum vér þau lǫg hafa, er hér ganga" ("Grœnlendinga þáttr" 273).

8. "hverr var maðr þessi, oss ókunnr, er stóð fyrir oss um hríð í blám kufli ok svarðreip mikit um sik ok spjót í hendi, eða hvaðan er hann?" ("Króka-Refs saga" 154).

9. "Eiríkr tekr vel við honum, með blíðu, ok kvað þat vel, er hann var þar kominn" ("Eiríks saga rauða" 209).

10. "fásinni er mikit með mér at vera...því at ek em einþykkr mjǫk; annan sið hefi ek ok en þér hafið" ("Grœnlendinga saga" 258).

11. "um vetrinn kómu troll ok óvættir ofan í Eiríksfjörð ok gerðu mönnum it mesta mein" ("Bárðar saga" 116).

12. "hon þótti ok með undarligu móti þar hafa komit, ok fyrir þat var hon tröll kölluð af sumum mönnum" ("Bárðar saga" 115).

13. In this saga, Snæfellsnes in western Iceland is also populated by strange creatures, insofar as it is home to the trollish Bárðr, his kin, and several other non-human inhabitants. However, the saga's treatment of Snæfellsnes is as a geographically complex, realistic location full of place-names, as may befit the purpose of the story (see Barraclough, "Following," esp. 34–5). By contrast, Greenland's Eastern Settlement is presented as vague and sketchy, with little sense of realism. This stands in stark contrast to older texts such as *Grœnlendinga þáttr*, which includes the names of several places and farmsteads (see earlier in this discussion).

14. "þar sem sjóvarstraumr brast í björgum,— 'í slíkum bylgjum skaltu vera ok aldri ór komast'" ("Flóamanna saga" 279).

15. "máttu þeir eigi burt leita fyrir ísum" ("Flóamanna saga" 286).

16. "ófrýnligar, nefsíðar, og hekk vörrin ofan á bringu" ("Jökuls þáttr" 49).

17. "burt leita ór óbyggðum, ef þeir mætti" ("Flóamanna saga" 287).

18. "eigi yfir þat sjá" ("Flóamanna saga" 287).

19. "óbyggðum í Grænlandi" ("Jökuls þáttr" 50).

20. "konungr er yfir öllum óbyggðum í Grænlandi, og allir jötnar eru hræddir við hann" ("Jökuls þáttr" 54).

21. "vikrki stóð nær á framanverðum sævarbakkanum. Þeir gengu þangat til ok umhverfis ok hyggja at því vandliga ok þykkjast eigi sét hafa jafnfagrt smíði" (Króka-Refs saga" 140).

22. Irrigation systems were a feature of many farms in Norse Greenland. The bishop's residence at Garðar (now called Igaliku) boasted an impressive network of water

channels that can still be seen today, running down the mountainside to the flat fields by the fjord. For more information see Arneborg ("Greenlandic Irrigation").

23. Building on discussions that came from the ICASS 2011 "Supernatural North" panel, I have explored this subject within the context of saga depictions of sea journeys to and from Norway, Iceland, and Greenland, where I argue that many of the same meteorological and socio-political factors are responsible for the increasingly ferocious storms and shipwrecks experienced by Norse voyagers heading west. See Barraclough, "Sailing."

WORKS CITED

Arneborg, J. "Greenland and Europe." Fitzhugh and Ward. 304–17.

———. "Greenlandic Irrigation Systems on a West Nordic Background: An Overview of the Evidence of Irrigation Systems in Norse Greenland c. 980–1450 AD." *Water Management in Medieval Rural Economy*. Ed. J. Klápste. Prague: Institute of Archaeology, Academy of Sciences of the Czech Republic, 2005. 137–45. Památky Archeologické, Supplementum 17 / Ruralia 5.

"Auðunar þáttr Vestfirzka." *Vestfirðinga sögur*. Eds. B.K. Þórólfsson and G. Jónsson. Reykjavík: Hið íslenzka fornritafélag, 1943. 119–276. Íslenzk fornrit 6.

Barlow, L.K., et al. "Interdisciplinary Investigations of the End of the Norse Western Settlement in Greenland." *The Holocene* 7 (1997): 489–500.

Barraclough, E.R. *Beyond the Northlands: Viking Voyages and the Old Norse Sagas*. Oxford: Oxford UP, 2016.

———. "Following the Trollish Baton Sinister: Ludic Design in *Bárðar saga Snæfellsáss*." *Viking and Medieval Scandinavia* 4 (2008): 15–43.

———. "Sailing the Saga Seas: Narrative, Cultural and Geographical Perspectives in the North Atlantic Voyages of the Íslendingasögur." *Journal of the North Atlantic* 18 (2012): 1–12.

"Bárðar saga." *Harðar saga*. Eds. B.K. Þórólfsson and G. Jónsson. Reykjavík: Hið íslenzka fornritafélag, 1991. 99–172. Íslenzk fornrit 13.

Ciklamini, M. "*Exempla* in an Old Norse Historiographic Mold." *Neophilogus* 81 (1997): 71–87.

Ebel, E. "Der Grœnlendinga þáttr—aktuelle oder antiquarische Geschichtsperspektive?" *Die Aktualität der Saga: Festschrift für Hans Schottmann*. Ed. S.T. Andersen. Berlin: De Gruyter, 1999. 13–25. Ergänzungsbände zum Reallexikon der Germanischen Altertumskunde 21.

Eggertsdóttir, M. "Gunnars saga Keldugnúpsfífls." Pulsiano 250.

"Eiríks saga rauða." *Eyrbyggja saga*. Eds. E.Ó. Sveinsson and M. Þórðarson. Reykjavík: Hið íslenzka fornritafélag, 1935. 195–237. Íslenzk fornrit 4.

Fitzhugh, W.W., and E.I. Ward, eds. *Vikings: The North Atlantic Saga*. Washington, DC: Smithsonian, 2000.

"Flóamanna saga." *Harðar saga*. Eds. B.K. Þórólfsson and G. Jónsson. Reykjavík: Hið íslenzka fornritafélag, 1991. 229–327. Íslenzk fornrit 13.

"Fóstbrœðra saga." *Vestfirðinga sögur*. Eds. B.K. Þórólfsson and G. Jónsson. Reykjavík: Hið íslenzka fornritafélag, 1943. 119–276. Íslenzk fornrit 6.

Grove, J. "The Place of Greenland in Medieval Icelandic Saga Narrative." *Journal of the North Atlantic* Special Vol. 2 (2009): 30–51.

"Grœnlendinga þáttr." *Eyrbyggja saga*. Eds. E.Ó. Sveinsson and M. Þórðarson. Reykjavík: Hið íslenzka fornritafélag, 1935. 271–92. Íslenzk fornrit 4.

"Grœnlendinga saga." *Eyrbyggja saga*. Eds. E.Ó. Sveinsson and M. Þórðarson. Reykjavík: Hið íslenzka fornritafélag, 1935. 243–69. Íslenzk fornrit 4.

"Gunnars saga Keldugnúpsfífls." *Kjalnesinga saga*. Ed. J. Halldórsson. Reykjavík: Hið íslenzka fornritafélag, 1959. 341–79. Íslenzk fornrit 14.

Halldórsson, Ó. "Einars þáttr Sokkasonar." Pulsiano 160.

Ingstad, H. *The Norse Discovery of America. Volume II. The Historical Background and the Evidence of the Norse Settlement Discovered in Newfoundland*. Oslo: Norwegian UP, 1985.

Jesch, J. "Geography and Travel." McTurk 119–35.

"Jökuls þáttr Búasonar." *Kjalnesinga saga*. Ed. J. Halldórsson. Reykjavík: Hið íslenzka fornritafélag, 1959. 45–59. Íslenzk fornrit 14.

"Króka-Refs saga." *Kjalnesinga saga*. Ed. J. Halldórsson. Reykjavík: Hið íslenzka fornritafélag, 1959. 117–60. Íslenzk fornrit 14.

Kuijpers, A., et al. "Impact of Medieval Fjord Hydrography and Climate on the Western and Eastern Settlements in Norse Greenland." *Journal of the North Atlantic* 6 (2014): 1–13.

Lynnerup, N. "Life and Death in Norse Greenland." Fitzhugh and Ward 285–94.

Magnusen, F., and C.C. Rafn, eds. *Grønlands Historiske Mindesmærker*. Tredje bind. Kjøbenhavn: Möller, 1845.

McGovern, T.H. "The Demise of Norse Greenland." Fitzhugh and Ward 327–39.

McTurk, R., ed. *A Companion to Old Norse-Icelandic Literature and Culture*. Oxford: Blackwell, 2005.

Ólason, V. *Dialogues with the Viking Age: Narration and Representation in the Sagas of Icelanders*. Reykjavík: Heimskringla, 1998.

———. "Family Sagas." McTurk 101–18.

Pulsiano, P., ed. *Medieval Scandinavia: An Encyclopedia.* New York: Garland, 1993.
Garland Encyclopedias of the Middle Ages 1.

Rowe, E.A. "Króka-Refs saga." Pulsiano 369.

Schach, P. "Fóstbrœðra saga." Pulsiano 216–8.

Seaver, K.A. *The Frozen Echo: Greenland and the Exploration of Norse America ca. A.D. 1000–1500.* Stanford: Stanford UP, 1996.

Wolf, K. "The Color Blue in Old Norse-Icelandic Literature." *Scripta Islandica* 57 (2006): 55–78.

6 Winter's Flesh

Septentrio *and the Monstrous Female Body in Late Medieval Medicine and Theology*

BRENDA S. GARDENOUR WALTER

IN 1589 AND 1590, James VI of Scotland, soon to be James I of England, found himself crossing the perilous North Sea on errands relating to his engagement and subsequent marriage to Anne of Denmark. In each instance, raging storms pinned his ship to the coast of Norway, preventing his return home. Following the specific rationality of late medieval and early modern Christian demonology espoused by his Dutch colleagues, James attributed the storms to the maleficence of treasonous Scottish witches who sought his death. Under pain of torture, Anna Koldings, one of the accused witches of North Berwick, confessed that she and her fellow witches had indeed raised the storm winds through the power of demons, which travelled on the cold air and climbed the keel of James' ship to toss it to and fro (Normand and Roberts). Although Anna and her sisters were merely women, falsely accused and executed as traitors to the crown, we might imagine them as James did in the second book of his *Daemonologie*: evil creatures who could suddenly and violently "raise stormes and tempests in the aire, either upon Sea or land," an act made "very possible" because of their master Satan's "affinitie with the aire as being a spirite, and having such power of the forming and mooving thereof" (James 46). Likewise in *Macbeth*, Shakespeare described the weird sisters, themselves a commemoration of the North Berwick witches, as commanders of the tempestuous storm and "the fog, the filthy air" (I.i.12; cf. Thompson).

This imaginary but deadly female was often depicted as a desiccated woman in the winter of her life, enrobed in black rags and with a sickly pallor, who could raise the storm winds and commit acts of maleficence through her association with demons. She was not a creation of the sixteenth century, although the witch hunts during this period did much to confirm her existence and enhance her mystique. Instead, the aged witch was a monster stitched together by theologians in the academic milieu of the thirteenth and fourteenth centuries. Many of these scholars were members of the Dominican Order, who applied the authoritative languages of Aristotelian natural philosophy, categorical logic, and learned medicine to theological discourse on women's bodies and souls. What began as an academic exercise in the medieval universities would become the theoretical substance of a practical inquisitors' handbook, the fifteenth-century *Malleus Maleficarum* ("The Hammer of the Witches"), which defined the physical and spiritual characteristics of the witch and her diabolical powers in concrete terms. This authoritative text served as the foundation for the European witch hunts, and it was undoubtedly this text, and the icy witch that crept through its pages, that kept James and his Dutch confidants shaking in their pyjamas when the cold, dry north wind rattled their windowpanes at night.

The theological construction of the icy flesh of the witch and her affiliation with the wind—particularly the North wind, or *Septentrio*—is rooted in learned conceptions of the cosmos and the microcosmic human body that functioned within it, both of which were shaped by the natural philosophy of Aristotle. The Aristotelian cosmos, the closed system within which the laws of physics and metaphysics might function, was a concept shared across the academic disciplines in the late medieval universities, from the *trivium* and *quadrivium* through the graduate fields of law, medicine and theology. According to Aristotle, the cosmos was composed of several concentric crystalline spheres, nesting like *matryoshka* dolls: beyond the outermost sidereal sphere lay the realm of the Prime Mover, understood to be God by late medieval theologians, who created the cosmos and set it into motion out of love (Metaph. 6:7). Below the sidereal sphere lay those of the planets, ever spinning in perfect, circular harmony through the fifth element: ether. In the planetary realm above the moon, all movement was circular and eternal, and change—in any form—could not exist. Below the moon, however, the cosmos became a very different place, a world of chaotic and often violent motion. Following Empedocles and Plato, Aristotle held that the world below the moon was composed of four elements, each of which had its own set of qualities and natural place of rest (Metaph. 1:3,7, Gen. corr, 1:1 and 2:1). At the centre of the cosmos lay cold and dry earth, the most corrupt, unstable, and therefore heaviest of all elements, upon which ran elemental water, cold and wet. Above earth and water rose the lighter elements: air, which was hot and moist and extended into the sky far beyond human vision, and fire, which was hot and dry and burned in a fiery ring at the outermost perimeter of the earth's atmosphere. It was here that the lightest element on earth—fire—came into contact with the ethereal realm of the divine.[1] For Aristotle, and those who would adopt his natural philosophy, purity and goodness would come to be associated with that which was warm, while corruption and evil would forever be linked with coldness.

Of the natural forces at work below the moon, medieval natural philosophers and theologians found the nature of the wind extremely perplexing. According to Aristotle, the earth's atmosphere was composed of elemental air made manifest in physical phenomena, including rain, clouds, and wind.[2] Atmospheric air was a product of water vapour and a "dry exhalation from the earth," which produced clouds as it warmed and rain as it cooled. Aristotle postulated that air circulated not only vertically because of continual elemental transformation and the laws of sublunary physics, but also horizontally because of the spherical rotation of the Prime Mover, for "it is the revolution of the heaven which carries the air with it and causes its circular motion" (Mete. 1:3). Problematically, however, atmospheric air did not maintain its circular path, but instead moved erratically across the face of the earth in the form of wind. Aristotle argued that terrestrial winds were in part "earthy exhalations" that rose from the four cardinal directions,[3] with the North wind, or Boreas (Gr. Βορέας, Lat. *Septentrio*), being cold and dry, followed by the south wind, or Notus (Gr. Νότος, Lat. *Meridies*), which was hot and wet, the east wind Eurus (Gr. Εὖρος, Lat. *Oriens*), which was cold and wet, and Zephyrus (Gr. Ζέφυρος, Lat. *Occidens*), the west wind, which was hot and dry.[4] For medieval theologians, the long-distant heirs of Aristotle, the winds had a multi-factorial genesis and were as much supernatural as natural, being laden with unseen forces. The cardinal winds, for example, were named after the Greek *Anemoi* (Ανεμοι), or wind gods, who directed the gales according to their temperament. In medieval manuscripts, *Septentrio*, so named after the seven-star oxen constellation associated with the northern sky, is also known as *Boreas*, Greek god of the North wind. This name translates as "The Devouring One," a reference to his biting breath as well as his violent and unpredictable temper. Medieval wind diagrams reveal another, less obvious, link to the supernatural world of antiquity: the belief that the winds carry demons. In the ancient world, the wind was believed to be teeming with spirits or δαίμονες, which might be good (εὐδαίμονες), bad (κακοδαίμονες), or neutral. Medieval Christian theology, of course, did not allow for either good or neutral demons, only evil ones. In wind diagrams, therefore, the demons of the air were often drawn as dark, winged creatures that were both the source and substance of the tempestuous winds that flew from their mouths (Obrist). By the thirteenth century, theologians argued that *Septentrio*—being the coldest and driest wind—carried the wickedest and most deadly of demons.[5]

According to medieval medical theory, the wicked North wind could penetrate the body and influence one's physical health and, through the pneuma, change the very shape of one's being. The human body, constructed of fire, air, water, and earth, was a microcosm unbounded and open to superlunary forces—such as the movement and influence

of the stars—and sublunary forces—not least of which was the wind—
which could disrupt a healthy humoral balance, thereby causing illness.[6]
The Hippocratic treatise, "Airs, Waters and Places," details the four winds
and their influence on the body. Because the south wind, or the plague
wind, was hot and moist, it caused the body to swell with moist humours.
Septentrio, on the other hand, was cold and dry and engendered the
production of the cold and dry humour, black bile, resulting in melancholia, as well as acute coughs and colds. Although the north and south
winds were equally dangerous, Hippocrates argued that the sporadic
blowing of both in a given region was deadly, for the body would swell
and dry, heat and cool too rapidly and become radically imbalanced.[7]
Building on the Hippocratic construction of the terrestrial winds and
their effect on the physical body, Galen elaborated a theory of pneuma,
by which the winds might enter the body through the breath and change
the nature of the human soul.[8] According to Galen, air entered the spongy
tissue of the lungs, where it was converted to a more subtle form of air, or
pneuma. This pneuma was then drawn to the left ventricle of the heart,
where it came into contact with superheated blood that rarified it into
vital pneuma. From there it was drawn to the brain where it was transformed into two varieties of psychic pneuma: sensory and kinetic. In
Galenic theory, pneuma functioned not only as the life force responsible
for sense perception and motion, but also as the fundamental essence of
the human soul, which he divides into three elements, following Aristotle:
the spiritive soul, which dwells in the heart; the appetitive soul, which
dwells in the liver; and the rational soul, which resides in the brain.[9] The
rational soul not only governed cognitive functions, such as imagination,
reason, and memory, and physical functions, such as sense perception and
motion, but it also determined the very nature and shape of an
individual's human body.[10]

While bitter *Septentrio* might corrupt any human being, late medieval
theologians argued that the bodies and souls of women were far more
susceptible to the destructive power of the North wind—and the demonic
beings that rode upon it—than those of men. Following Aristotle, the

male body was held to be the paradigm of physical perfection. Hot and dry with firm and powerful flesh, the male physiological system functioned at peak efficiency. Because of its innate heat, the male body digested its food completely into humoural blood, which was then refined into muscle, hair, and sperm, while any excess toxins were purged through sweat. Just as the strength and heat of the properly formed male body protected it from cold dry winds of the north, so too did fortitude and ardent prayer protect him from the influence of cold-bodied demons, themselves composed of air, that dwelled within it. Women, however, were not so blessed. Through the process of Aristotelian categorical inversion, theologians constructed the female body in opposition to male perfection: cold and moist with loose and spongy flesh, female physiology was completely inefficient.[11] Her lack of heat made it impossible to fully refine the blood that resulted from imperfect digestion into hair or muscles, and so she required a receptacle for the storage and periodic disposal of bodily toxins and waste blood (Dean-Jones). The womb, unique to a woman's anatomy, became the locus of her toxicity, a sign of her imperfection and corruption. Cold and moist, a woman's body could not properly heat the air that entered her lungs and convert it to vital pneuma; for this reason, her mind was as slow and irrational as her flesh, her soul corrupt and longing for completion.

According to medieval theologians, a woman's only hope for protection against cold corruption was a chaste life of ardent prayer: the life of a holy woman. As the paradigm of female perfection, the holy woman is depicted in hagiographical sources as young and virginal, her rosy cheeks a sign of a body and soul warmed by prayer and communion with the divine. One holy woman, Lutgard of Aywières, became so fervent in her devotions that she achieved ecstatic union with Christ, a fiery experience that burned off the dross within her, rarefied her soul, and purified her flesh. In his account of Lutgard's life, the thirteenth-century Dominican theologian Thomas Cantimpré writes that she became so pure that she produced thaumaturgic oil from her breasts and ceased menstruating (Newman and King). Infused with divine pneuma, Lutgard's miraculous flesh became so

light as to float on air like warm and dry elemental fire and, in this levita-
tion, rise closer toward the divine ether that was her mystical home. The
warmth of prayer and the fire of the Holy Spirit, then, had the power to
heal women of their fundamental coldness, the source of their physical,
mental, and spiritual corruption. While devout women in controlled environments might attain the purity of the divine, most women left to their
own devices were likely to fall victim to their cold, moist natures and the
temptations of the flesh (Caciola).

The corrupt nature of female flesh, its toxicity, rapacious desire, and
openness to cold and dark evil forces is detailed in *De Secretis Mulierum*
("On the Secrets of Women"), a thirteenth-century medico-theological
treatise attributed to Pseudo-Albertus Magnus (Lemay). Written as an
exposé on the secret workings of the female body, the treatise focuses on
the toxic nature of the menses. Of particular concern is fetid menstrual
blood, which, retained too long in the uterus, corrupts and produces cold
and dry poisonous fumes that permeate the flesh. These toxic fumes
fused with the pneuma and might rise to the brain, causing melancholia
or mania; they might also escape the body through the breath, sweat,
and saliva. Since medieval theories of vision postulated that the act of
seeing was accomplished through the projection of one's pneuma, toxic
vapours might even be communicated through a woman's cold glance,
or the evil eye (Smith xi). As a result of their cold and moist natures,
younger women constantly craved contact with warm and dry males as a
means of balancing out their systems. Should their uteruses become dry,
our author argues, women must seek warm, moist sperm to placate that
wandering and thirsty animal, the womb. Even more dangerous than the
body of an irrational, carnal, and hungry young woman was that of the
aged woman, still rapacious in her desires but unable to seduce any man,
who had ceased menstruating and whose body had become desiccated and
intensely cold. With neither the vital heat necessary to burn off poisonous
humours nor the process of menstruation to remove toxins from the body,
nor even the ability to abscond with male moisture and heat through
sexual contact, the older woman became the most poisonous creature of

all. The glance, the touch, the breath of the hungry and haggard crone might kill upon contact, much like the icy, demon-laden north wind.

The *De Secretis Mulierum* of Pseudo-Albertus, combined with the authoritative demonology of the thirteenth-century Dominican, Thomas of Aquinas, facilitated the development of medico-theological theories of witchcraft. Aquinas argued that women, weak and wanton, would offer themselves sexually to demonic beings, which tempted them in the guise of men. In his homily notes on Matthew 8:23 (Fretté 208–9), Aquinas argues that there are four winds of temptation, the strongest of which is the "infestation of demons," which he claims is the icy wind of Sirach, in which the "cold north wind bloweth, and the water congealeth into crystal" (Sir. 43:22). Composed of coagulated cold air, demons and their master, Satan, could be discerned by their icy flesh and foul breath. Also like their master, demons were cold and dry and therefore associated with elemental earth, black bile, the season of late autumn, and the coming of winter, and death, both spiritual and physical. Late medieval demonology combined with theologized medical authority served as the foundation for treatises such as Johannes Nider's *Formicarius* of 1437 (Tschacher), in which we find the first explicit connections between corrupt female physiology, female wantonness, and irrationality, and collusion with demons and the devil. In the clerical imaginations of men like Nider, the evil woman—no longer merely the victim of temptation—was ever surrounded by hovering demons, icy and cold, awaiting her command (Bailey 978). Through her demonic pact, the witch—who was otherwise powerless save for her toxicity—became the master of natural forces such as storms and wind. She also craved the warm, moist Christian blood of children, a parody of the Eucharist and integral part of the Black Mass. Her corrupt physiology and her demonic pneuma commanded it.

Nider's ideas were reified in Kramer and Sprenger's *Malleus Maleficarum*, an inquisitorial manual that came to define witchcraft for a clerical and lay audience. While questioning the witchcraft paradigm set out in these earlier texts, skeptical sources such Martin Castañega's *Treatise on Witchcraft* and Reginald Scot's *The Discoverie of Witchcraft* did much to proliferate and reinforce deeply held cultural ideas of witches and their strange natures. In all of these texts, the crone's body, already frigid and dry, is assumed to be not only the most toxic, but also the most susceptible to the wiles of Satan and his demons. Having entered into a Satanic pact, often through sexual communion with the Devil and his icy cold member, the witch's pneuma would become imbued with the icy air of which evil spirits were made. Since pneuma shaped the form of the flesh, the witch's physical being reflected her demon-winded interior: pale, twisted, swathed in black, and cold to the touch, a haggard creature approaching winter. Composed of demonic air, she herself became as a demon, a rider of the wind and commander of icy cold, crystal-laden *Septentrio*, the winter wind, the end of life. Little wonder that King James feared the power of witches and their command of the North wind, all those centuries ago.

Bubble, bubble, toil, and trouble. The frigid witch born beneath the quills of thirteenth- and fourteenth-century clerics still rides the winds of our imaginations. From the old New England saying, "colder than a witch's teat," to the White Witch of Narnia, the icy enchantress of the North remains with us—even if only to ride the cold October winds as they twist through the trees, heralding the coming of the North wind of winter, with its promise of darkness and snow.

NOTES

1. Where Greek philosophers such as Anaximenes, Empedocles, and Plato had postulated that ether was also a form of clear air, a fifth element located in the terrestrial realm below the fiery ring, Aristotle argued that ether was unique from the four earthly elements and existed only in the celestial realm. The "first element" from which all others sprang, divine ether, was the immaterial material of the cosmos; "unaffected by change and decay," it revolved "by nature in a circle—eternally" (Wildberg 12). Although ether, because of its perfect and eternal nature, could not actively interact with the earthly elements, it did, however, come into physical contact with the ring of fire that brushed along its underbelly. Here, at the boundary, the atmosphere of the divine celestial realm and that of the earthly

realm made a connection that facilitated the conceptualization of an elemental gradient that rose from heavy, dross earth to lightest air and fire and ultimately to divine ether. For later medieval theologians, this atmospheric matrix of ether, fire, and air would become the conduit through which moved celestial beings such as angels, divine spirits, and even demonic entities.

2. On the complex names for the variety of winds and airs, see Lloyd 136.

3. There are several names for the winds in Greek; the ones given here are the most standard. For instance, Aristotle gives *Aparctias* (ἀπαρκτίας) as well as *Boreas* for the north wind, and Timosthenes uses *Aparctias* for the north wind and *Boreas* for the northeast, whereas Theophrastus uses only *Boreas*. For the east, Aristotle uses *Apeliotes* (ἀπηλιώτης), while *Eurus* is a southeasterly wind for him, Theophrastus, and Timosthenes. For clarity, throughout this chapter Aristotle's terms have been used for the Greek.

4. Aristotle, Mete. 1:3. Between each of the cardinal winds blew a total of twelve intermediate winds. The qualities of these winds, however, are less than clear. It would seem that two distinct models were at work in determining the qualities of the cardinal winds. In *Airs, Waters and Places*, Hippocrates asserts that the north wind is cold and dry, while the south wind is cold and moist. This contradicts the *annus–mundus–homo* model preserved in the *De Medicina* of Isidore of Seville and embraced by late medieval academic medicine.

5. According to a thirteenth-century *Etymologia*: "...unde que merito diaboli forman inducit qui ab...frigore...corda constringit." Online at: http://www.henry-davis.com/MAPS/EMwebpages/205L.html

6. The wind, along with other sublunary factors such as diet, sleeping and waking, retention, and excretion would come to be known as the Galenic "non-naturals," which worked in conjunction with the "naturals" (humours, organs, elements) to prevent or promote the "contra-naturals," namely disease. See Ballester and Arrizabalaga.

7. Hippocrates, Morb. Sacr.: "Therefore, they are attacked during changes of the winds, and especially south winds, then also with north winds, and afterwards also with the others. These are the strongest winds, and the most opposed to one another, both as to direction and power. For, the north wind condenses the air, and separates from it whatever is muddy and nebulous, and renders it clearer and brighter, and so in like manner also, all the winds which arise from the sea and other waters; for they extract the humidity and nebulosity from all objects, and from men themselves, and therefore it (the north wind) is the most wholesome of the winds. But the effects of the south are the very reverse."

8. Because the Hippocratic tradition—rather than the Galenic tradition—was transmitted to the early Middle Ages in truncated form through encyclopedic works such as the *Etymologia* of Isidore of Seville, the influential nature of terrestrial winds on the body and the noxious powers of infected air became salient features of medieval intellectual culture. The Galenic tradition, with its emphasis on pneuma, did not influence medical thinking in the West until the translation movements of the twelfth century and the subsequent introduction of Galenic texts, as well as Arabic commentaries and new compositions, into the burgeoning universities of medieval Europe. In the academic milieu of the thirteenth century, theologians would use Galenic theories of pneuma in conjunction with humoural theory and Aristotelian natural philosophy to argue that internal air might be of divine or demonic origin, and that the toxic pneuma of the spiritually corrupt might infect the air and bodies of those surrounding them.

9. Later medieval natural philosophers working from Latin translations of Greco-Arabic medical texts added Aristotle's vegetative soul to Galen's system, thereby creating a hierarchy of souls; in human beings, the functions of all of these pneumatic entities were governed by the rational soul.

10. For Aristotle and Galen, the pneumatic soul provided the formal cause of the physical self, thereby acting as an organizing principle that maintained the ever-shifting elements and humours in their primary bodily form.

11. For a post-modernist discussion of Aristotle and the creation of categories, see Hacking 2001.

WORKS CITED

Aristotle. "Metaphysics." Trans. W.D. Ross. *The Internet Classics Archive.* <http://classics.mit.edu/Aristotle/metaphysics.html> 26 May 2012.

———. "Meteorlogy." *The Internet Classics Archive.* Trans E.W. Webster. <http://classics.mit.edu/Aristotle/meteorology.html> 26 May 2012.

———. "On the Heavens." Trans. J.L. Stocks. *The Internet Classics Archive.* <http://classics.mit.edu/Aristotle/heavens.1.i.html> 26 May 2012.

———. "On Generation and Corruption." Trans. H.H. Joachim. *The Internet Classics Archive.* <http://classics.mit.edu/Aristotle/gener_corr.html> 26 May 2012.

Bailey, M. "From Sorcery to Witchcraft: Clerical Conceptions of Magic in the Later Middle Ages." *Speculum* 76 (2001): 960–90.

Ballester, L.G., and J. Arrizabalaga, eds. *Galen and Galenism: Theory and Medical Practice from Antiquity to the European Renaissance.* Burlington: Ashgate, 2002.

Broedel, H.P. *The Malleus Maleficarum and the Construction of Witchcraft: Theology and Popular Belief.* Manchester: Manchester UP, 2003.

Caciola, N. *Discerning Sprits: Divine and Demonic Possession in the Middle Ages.* Ithaca: Cornell UP, 2003.

Dean-Jones, L. *Women's Bodies in Classical Greek Science.* Oxford: Oxford UP, 1996.

Fretté, S.E., ed. *Doctoris Angelici Thomae Aquinatis opera omnia.... Vol. 29. Opuscula theologica.* Parisiis: Vivès, 1876.

Hacking, I. "Aristotelian Categories and Cognitive Domains." *Synthese* 126 (2001): 473–515.

Hippocrates of Cos. "On Airs, Waters, Places." Trans. F. Adams. *The Internet Classics Archive.* <http://classics.mit.edu/Hippocrates/airwatpl.html> 26 May 2012.

———. "On the Sacred Disease." Trans. F. Adams. *The Internet Classics Archive.* <http://classics.mit.edu/Hippocrates/sacred.html> 26 May 2012.

James VI. *Dæmonologie, in Forme of a Dialogue....* 1597. London: 1603.

Lemay, H.R. *Women's Secrets: A Translation of Pseudo-Albertus Magnus' De Secretis Mulierum.* Chicago: Chicago UP, 1992.

Lloyd, G. "Pneuma between Body and Soul." *Journal of the Royal Anthropological Institute* 13 (2007): 135–46.

Newman, B., and M.H. King, trans. *Thomas of Cantimpré: The Collected Saints' Lives: Abbot John of Cantimpré, Christina the Astonishing, Margaret of Ypres, and Lutgard of Aywières.* Turnhout: Brepols, 2008.

Normand, L., and G. Roberts *Witchcraft in Early Modern Scotland: James VI's Demonology and the North Berwick Witches.* Exeter: U of Exeter P, 2000.

Obrist, B. "Wind Diagrams and Medieval Cosmology." *Speculum* 72 (1997): 33–84.

Shakespeare, W. "The Tragedy of Macbeth." 1623. *The Complete Oxford Shakespeare: Tragedies.* Vol. 3. Eds. S. Wells and G. Taylor. Oxford: Oxford UP, 1987. 1307–35.

Sharpe, W.D., trans. *Isidore of Seville: The Medical Writings.* Philadelphia: American Philosophical Society, 1967. Transactions of the American Philosophical Society 54.

Smith, M. *Alhazen's Theory of Visual Perception: A Critical Edition, with English Translation and Commentary, of the First Three Books of Alhacen's De aspectibus, the Medieval Latin Version of Ibn al-Haytham's Kitāb al-Manāz ir.* Vol. 1. Philadelphia: American Philosophical Society, 2001. Transactions of the American Philosophical Society, New Series 91/4.

Thompson, E.H. "Macbeth, King James and the Witches." 1993. University of Dundee: Scotland. <http://www.faculty.umb.edu/gary_zabel/Courses/Phil%20281b/Philosophy%20of%20Magic/Arcana/Witchcraft%20and%20Grimoires/macbeth.htm>. 26 May 2012.

Tschacher, W. *Der Formicarius des Johannes Nider von 1437/38: Studien zu den Anfängen der europäischen Hexenverfolgungen im Spätmittelalter.* Aachen: Shaker Verlag, 2000.

Wildberg, C. *John Philoponus' Criticism of Aristotle's Theory of Aether.* Berlin: De Gruyter, 1988.

7 The Supernatural Image of Iceland in Johannes Kepler's *Somnium* (1634)

STEFAN DONECKER

Et Septentrionalibus populis magiam familiarem tradunt scriptores.
"Writers say that magic is common among the people of the north."
(Kepler, Somnium *336)*

THE MAGICAL NORTH and its sorcerous inhabitants provided the
setting for one of the most unusual writings of Johannes Kepler (1571–
1630), Imperial Mathematician, pioneer of astrophysics, and one of the
most brilliant minds of the early modern age. *Somnium,* "The Dream,"
his only attempt at prose fiction (Lemcke 25), was composed in a long,
laborious, and discontinuous writing process between 1593 and 1630
and finally published posthumously in 1634. Since the late 1990s, the
"Lunar Dream" has received considerable attention from literary scholars
(Luminet; Swinford; Poole; Parrett 38–50; Bezzola Lambert 66–105;
Campbell; Paxson, "Revisiting"; Paxson, "Kepler's"). However, the role of
Iceland and the North in the context of Kepler's narrative has only been
mentioned in passing. In the following, I would like to address this aspect

and draw attention to Kepler's *imaginatio borealis*. His short narrative can be considered a representative expression of the attitude toward the North, and toward Iceland in particular, among scholars and intellectuals of the seventeenth century. Even a superficial reading makes apparent that the wonders and mysteries of the North, as well as the resident witches and demons, feature prominently in Kepler's tale. In a nutshell, *Somnium* presents the full scope of the supernatural North, as it was envisioned during the early modern period.

AUTHOR AND TEXT

The author of *Somnium*, Johannes Kepler, hardly requires a detailed introduction.[1] Together with Nicolaus Copernicus and Galileo Galilei, he is commonly regarded as one of the key protagonists in the scientific revolution that overcame the geocentric cosmology of the Middle Ages and established the foundations of modern astronomy. Kepler was a native of the Imperial Free City Weil der Stadt in southwestern Germany. During his studies at Tübingen, he established his reputation as an outstanding mathematician and astrologer. Kepler later became assistant to the great Danish astronomer Tycho Brahe and, after Brahe's death in 1601, succeeded him as Imperial Court Mathematician at Prague. As a Protestant, Kepler had to work under constant pressure from Catholic authorities (see List). He spent most of his life in Bohemia and Austria, repeatedly troubled by the religious turmoil that culminated in the Thirty Years' War. Among his numerous scientific achievements, Kepler is undoubtedly best known for his laws of planetary motion, based on the observations of his mentor Brahe and published in 1609 and 1619, which are considered the foundation of modern astrodynamics.

Four years after Kepler's death, his son Ludwig (see Rosen, *Kepler's Somnium* 194–206) published a book under the title *Ioh. Keppleri Mathematici olim Imperatorii Somnium, seu opus posthumum de astronomia lunari* ("The Dream, or Posthumous Work on Lunar Astronomy of Johannes Kepler, late Imperial Mathematician").[2] *Somnium* has been labelled as "the first piece of authentic science fiction" by no less an authority than Isaac Asimov (99), one of the undisputed masters of the genre. The text indeed has to be understood as science fiction in the strict sense of the word (Bozzetto 375; cf. Menzel; Poole): Kepler embedded his scientific theories on the movements of celestial bodies in a fantastic tale of witches, spiritistic séances, and lunar demons.[3]

However, modern readers expecting a linear and balanced narrative and a pleasant science-fiction story from one of the great minds of the early modern period might end up disappointed. One of the most distinctive features of Kepler's *Somnium* is its extremely complicated structure (see Poole 60–1; Bezzola Lambert 69–72; Bozzetto 373–4; Hallyn 334–5). The first-person narrator, presumably Kepler himself, tells how he spends a day reading the story of the legendary Bohemian queen Libussa, a renowned sorceress, and afterwards observes the moon and the stars until late at night. These two elements, sorcery and astronomy, inspire a rather peculiar dream. In this dream, he visits the book fair at Frankfurt and acquires a book written by a fellow astronomer, a certain Duracotus. In addition to Duracotus' autobiography, the tome contains an account of a séance he and his mother performed, in which they summoned a spirit, identified as a Dæmon from Levania, to consult him on life on the moon.[4] The Dæmon provided them with a detailed description of the various beings who inhabit the lunar realm, explained how it would be possible to travel there, and devoted particular attention to the question of how the skies and the celestial bodies would appear to an observer standing on the moon. Before the dreaming narrator can learn the last secrets about the moon from Duracotus' book, he is woken by a storm rattling against the windows and the story ends on a rather abrupt and anticlimactic note. Neither the Dæmon's account nor the story of Duracotus' life is brought to a conclusion.

Somnium displays an intricate narrative structure for a comparatively short text. Three different first-person narrators—the authorial narrator, i.e., Kepler himself, Duracotus, and the Dæmon—succeed each other with their interlaced tales. Kepler could have written a story about a journey to the moon (see Reiss 154); instead, he chose to write a story about someone who dreams about a book whose author retells the speech of a demon on how it would be like, theoretically, to travel to the moon. To make things even more complicated—and scholarly—Kepler added extensive endnotes to his text, which turned out to be far longer than the story itself. *Somnium* is a scientist's dream, and conveys a very academic feeling.

The complex structure is, to a certain degree, the result of the story's long development (G.E. Christianson 81–2, 88). *Somnium* did, in fact, accompany Kepler for most of his adult life: the Dæmon's lecture is essentially a revised version of an academic disputation that Kepler prepared in 1593 as a student at Tübingen, a hypothetical consideration on how the earth and the stars would look when observed from the moon.[5] Kepler added the frame story of Duracotus, his mother, and the dreaming narrator sixteen years later, after a discussion with a learned colleague, Johann Matthäus Wacker von Wackenfels (1550–1619), caused him to reconsider his student oration (Granada 480, 490; Horsky 273–4). The substantial endnotes were added during the 1620s, in preparation for publication (Rosen, *Kepler's* Somnium xix–xx). Thus, the multi-layered narrative is partially attributable to *Somnium*'s complicated development history. Yet to a certain degree it has to be considered a deliberate literary device employed by Kepler to establish a sense of distance between himself as the author and the events he described (see Poole 61; Reiss 147; G.E. Christianson 83).

DURACOTUS, THE ASTRONOMER: KEPLER'S ICELANDIC *ALTER EGO*

Kepler felt obliged to present himself as detached from the fantastic elements of his story, since the similarities between his own life and that of his protagonist, Duracotus, would otherwise be difficult to overlook (Nicolson, "Kepler" 261–2). Duracotus is an astronomer and a former pupil of Tycho Brahe, just like Kepler himself.[6] Duracotus' mother Fiolxhilde is a witch, and although it might seem unlikely, even this detail is, in a way, autobiographical. In 1620, Kepler's own mother Katharina was arrested by the magistrate of her home town Leonberg, Lutherus Einhorn, a well-known witch-hunter, after a local woman had denounced her as a poisoner and a witch (Sutter 35–116).[7] Katharina Kepler was saved by the intervention of her prominent son who managed to effect her release after a fourteen-month imprisonment. However, she died half a year later; it seems that, at the age of seventy-three, she did not recover from the treatment she received during the trial.

Despite the obvious similarities between the two learned astronomers, Kepler and Duracotus, the latter is portrayed as an Icelander. His enigmatic book, which the authorial narrator buys and reads in his dream, begins with the simple, straightforward statement: "My name is Duracotus. My country is Iceland, which the ancients called Thule" (Kepler, *Somnium* 321). Throughout the tale, Duracotus' Icelandic heritage is much more than mere background information. It is repeatedly stressed and constitutes one of the defining traits of the character. Why, then, did Kepler decide on an Icelandic origin for his literary *alter ego*?

In the narrative of *Somnium*, Iceland serves as a contrast to the scientific, academic world that Kepler belonged to (Swinford 100). He describes "this remote island" as "a place where I might fall asleep and dream" (Kepler, *Somnium* 332). The inhabitants of this otherworldly dream-land are described as primitive, almost savage people, who nevertheless possess extraordinary knowledge in occult and supernatural matters. However, they refuse to commit their lore to writing.[8] The savage, sorcerous, and exclusively oral society of Iceland, as Kepler imagines it, stands diametrically opposed to the civilized, scientific, and literate world of European scholars. The two opposing spheres of knowledge are personified by the two parent figures in Duracotus' life: his mother, the Icelandic witch Fiolxhilde, and his mentor, the erudite astronomer Tycho Brahe.

Duracotus manages to bridge these two very different settings. At the age of fourteen, he accidentally ruins one of his mother's magic charms. In a fit of anger, the witch sells her son to a sailor who takes the boy to Denmark, where he eventually becomes a pupil of Brahe. "I was delighted beyond measure by the astronomical activities," Duracotus recalls, "for

Brahe and his students watched the moon and the stars all night with marvelous instruments.... Through this opportunity, then, I, who had come from an entirely destitute background in a half-savage country, acquired knowledge of the most divine science" (Kepler, *Somnium* 332). After several years, he returns to Iceland and is reunited with his mother, who has come to regret her rash decision. Together, Fiolxhilde and Duracotus seek to unravel the mysteries of the moon and the beings that dwell there. In his unpretentious prose, Kepler sketches an interesting image of Duracotus caught between the scholarly erudition he has gained abroad and the supernatural customs of his homeland. He is an Icelander who learned occult lore from his sorcerous mother, but he is educated among the elite of European astronomers.

Thus, Duracotus has access to both spheres of knowledge, the occult and the scientific, and eventually manages to reconcile the two traditions. In doing so, he allows the reader to discover that the supernatural lore of the Icelanders and the academic knowledge of Tycho Brahe and his pupils are not as incompatible as they seem. The Dæmon who teaches Fiolxhilde the secrets of the moon is not a demon in the Christian sense, no agent of diabolical forces, but essentially the Genius of Astronomy itself.[9] In the text, Kepler conveys a sense of arcane mystery when he claims that the Dæmon "is evoked by one and twenty characters" (Kepler, *Somnium* 322), without explaining what these occult sigils might be. However, in the notes he solves the riddle and explains that the twenty-one letters needed to summon the Dæmon are "ASTRONOMIA COPERNICANA," "Copernican astronomy" (336). Instead of being occult, they turn out to be the creed of Kepler's rational science. Thus, the magic performed by Fiolxhilde becomes an allegory of astronomy. Although they seem to be the antithesis of one another, Kepler has Fiolxhilde and Brahe follow the same path to astronomical knowledge, expressed through very different metaphors and symbols (Campbell 240–1; Hallyn 339–41; Reitlinger 163–4).

Interestingly enough, there is no indication that Kepler regarded the occult approach of the savage Icelanders as inferior to the civilized science of the European *res publica litterarum*.[10] He points out that the Icelanders are known to be *perquam ingeniosi*, "extraordinarily intelligent" (Kepler, *Somnium* 336). In his text, the Icelandic witches learn as much about the universe from their conversations with their demons and familiar spirits as the astronomers deduce from their scientific observations. Fiolxhilde, the witch, stresses the strength of her native tradition after her son returns from Denmark, full of academic knowledge: "Advantages have been conferred, Duracotus my son, not only on all those other regions to which you went but also on our country, too. To be sure, we are burdened with cold and darkness and other discomforts.... But we have plenty of clever persons. At our service are very wise spirits who detest the bright light of other lands and their noisy people. They long for our shadows, and they talk to us intimately" (322).

IMAGINATIO BOREALIS

Duracotus' origins in mysterious Iceland notwithstanding, the wonders of the North are not at the core of Kepler's *Somnium*. The text is, after all, primarily speculative science fiction about possible journeys to the moon, framed by a story of northern mysteries. But despite their marginal importance for the text, Kepler devotes considerable attention to the various supernatural and extraordinary phenomena connected to Iceland.

He points out that the witches and sorcerers of Iceland consort with familiar spirits, who are attracted by the dark polar nights (Kepler, *Somnium* 336). These spirits or demons are not only willing to disclose secrets about the universe, but also enable the witches to undertake spiritual journeys to distant lands. "By [the Dæmon's] help," Fiolxhilde explains, "I am not infrequently whisked in an instant to other shores, whichever I mention to him" (322). As befits a being with such a strong connection to Iceland, Fiolxhilde's familiar prefers to recite his lunar lore *idiomate Islandico*, in the "Icelandic language" (323). Kepler also reports that the Icelanders are said to be capable of summoning the wind and imprisoning it in certain bags, which they then sell to foreign sailors:[11]

"The geographers commonly say, whether rightly or wrongly, that the pilots of ships sailing from Iceland produce whatever wind they want by opening a wind bag" (335).

The Icelanders in Kepler's story appear to be extraordinarily long-lived: "My mother never told me my father's name," Duracotus recalls. "But she said that he was a fisherman who died at the ripe old age of 150 (when I was three) in about the seventieth year of his marriage" (Kepler, *Somnium* 321). Together with her son, the widowed witch lives in the vicinity of the infamous volcano, Mount Hekla. In *Somnium's* opening paragraphs, Kepler merely provides a cryptic remark that Hekla is a place of punishment and damnation.[12] In the endnotes, however, he explains that "Pluto's court," that is, the underworld, "is entered...through the chasms of Hekla," and that Saint Patrick's Purgatory (*Purgatorium Patricianum*) is to be found "in the earth beneath Mt. Hekla, the Icelandic volcano" (332, 334).

The most important source for these images of wondrous Iceland was Olaus Magnus (1490–1557), a Swedish humanist and clergyman, whose "History of the Northern Peoples" (*Historia de gentibus septentrionalibus*, 1555) was the quintessential early modern textbook on northern Europe and its inhabitants.[13] Olaus wanted to educate his learned contemporaries on the lands of the North, but he also wanted to amaze and astonish them. Accordingly, he devoted particular attention to the wonders of the North, from the enormous sea monsters that allegedly threatened ships and sailors in northern waters to the exquisite beauty of snowflakes. He also commented extensively on the extraordinary sorcerous abilities of the Northerners, who "exercise this Divelish Art, of all the Arts of the World, to admiration" (Magnus 47). Several of the phenomena described in Kepler's *Somnium*—the abundance of demons and familiar spirits, the witches' wind-summoning, including the sale of imprisoned winds to foreign sailors, and their out-of-body experiences and spiritual journeys to distant lands—are directly taken from Olaus' *Historia*.[14] According to Olaus Magnus, magic is common everywhere in the North, but he does not single out the Icelanders as particularly notorious sorcerers. Instead, he emphasises the supernatural abilities of the Finns and Sámi, who are said to excel both at wind-summoning (see Moyne) and at extra-corporeal spirit journeys. Kepler (*Somnium* 337) is aware of the Finns' reputation as the supreme sorcerers of Europe, but chooses to transfer their abilities to the Icelanders.

It is likely that Kepler relied on additional information from a native Icelander. Oddur Einarsson (1559–1630), who later became bishop of Skálholt, had been one of Tycho Brahe's students in Denmark approximately fifteen years before Kepler was introduced to Brahe's circle in Prague (J.R. Christianson 271–2; Rosen, *Kepler's* Somnium 216–7). Oddur seems to have been keenly interested in the supernatural phenomena allegedly occurring in Iceland, and if he narrated such stories to his fellow students, it is indeed possible that they were still circulating among Brahe's *famuli* fifteen years later when Kepler might have heard them.[15] In Kepler's notes to *Somnium*, Oddur Einarsson remains unnamed, but is repeatedly mentioned as *Episcopus Islandicus*, an Icelandic bishop who provided Brahe with knowledge about his native land (Kepler, *Somnium* 334–5).

Yet another source of inspiration was the *Rerum Scoticarum historia* ("Scottish History," 1582), one of the major writings of Scottish humanist George Buchanan (1506–82). Kepler explains that he borrowed both the name "Duracotus" and the story of a 150-year-old fisherman who fathers a son at that biblical age from Buchanan's work (Kepler, *Somnium* 332, 334, cf. Rosen, *Kepler's* Somnium 30, 43). In *Rerum Scoticarum historia*, the extraordinary fisherman is a Shetlander named Laurentius, who is said to have married when he was hundred years old and still went to sea at an age of 140 (Buchananus 13ᵛ). Buchanan, however, does not claim that Laurentius became a father at that age; only his late marriage and his vitality are mentioned.

The name "Duracotus" seems to be inspired by a list of toponyms in the second book of the "Scottish History." Buchanan notes that the syllable *Dur*, which supposedly meant "water," was common in ancient Gallic and Britannic place names, and gives *Durocortorum in Gallia* (present-day Reims) as an example (Buchananus 23ᵛ). Thus, neither of the two motifs is, in any way, connected to Iceland. Kepler (*Somnium* 332), almost apologetically, reminds his readers that Scotland is a country that "looks out upon the Icelandic Sea," implying that it is appropriate to model his version of Iceland on details from a Scottish chronicle.[16]

However, Kepler was generally not particularly selective in his choice of sources (see Bezzola Lambert 78). He frankly admits that some elements of his story are curious details picked up by chance. In one of the endnotes, for example, he explains the origin of the allegedly Icelandic name Fiolxhilde: "On a wall in the house which I used by permission of Martinus Bacchatius [Martin Bachaczek], rector of Charles University [in Prague], there used to hang a very old map of Europe, on which the word 'Fiolx' was attached to localities in Iceland.[17] Whatever it signified, its harsh sound delighted me, and I appended 'Hilde', a familiar designation of women in the ancient tongue, whence the names Brunhilde, Mathilda, Hildegard, Hiltrud and the like are derived" (Kepler, *Somnium* 333).

Kepler's eclectic and associative use of random northern oddities resulted in a rather convoluted image of supernatural Iceland. Most of the phenomena he copied from literature had little, if anything, to do with Iceland. The witches' mastery over the wind and their aptitude for extracorporeal journeys are typical attributes of Finnish sorcerers, as the authoritative Olaus Magnus testifies. The extraordinary longevity of the Icelanders, evinced by the virility of Duracotus' 150-year-old father, is borrowed from the Scots. Kepler's image of mysterious Mount Hekla is at least partially in line with common assumptions of the sixteenth and seventeenth centuries. It was often claimed that the summit of the volcano marked an entrance to hell or purgatory (Maurer), and these rumours caused considerable embarrassment to the few Icelandic scholars of the early modern era, who objected to the idea that they lived at the doorstep of purgatory (Morgan). There is, however, no indication that anyone apart from Kepler located St. Patrick's Purgatory—a sanctuary in County Donegal, Ireland, where Saint Patrick allegedly received a vision of the torments that awaited sinners in the afterlife—in Iceland. It seems that Kepler simply confused the two famous gateways to the underworld.

Emphasising the two spheres of knowledge in his protagonist's life, Kepler created an associative image of the northern periphery, contrasted to the learned centre further to the south. To flesh out Duracotus' background, he collected supernatural phenomena from all over northern Europe[18]—the abilities of Finnish sorcerers, the putative longevity of Scottish fishermen and the Irish pilgrimage site of St. Patrick's Purgatory—and transferred them, arbitrarily and slightly carelessly, to Iceland. In the frame story of *Somnium*, Iceland becomes the essence and epitome of the supernatural North.[19]

THE GOOD WITCH OF THE NORTH

Kepler's image of the North was deeply indebted to Olaus Magnus and other authoritative texts, but he nevertheless gave it a personal note. In the early seventeenth century, during the heyday of the early modern witch hunts, the malevolence of Scandinavian witches was notorious (cf. Willumsen)—yet Kepler chose to depict his Icelandic sorceress, Fiolxhilde, as a kind and sympathetic character. She does, admittedly, appear unpredictable and irascible, and banishing her son Duracotus for a trivial misdemeanour is clearly a disproportionate overreaction. But Kepler (*Somnium* 322) is quick to explain that Fiolxhilde deeply regretted her impetuosity, and describes her as "deliriously happy" when her son returns safely from Denmark. After the fortunate reunion of mother and son, the enigmatic witch, herbalist, and demon-summoner is portrayed as a kind and lovable elderly woman.

Kepler provided his literary *alter ego*, Duracotus, with an idealized image of his own biography. The relationship between Duracotus and his mentor Tycho Brahe is presented as far more harmonious and amiable than Kepler's own complicated and sometimes strained cooperation (see Ferguson 249–81) with the renowned Danish astronomer. Likewise, Fiolxhilde appears to be a far gentler person than Kepler's mother Katharina, who seems to have been a rather difficult character (see Rosen, "Kepler's Attitude"). In private letters and confidential manuscripts,

Kepler described her as garrulous, quarrelsome, and malicious (Frisch 672) and complained about her "tomfoolery and noseyness, her irascible temper, her foul-mouthedness and her insistent obstinacy" (Kepler, "Letter" 214). His annoyance notwithstanding, Kepler remained loyal to his mother and was apparently fond of her despite her shortcomings (Rosen, "Kepler's Attitude" 347). When he wrote the final version of *Somnium*, Katharina Kepler had been dead for several years, and it is plausible that he had developed a somewhat idealized memory of her. Katharina's pitiable suffering during her witch trial certainly mellowed her son's attitude as well.

Even without resorting to psychoanalytical arguments, it seems understandable that Kepler wanted to portray Fiolxhilde as a likeable character. Bearing in mind that Fiolxhilde and her Dæmon are, essentially, avatars of astronomy, they could not possibly be depicted as malevolent beings. The northern sorceress appears as a dubious character at a cursory glance, just as early modern astronomy might appear suspicious and arcane to uninitiated minds. But this first impression is misleading: to Kepler, neither astronomy nor her personification is tainted by evil. Thus, his reason for depicting a "good witch" goes beyond a mere personal idealizing of his own mother. Toying with the motif of the northern sorceress, he found a way to express the ambiguous reputation of astronomical science.

In doing so, he inverted the stereotypical image of Scandinavian witchcraft. As a disciple of the devil, a murderer of children and a sexual deviant, the witch was commonly envisioned as an embodiment of evil, the quintessential criminal of the early modern period. Like any of his contemporaries, Kepler was familiar with these images. In *Somnium*, he mockingly referred to "dried-up old women, experienced from an early age in riding he-goats at night or forked sticks" (323). His Icelandic wise woman, on the other hand, is a frail, kind old lady, who affectionately clings to her son wherever he goes and gleams with maternal pride over his achievements—a thoroughly sympathetic character and, as such, the antithesis of the stereotypical northern witch.

CONCLUSION

Among the scholarly elite of early modern Europe, it was a well-known fact that the North was a realm of sorcery and an abode of witches (see Donecker). The famous French jurist and demonologist Jean Bodin, for example, stated that "most witches and sorcerers are to be found in the northern lands,...because the devil holds more power over Septentrio. There are more warlocks in Norway and Livonia and other Septentrional areas than in the entire rest of the world" (Bodin 113–4). Johannes Kepler was certainly aware of the supernatural and diabolic connotations of the North, but he was definitely no expert on this topic. In the context of his scientific considerations on Copernican astronomy and lunar voyages, Iceland was of no particular importance. He merely required a suitably exotic setting to provide a backdrop to his story and a supernatural contrast to the scientific world of the astronomers. Judging from his own endnotes and comments, Kepler made no efforts to be particularly creative and did not do any research; instead, he merely gathered random peculiar details he encountered.

However, I believe that Kepler's image of supernatural Iceland is particularly interesting precisely *because* he was not an expert. The account of Iceland in *Somnium* represents, essentially, the knowledge one may expect from a well-read European intellectual of the seventeenth century: motifs based primarily on Olaus Magnus' *Historia de gentibus septentrionalibus*, supplemented with additional details collected from various other written sources that were available to him. The North was, to Kepler, a locus of extraordinary phenomena, speculative rumours, and alleged facts, all of which could be employed to construct the notion of otherness that *Somnium*'s plot and purpose required. These topoi of Northernness could also be subverted, as Kepler demonstrated with the character of his sympathetic witch, Fiolxhilde, the literary stand-in for his mother and representative of enigmatic astronomy.

In her pioneering book *Voyages to the Moon*, published at the dawn of the space age in 1948, Marjorie Nicolson emphasised the dual nature of Kepler's *Somnium*: "No important later voyage will employ so fully the

supernatural, yet none will be more truly 'scientific' than that 'Dream'"
(Nicolson, *Voyages* 41). That the supernatural aspects of the Lunar Dream
are so unmistakably associated with the North is indicative for the worldview of Kepler and his contemporaries. To present-day readers interested
in the past constructions of Northernness, the *imaginatio borealis* of
previous centuries, *Somnium* serves as a reminder of what an educated
man of the seventeenth century simply had to know about the supernatural North.

NOTES

1.   For a concise overview of Kepler's biography and the state of research, see Lemcke.

2.   In addition to the annotated text of *Somnium* itself, the edition (182 pages in
     quarto) contains a dedication to Landgrave Philip III of Hesse-Butzbach, an
     appendix to *Somnium* in the form of a letter by Kepler to the Jesuit mathematician
     Paul Guldin (1577–1643), written in 1623, and finally Kepler's own translation of
     Plutarch's *De facie quae in orbe lunae apparet* ("On the face which appears in the orb
     of the moon") (Bezzola Lambert 69).

3.   In Kepler's own words: "The purpose of my Dream is to use the example of the
     moon to build up an argument in favor of the motion of the earth" (*Somnium* 333).
     Parrett (38–9) explains Kepler's motivation in the following way: "The idea was
     that many of the phenomena we witness from the earth that convince us of the
     geocentric system would, from the moon, appear in a quite different context, thus
     casting doubt on the centrality of the earth.... Once it was established that the rela-
     tivity of the observer's viewpoint was the most important factor in determining the
     apparent motions of the celestial bodies, the next step would be to demonstrate
     how Copernicanism could explain both apparent phenomena."

4.   In Kepler's text, *Levania* is the name used for the moon. In the course of the story,
     however, it becomes apparent that the *Daemon ex Levania* is no true inhabitant of
     the moon, but merely an expert on lunar voyages, a terrestrial spirit that regularly
     travels to the moon and consorts with the local demons that live there.

5.   Kepler was not allowed to present his theses in public, since the professor in
     charge of disputations at Tübingen's philosophical faculty was strongly opposed to
     Copernican astronomy. Accordingly, the text of the disputation was never printed
     and the manuscript of this earliest draft of *Somnium* has not been preserved
     (Rosen, *Kepler's* Somnium xvii–xviii).

6. Admittedly, Duracotus is said to have studied at Brahe's famous observatory on the Danish island of Hven as a very young man, while Kepler and Brahe collaborated during the latter's tenure at Prague, when Kepler himself was already an established scientist in his own right. Nevertheless, the parallel is obvious.

7. Kepler (*Somnium* 334) suspected that an early draft of *Somnium*, which was circulated without his authorization during the early 1610s, might have contributed to the accusations against his mother. Malicious gossipers could have interpreted the ominous character of Fiolxhilde as an oblique confession on Kepler's part that his mother was indeed a sorceress. Nicolson (267) argues that "Kepler unwittingly put into the hands of his enemy the most potent of all charges against his mother, the evidence of her own son." However, it seems that Nicolson overestimates the importance of the *Somnium* draft for the witch case. In Sutter's (35–119) detailed analysis of the trial, there is no indication that the accusers or the prosecutors were familiar with Kepler's writings, and they never referred to the *Somnium* draft as evidence. Like most witch trials of the seventeenth century, the Kepler case was the result of initially trivial neighbourhood squabbles that escalated in an atmosphere of fear and denunciation. It is very unlikely that any of the Leonberg locals involved in the accusations had access to a complicated academic text like *Somnium*. Kepler's guilty conscience was apparently unwarranted.

8. Duracotus explains that as long as his mother was alive he had to refrain from writing, lest his knowledge would become accessible to unworthy readers: "While she lived, she carefully kept me from writing. For, she said, the arts are loathed by many vicious people who malign what their dull minds fail to understand, and make laws harmful to mankind" (Kepler, *Somnium* 321).

9. *...in hoc loco Daemon sumitur pro scientia Astronomica* (Kepler, *Somnium* 339).

10. In one of his notes, Kepler (*Somnium* 333) explicitly asserts that Fiolxhilde is meant to represent *ignorantia*, "ignorance." This statement, however, is contradicted by her depiction as a particularly wise woman whose astronomical knowledge rivals Tycho Brahe's expertise (Campbell 238). Is seems that Kepler enjoyed toying with ambiguities and apparent contradictions. Mary Baine Campbell (239) singled out this aspect as a characteristic feature of *Somnium*: "Kepler's appetite for the hybrid, his ability to tolerate ambivalence, are high—higher perhaps than a fully rationalized science can express."

11. Although it is not mentioned explicitly in the story, it is implied that Fiolxhilde also participates in this trade. The "charm" that young Duracotus accidentally destroys, causing his mother to banish him from home, is most likely meant to be such a magical wind bag.

12. "Condemned by these laws [the laws of vicious men], not a few persons have perished in the chasms of Hekla" (Kepler, *Somnium* 321). The remark is difficult to interpret, and it remains uncertain what kind of condemnation Kepler was referring to. Traditionally, Hekla was seen as a gateway to hell or purgatory, but Kepler gives it another twist. He explains that he had the fates of Empedocles (a Greek philosopher who allegedly jumped into the flames of Mount Etna to achieve divinity) and Pliny the Elder (who, according to Kepler, was driven by curiosity when he died in the Vesuvius eruption of 79 CE) in mind when he wrote about Hekla. Thus, the victims of Hekla, in Kepler's imagination, seem to be no common sinners, but individuals who overstep the limits of scientific curiosity that have been set by narrow-minded men.

13. On Olaus Magnus and the *Historia* see, Mergner (2012), who also provides an overview of existing literature on the topic.

14. There are indications that Kepler used the abridged 1599 edition of the *Historia de gentibus septentrionalibus* (Rosen, *Kepler's* Somnium 48–9). He mentions his source at one point (Kepler *Somnium* 337), simply referring to the author as "Olaus," as if the name needed no additional explanation.

15. Oddur was most probably the author of an anonymous description of Iceland, entitled *Qualiscunque descriptio Islandiae*, which covers topics such as trolls, mermaids, water monsters, and sexual intercourse between humans and elves (Gunnell 1).

16. Kepler was aware of the historical connections between Scotland and Scandinavia and the Norse influence on the Gaelic world, since these topics are mentioned in Buchanan's Scottish history. These connections apparently prompted him to subsume the North Atlantic as part of his conception of the North.

17. Kepler's eyesight was notoriously bad, and he apparently misread the text on the "very old" map (Rosen, *Kepler's* Somnium 35). Attempts to identify the map Kepler used are rather pointless, although it is tempting to speculate that he might have misread *fiord*, which is indeed a word "attached to localities in Iceland," as *fiolx*.

18. In *Somnium*, there is only one single instance (Rosen, *Kepler's* Somnium 236–9) when Kepler refrains from transferring a wondrous northern phenomenon to Iceland. The people of *Lucumoria* are said to die each year at the onset of polar night, and revive as soon as the sun returns (Kepler, *Somnium* 363). In this case, Kepler does not use this strange semi-fatal hibernation to embellish his account of Iceland, but retains the original location of the Lucumorians in northern Russia/Scythia, in accordance with his source, the Jesuit theologian Martin Delrio (310) who, in turn, copied the tale from the *Rerum Muscovitarum commentarii* by the imperial ambassador to Russia, Sigismund von Herberstein (270–1).

19. At first glance, it seems difficult to understand why Kepler chose Iceland as
     the representative of the mysterious North, instead of Lapland, which had a
     far stronger reputation for sorcery among his contemporaries. In his notes, he
     explains that he was partially inspired by ancient Greek writers who used islands
     in the Atlantic Ocean as the setting for their literary speculations on the moon (and
     as the point of departure for imaginary lunar voyages) (see Bezzola Lambert 103).
     But the decisive incentive to use Iceland came from Tycho Brahe, who had, appar-
     ently, described it to Kepler as a particularly distant, almost otherworldly land
     (Kepler, *Somnium* 334).

WORKS CITED

Asimov, I. *Asimov's Biographical Encyclopedia of Science and Technology.* Newton Abbot:
     David & Charles, 1978.

Bezzola Lambert, L. *Imagining the Unimaginable: The Poetics of Early Modern Astronomy.*
     Amsterdam: Rodopi, 2002. Internationale Forschungen zur allgemeinen und
     vergleichenden Literaturwissenschaft 58.

Bodin, J. *Vom aussgelasnen wütigen Teuffelsheer.* 1580. Graz: Akademische Drucks- und
     Verlagsanstalt, 1973.

Bozzetto, R. "Kepler's *Somnium*; or, Science Fiction's Missing Link." *Science Fiction
     Studies* 17 (1990): 370–82.

Buchananus, G. *Rerum Scoticarum historia.* Edimburgi: Arbuthnetus, 1582.

Campbell, M.B. "Alternative Planet: Kepler's *Somnium* (1634) and the New World." *The
     Arts of 17th-Century Science: Representations of the Natural World in European and
     North American Culture.* Eds. C. Jowitt and D. Watt. Aldershot: Ashgate, 2002.
     232–49.

Christianson, G.E. "Kepler's *Somnium*: Science Fiction and the Renaissance Scientist."
     Science Fiction Studies 3 (1976): 79–90.

Christianson, J.R. *On Tycho's Island: Tycho Brahe and His Assistants, 1570–1601.*
     Cambridge: Cambridge UP, 2000.

Delrio, M. *Disquisitionum magicarum libri sex....* Coloniae Agrippinae, 1633.

Donecker, S. "The Lion, the Witch and the Walrus: Images of the Sorcerous North in the
     16th and 17th Centuries." TRANS. *Internet-Zeitschrift für Kulturwissenschaften.* 17
     Feb. 2010. <http://www.inst.at/trans/17Nr/4-5/4-5_donecker.htm> 24 Nov. 2012.

Ferguson, K. *The Nobleman and His Housedog. Tycho Brahe and Johannes Kepler: The
     Strange Partnership that Revolutionised Science.* London: Review, 2002.

Frisch, C. "Kepleri vita servato annorum ordine." *Joannis Kepleri astronomi opera omnia.* Vol. VIII. Part II. Ed. C. Frisch. Francofurti: Heyder & Zimmer, 1871. 668–933.

Granada, M.A. "Kepler and Bruno on the Infinity of the Universe and of Solar Systems." *Journal for the History of Astronomy* 39 (2008): 469–95.

Gunnell T. "Clerics as Collectors of Folklore in Iceland." *Study Platform on Interlocking Nationalisms (SPIN).* 2010. <http://spinnet.eu/images/2010-12/gunnell_folklore_in_iceland.pdf > 24 Nov. 2012.

Hallyn, F. "Le *Songe* de Kepler." *Bibliothèque d'Humanisme et Renaissance* 42 (1980): 329–47.

Von Herberstein, S. *Rerum Moscoviticarum Commentarii.* 1556. Ed. H. Beyer-Thoma et al. München: Osteuropa-Institut, 2007.

Horsky, Z. "Kepler's 'The Dream, or Lunar Astronomy' as a Predecessor of Space Research." *History of Rocketry and Astronautics: Proceedings of the Ninth, Tenth and Eleventh History Symposia of The International Academy of Astronautics. Lisbon, Portugal, 1975; Anaheim, California, U.S.A., 1976; Prague, Czechoslovakia, 1977.* Ed. F.I. Ordway. San Diego: AAS Publications Office, 1989. 269–75. AAS History Series 9.

Kepler, J. "Letter to Sebastian Faber." 1617. *Johannes Kepler: Gesammelte Werke. Band XVII. Briefe 1612–1620.* Ed. M. Caspar. München: Beck, 1955. 213–7.

———. "Somnium." 1634. *Johannes Kepler: Gesammelte Werke. Band XI, 2. Calendaria et prognostica. Astronomica minora, Somnium.* Eds. V. Bialas and H. Grössing München: Beck, 1994. 315–67.

Lemcke, M. *Johannes Kepler.* Reinbek: Rowohlt, 2007.

List, M. "Kepler und die Gegenreformation." *Kepler Festschrift 1971: Zur Erinnerung an seinen Geburtstag vor 400 Jahren.* Ed. E. Preuss. Regensburg: Naturwiss. Verein, 1971. 45–63. Acta Albertina Ratisbonensia 32.

Luminet, J.-P. "Autour du *Songe* de Kepler." *Alliage: Culture—Science—Technique* 70 (2012): 22–30.

Magnus, O. *A compendious history of the Goths, Swedes, & Vandals, and other northern nations.* 1555. London: Streater, 1658.

Maurer, K. "Die Hölle auf Island." *Zeitschrift des Vereins für Volkskunde* 4 (1894): 256–69.

Menzel, D.H. "Kepler's Place in Science Fiction." *Kepler Four Hundred Years: Proceedings of Conferences held in Honour of Johannes Kepler.* Eds. A. Beer and P. Beer. Oxford: Pergamon, 1975. 895–904. Vistas in Astronomy 18.

Mergner, A. "Elfentänze, Zwergenkämpfe, Menschenopfer: Die 'Erfindung' Skandinaviens in Olaus Magnus' 'Historia de gentibus septentrionalibus' (1555)." *Stereotype des Ostseeraumes: Interdisziplinäre Beiträge aus Geschichte und Gegenwart.* Eds. I. Sooman and S. Donecker. Wien: U Wien, 2012. 173–201.

Morgan, H. "The Island Defenders: Humanist Patriots in Early-Modern Iceland and Ireland." *Nations and Nationalities in Historical Perspective*. Eds. G. Hálfdanarson and A.K. Isaacs. Pisa: Ed. Plus, 2001. 223–45. Clioh's Workshop 3.

Moyne, E.J. *Raising the Wind: The Legend of Lapland and Finland Wizards in Literature*. Newark: U of Delaware P, 1981.

Nicolson, M. "Kepler, the *Somnium*, and John Donne." *Journal of the History of Ideas* 1 (1940): 259–80.

———. *Voyages to the Moon*. New York: MacMillan, 1948.

Parrett, A. *The Translunar Narrative in the Western Tradition*. Aldershot: Ashgate, 2004.

Paxson, J.J. "Kepler's Allegory of Containment, the Making of Modern Astronomy, and the Semiotics of Mathematical Thought." *Intertexts* 3 (1999): 105–23.

———. "Revisiting the Deconstruction of Narratology: Master Tropes of Narrative Embedding and Symmetry." *Style* 35 (2001): 126–50.

Poole, W. "Kepler's *Somnium* and Francis Godwin's *The Man in the Moone*: Births of Science-Fiction 1593–1638." *New Worlds Reflected: Travel and Utopia in the Early Modern Period*. Ed. C. Houston. Farnham: Ashgate, 2010. 57–69.

Reiss, T.J. *The Discourse of Modernism*. New York: Cornell UP, 1982,

Reitlinger, E. "Kepler's Traum vom Monde." *Freie Blicke: Populär wissenschaftliche Aufsätze*. Ed. E. Reitlinger. Berlin: A. Hofmann, 1875: 149–82.

Rosen, E. "Kepler's Attitude to his Mother." *The Psychoanalytical Review* 55 (1968): 342–8.

———. *Kepler's* Somnium: *The Dream, or Posthumous Work on Lunar Astronomy*. Mineola: Dover, 2003.

Sutter, B. *Der Hexenprozeß gegen Katharina Kepler*. Weil der Stadt: Kepler-Gesellschaft, 1979.

Swinford, D. *Through the Daemon's Gate: Kepler's* Somnium, *Medieval Dream Narratives, and the Polysemy of Allegorical Motifs*. New York: Routledge, 2010.

Willumsen, L.H. *Witches of the North: Scotland and Finnmark*. Leiden: Brill, 2013. Studies in Medieval and Reformation Traditions 170.

The Nineteenth Century

The Scientific and the Spiritual

8 Imagining the Celtic North
Science and Romanticism on the Fringes of Britain

ANGELA BYRNE

INTRODUCTION

Voyaging from London to Iceland in August 1772, the celebrated explorer and man of science[1] Sir Joseph Banks (1753–1820) paused to make meteorological, geological, and archaeological observations on the Inner Hebrides. Passing between Morvern and Mull, Banks grew excited at the sight of what he thought was "Morven the Land of Heroes once the seat of the Exploits of Fingal the mother of the romantick scenery of Ossian."[2] However, the Scottish headland that so excited Banks was not the same Morven as that immortalized in James Macpherson's controversial poems of the mythical Gaelic bard Ossian, published from 1762.[3] Conflating the mythical Morven with the actual headland of Morvern, Banks recalls the enchanting experience of reading the Ossian poems. He continues,

> I could not even sail past it without a touch of Enthusiasm...I lamented
> the busy bustle of the ship &, had I dard to venture the Censure of my
> Companions, would certainly have brought her to anchor. To have read
> ten pages of Ossian under the shades of those woods would have been
> Luxury above the reach of Kings. (Banks 34–5)

The following day, an Englishman living in the area brought Banks and his party to visit Staffa, an island he believed not even locals had seen, on which were basalt pillars "like those of the Giants Causeway." Banks was determined to visit to compensate for not having time to visit the Causeway itself (37–8). He describes the outing in detail, emphasizing the "highest expectations" and impatience the party harboured in anticipation of "the wonders we had heard so largely describd." His description of the basalt columns moves between breathless attempts to capture the scene and efforts to make scientific observations:

> [W]e were struck with a scene of magnificence which exceeded our expectations...the whole of that End of the island supported by ranges of natural pillars, the most above 50 feet high standing in natural Colonades according as the bays or points of Land formd themselves: upon a firm basis of Solid unformd rock.... Compard to this what are the Cathedrals or the palaces built by man, mere models or play things, imitations as diminutive as his works will always be when compared to those of nature. Where is now the boast of the Architect, regularity the only part in which he fancied himself to exceed his mistress? Nature is here found in her possession & here it has been for ages uncounted. Is not this the school where the art was originally studied[?] (Banks 34–5)

If this experience was not sufficiently wonderful, the party was then brought to "'the Cave of Fiuhn," which Banks thought "the most magnificent...that has Ever been described by travelers" (42).[4] Banks was thrilled at the circumstance: "[H]ow fortunate that in this cave we should meet with the remembrance of that chief whose existence as well as that of the whole Epick poem is almost doubted in England" (43). He concluded the day's adventures by avowing to "proceed to describe it & its productions more Philosophicaly" (43). Even the traveller, antiquary, mineralogist, and Ossian-cynic Edward Daniel Clarke (1769–1822) confessed that his feelings were stirred by the sight of the headland of Morvern in 1797:

Not feeling that internal evidence which the admirers of Ossian profess
to entertain, respecting the authenticity of those poems, and having
ever regarded them as an ingenious fiction, blended with a very scanty
portion of traditional information, I could not, nevertheless, avoid
feeling some degree of local enthusiasm, as I passed the shores on
which so vast a superstructure of amazing but visionary fable had been
erected. Mouldering fabrics, the undoubted residence of valiant chief-
tains in days of yore, were seen both on the coast of Morvern, and upon
the opposite shores of Mul. (cited in Otter 1: 294–5)

Banks' and Clarke's inscribing of the Ossian poems—mythical in
nature and mysterious in provenance—onto Gaelic landscapes provides
the cultural context for this examination of accounts of Scotland, Ireland,
and the Scottish islands in circa 1790–1830 by British men of science. These
accounts delineate the place of Gaels within the supernatural North by
integrating scientific knowledge, Romantic literature, local folklore and
mythology, and antiquarian analysis. While travelling men of science
attempted to focus on empirical information in their descriptions of the
Gaelic fringes of the United Kingdom, few could avoid referring to local
traditions, "superstitions," and mythologies of place. Indeed, this integration of environment and culture reflects the broad contemporary
appreciation of what constituted "the North." The Romantic North was
not so much a geographically delineated space as it was a culturally
contingent imagined geography, a set of socio-cultural, climatic, ethnographical, topographical, linguistic, and historical characteristics considered
representative of "Northernness" (Wawn; Fjågesund and Symes; Davidson;
Fielding; Byrne). Therefore, "the North" (in the European context) could
encompass Scandinavia, Iceland, and Britain, the Scottish islands, and
Ireland.

This chapter builds on the developing historiography of Romantic
science (Cunningham and Jardine; Fulford, Lee, and Kitson; Heringman,
Romantic Science; Heringman, *Romantic Rocks*; Wilson). Romanticism and
the sciences operated in complementary roles in imaginings, experiences,

and perceptions of the North (Byrne). This Romantic–scientific context led the travellers under study here to conceive of the North through encounters with and interpretations of landscapes, histories, and peoples. Acknowledging the Romantic context of scientific observations permits engagement with the literary, mythological, and scientific subjectivities of exploration narratives.

THE "GREAT CELTIC FAMILY," MYTHOLOGY, AND GAELIC ORIGINS

Today, Gaels are not generally considered Northern, possibly due in part to early Christianization. However, they have been long associated with the mysticism and deep connection with the natural world typically attributed to Northern peoples.[5] The historical and anthropological obscurity of Gaelic origins, the mystery surrounding the provenance of round towers in Ireland, and the Romantic "discovery" and publication of Gaelic myths and poetry, together with the still-imperfect nature of the geographical knowledge of such peripheral areas, contributed to the portrayal of Britain's Gaelic fringe in supernatural terms in the late eighteenth and early nineteenth centuries.

The period saw a lively and politically charged debate on the origins of the peoples of Britain and Ireland and their places within the United Kingdom and the British historical narrative (Leerssen; Kidd; Carruthers and Rawes; O'Halloran; Fielding). Opinions on the origins of the umbrella groupings of "Celts" and "Goths" were sorely divided and fiercely politicized among Irish and Scottish antiquaries in particular, for whom the debate on origins provided a vehicle for political arguments. Opinions varied too widely to be presented in detail here, but broadly speaking they represented the religious opposition between dissenting and established religions as well as the political division between Whig and Tory. Some argued for a progressive northerly migration—that Britain's original inhabitants were, with each new wave of immigration, pushed farther north into the Highlands and Scottish islands. Consequently, by the early nineteenth century, "Celts" (in general) were considered either entirely separate from Anglo-Saxons, or as "expressive of a certain ancient Britishness" (Fielding 103).

Origins debates created ethnographical alignments that reflected contemporary imagined hierarchies best elucidated in scientific terms by Enlightenment stadial theory, which graded the peoples of the world on a developmental basis (Jacques; Wolloch). The terms *Goth* and *Celt* were indiscriminately conjoined in many ethnographies and, as discussed below, connections were made between various peoples inhabiting the North. These origins debates provide part of the scientific and cultural context for characterizations of Britain's Gaelic fringe as supernatural in character.

The supernatural, and fairy lore in particular, was an important aspect of English identity from the 1790s (Silver 141–2). Well-established associations between the North and the supernatural were further perpetuated, and formed part of the basis for aligning the various people of Britain with other Northern cultures; particular connections were made between English culture and Norwegian culture (Byrne; Fielding; Wawn). Hotly contested origins debates were infiltrated by conjecture on the role of mythic races and supernatural beings. Debates on the origins of the Picts, for example, were informed by local lore and early modern hypotheses on the role of fairies in the British Isles in the distant past. Some theorists held the view that Picts were diminutive "Lapps" who had populated the ancient ring-forts and passage graves of Britain and Ireland (Grydehøj; Silver).

Dublin historian Thomas Keightley (1789–1872) opened his chapter on what he classified as "Celtic" myths by stating his belief that Celts had been displaced by Goths, indicating that they were a weaker people (not an uncommon idea at the time):

Under the appellation of Celts we include the inhabitants of Ireland, the Highlands of Scotland, Man, Wales, and Brittany. It is not, however, by any means meant to be asserted that there is in any of these places to be found a purely Celtic population. The more powerful

*Gothic race has, every where that they have encountered them, beaten
the Celts, and intermingled with them, influencing their manners,
language, and religion. (Keightley 1: 175–6)*

Keightley posited that "Celtic" myths were adapted from those of
immigrant Northmen, on the basis that no "Celtic" myth appeared
to predate the Nordic myths. His use of mythology as an indicator of
common origins illustrates the importance of popular culture not only
directly in national processes of self-fashioning, but also in origins
debates.

Others found differences between the various inhabitants of
Scandinavia and drew hierarchical correlations between them and the
population groups of the British Isles. Edward Daniel Clarke asserted,
"The Finns are to the Swedes and Lapps [Sámi] what the Irish are to the
English and Scotch" (2: 37). The phrenologist Robert Everest, for example,
found that the inhabitants of mountainous Telemark "reminded us of
what we had heard of the wild Irish.... Certainly there is a difference
between them and the rest of the Norwegians" (26; see also Fjågesund and
Symes 117–20). The Orcadian scholar Samuel Laing (1780–1868) argued
that another Northern colonized people, the Sámi, were "a branch of the
great Celtic family which seems to have occupied Europe before the immigration of the Gothic people from Asia" (314). Such observations served
to place England and Sweden on a similar footing as Northern imperial powers, despite English protest at the annexing of Norway to Sweden
from Denmark in 1814. The seemingly powerless and "backward" Gaels
and Sámi were "other" to the English and Swedes. These peoples were both
represented in supernatural terms, both drawn into Northern empires and
both the "other" within intra-European colonies, representing gradations
of civilization within Europe itself.

THE NORTH, "GEOLOGY, SCENERY, ANTIQUITIES, AND SUPERSTITIONS"

In the early nineteenth century, metropolitan knowledge of the more remote Gaelic fringes of Britain and Ireland remained poor. The Welsh naturalist and antiquary Thomas Pennant (1726–98) noted in 1776 that Snowdon had only recently lost the title of Britain's highest peak to Ben Nevis, and wondered whether Beinn a'Bhuird was not higher again (1: 227). Similarly, in 1807, the Anglo-Irish topographical writer Isaac Weld (1774–1856) wrote, "Magillicuddy's reeks are generally supposed to be the most lofty mountains in Ireland; although their exact height does not appear to have been ascertained" (147, 151).[6] Weld was aware of the importance of his work as "descriptive of a part of the United Kingdom, which, though confessedly interesting, has hitherto remained imperfectly known" (i). Other commentators made similar remarks in relation to the Shetland Islands. In 1809, Arthur Edmondston noted that while the islands had "long constituted an integral part of Great Britain...yet their production, resources, and internal economy, are less generally known than those of the most distant colony of the empire" (1: v–vi). Little had changed by 1820: the geologist Samuel Hibbert (1782–1848) was put to "great pains" to assemble a "new draught [map] fit for my purpose" in composing his geology of the islands (viii). While it should be noted that writers needed to emphasize the newness of the information contained within their books to promote sales in a period of profuse publication of travelogues, the fact remains that detailed and accurate geographical knowledge of Ireland, for example, was not available until the completion of the first Ordnance Survey maps between 1829 and 1842 (the first large-scale survey of an entire country). In the context of this knowledge deficiency, mythology and folklore made up the shortcoming. The image of Britain's Celtic fringe as supernatural and northern in nature was reinforced in the scientific and antiquarian accounts of the age.

The Manchester antiquary and geologist Samuel Hibbert's *A Description of the Shetland Islands, Comprising an Account of their Geology, Scenery, Antiquities, and Superstitions* (1822), was one of the first comprehensive accounts of those islands. Tellingly, his account not only covered geology, topography, and antiquities, but also local traditions; the title of his work encapsulates the complexity of contemporary perceptions of the North. The physician Arthur Edmondston's *A View of the Ancient and Present State of the Zetland Islands* (1809) also laid side-by-side the "Civil, Political, and Natural History; Antiquities; and...Agriculture, Fisheries, Commerce, and the State of Society and Manners" of his native islands. Edmondston acknowledged that the early history of Shetland was "involved in mystery and conjecture" and emphasized "[i]ts classical name Thule...expressive of this obscurity" (1: 13).

Samuel Hibbert excused his book's indulgence in local traditions and folklore by stating that these provided relief from "the monotonous labours of the hammer" (175–6). The pattern is repeated in other Northern travelogues authored by contemporary men of science. The unsuccessful determination of one observer to ignore such unscientific information only highlights the extent to which local myths and folklore permeated scientific texts. The Scottish natural historian and geologist Robert Jameson (1774–1854) resolved to steer clear of mythology and legend as "not worthy of serious attention" in *Mineralogy of the Scottish Isles* (2: 2–3), but he acknowledged the "general obscurity which veils the ancient history of Scotland." Led by the local pastor to Massacre Cave on the Isle of Eigg, Jameson admitted that the cave's story was "not uninteresting."[7] The local authority of the pastor may have assured Jameson of the site's importance. He was awakened to the (possible) reality of the legendary massacre by visiting the bone-strewn scene, and finding his "sensibility increased by the sequestered and dreary place in which the deed was done" (2–3, 41–3). Later in his tour, en route to Elgin, Jameson submitted to the *genius loci* of Scotland: "The solitary hour of the night, the melancholy noise of the wind rushing across the heath, the glimmering of the Will-o'-the-wisp, excited in us that strange feeling of superstitious alarm of which every man must at some time or other have been conscious" (266). Jameson's intended (albeit unsuccessful) avoidance of unscientific information reflects a division between metropolitan and local or provincial ways of knowing, rather than a division between

Romanticism and the sciences. This division collapses upon engagement with the landscape, because the landscape demands engagement
with local tradition. Once more, the interdependency of environment and
culture is evident.

Thomas Pennant made a merit of recording apparently fast-disap-
pearing Highland traditions in his *Tour of Scotland and the Hebrides* (1776).
He noted a rapid decline in the practice of "ancient customs and superstitions" in the Scottish Highlands and determined to record those he
encountered "least their memory should be lost" (Pennant 1: 108). He
noted in both the Scottish Highlands and in Ireland a continued belief
in ghosts and fairies (115–6); the continued celebration of the Celtic
summer festival, *Bealtaine* (110–1); continuing practices of wakes and
keening (112–5); and the enduring memory of "fragments of the story of
Fingal and others, which they carrol as they go along" (215). Isaac Weld's
Illustrations of the Scenery of Killarney and the Surrounding Country (1807)
also combines detailed geological and natural historical information with
popular culture and antiquities.

THE LITERATURE OF THE GAELIC LANDSCAPE

An important thread in Romantic imaginative connections with the North
is the contemporary "rediscovery" of Nordic and Celtic myth and traditional Gaelic and Icelandic poetry. This is epitomized by the popularity
of Macpherson's series of Ossian poems (from 1762), Southey's *Icelandic
Poetry or The Edda of Sæmund* (1797), and Walter Scott's novels, which
fuelled interest in the still relatively poorly known Northern regions
(Lönnroth). The popularity of such literature in the period embedded an
association between the North and mythology, identifying it as the site
of heroic deeds, bloody battles, and sorcery. Romantic scientific travellers encountered and constructed the North through mythologies,
stories, and histories rooted in local landscapes. These landscape mythologies created an alternative world that challenged scientific explanation.
Their rich portrayals of supernatural agency on the landscape offered

explanations for unusual features. In Ireland, the astronomer and anti-quary John Lee (né Fiott, 1783–1866) encountered geological formations to which local traditions attributed a superhuman history, such as a rock named the "Giant's Rock," reputed washing place of the giant, hunter, and warrior of Irish folklore, Fionn Mac Cumhaill (137). On the Scottish island of Unst, at Lamba Ness, Samuel Hibbert noted a circular rock cavity known as the Saxe's Kettle, traditionally thought to have been used by the "Shetland Giant" (403). On Shetland, he found a "rude inclosure" styled the Giant's Garden, the place where a plundering giant had kept his bounty (504), and described Trolhouland as a "Wild abode of man, a knoll shrouded in clouds and mists...long...dreaded as a domicile for unclean spirits; hence its name of Trolhouland, or the Hill of Demons or Trows" (444). He noted that other parts of the Shetlands were similarly considered the residences of "evil genii," similar to Norway's trolls, and that Iceland featured a number of craters known as *Trölla-dyngiar* and one known as the *Trölla-kyrkia* (translated by Hibbert as "magic heaps" and "Giant's Church," respectively, 445). He concludes by drawing all of these regions together as "Thule," a cultural geography based on intertwining landscape and mythology: "In no country are there more habitations remaining of unclean spirits than in Thule. All these had their origin in the mythology of the ancient Scandinavians" (451).[8]

Poetry could also be used to convey Romantic scientific perspectives on natural wonders. William Hamilton Drummond's (1778–1865) topograph-ical poem *The Giant's Causeway* (1811) is prefaced by the local author's assertion that "[t]he coast of Antrim has long been a subject of laudable curiosity, as it furnishes a fine field for geological enquiry, and presents a grand and novel spectacle to the eye of taste, in the wild sublimity of its promontories, the fantastic winding of its bays, and the romantic variety of its cliffs and rocks" (v). As a natural wonder and puzzling curiosity, the Causeway was the subject of scientific enquiry from the late seventeenth century (Kennedy), and by 1800 it was a site of scientific importance and Romantic sensory indulgence. Drummond's poem contains the strands evident in the prose works studied here: wild scenes in keeping with the standard Romantic aesthetic, detailed geological information and references to geological research (xxii–xxiv), and information on the myths and legends of the "simple inhabitants of the coast" (xix–xx). The poem once again emphasizes the relationship between landscape and culture, as science and Romanticism intersect in assessments and perceptions of the Gaelic cultural landscape.

Following the geological account, Drummond recounts the legend of Fionn Mac Cumhaill—the giant credited in Irish lore with having built the "causeway"—and contemplates the widespread popular belief in giants of old among Northern peoples (Drummond xx). The poem itself is a patchwork of Northern mythologies and aligns Mac Cumhaill's Scottish rival, Benandonner, with the Nordic world as he appeals to Odin for assistance in battle. Indeed, comparisons between Nordic and Celtic mythologies were not uncommon in the period. Other examples include Hibbert's comparisons of Celtic, Scandinavian, and Shetland gods of the waters (524–6) and Keightley's assertion that "in the popular creed" of "Celtic" peoples (in which he included the Irish, Scottish Highlanders, Manx, Welsh, and Breton) were "beings exactly corresponding to the Dwarfs and Fairies of the Gothic nations" (1: 175–6).

Manmade aspects of the Gaelic landscape also presented puzzles to scholars. The inscrutability of the origins and purposes of so-called "round towers" added to the mystery surrounding Gaelic origins, the towers themselves forming the subject of much confusion, conjecture, and debate. While the purpose of these iconic features of the Irish landscape remains obscure,[9] they are now thought to date from the early tenth to mid-thirteenth centuries (Corlett 25). "Those singular round towers... whose use has so long baffled the conjectures of antiquaries" (Pennant 2: 161–2) became points of contention, subject to manipulation by various political agendas. In the late eighteenth and early nineteenth centuries, round towers reflected the political divisions in Irish antiquarian study (O'Halloran 60–1). In the nineteenth and early twentieth centuries, they came to symbolize a great Irish past that was drawn upon by the nationalist movement. The roles of other historic sites in later nineteenth-century Irish and British national identities have been examined elsewhere (Harvey).

Debates on the provenance of round towers developed alongside debates on Celtic origins. Some contemporaries attempted to explain round towers as indicative of an advanced, Asiatic, sun- or fire-worshipping colony in ancient Ireland. In his discussion of round towers and the various hypotheses on their purpose, Weld agreed with the view of his fellow Irish antiquary, Charles Vallancey (c. 1726–1812), that an "oriental colony" had been established in Ireland that used round towers to display sacred fires "in honour of the pagan deities" (Weld 55; O'Halloran 60). Another Anglo-Irish antiquary, John D'Alton (1792–1867), agreed, writing that the lack of such structures in other druidical societies indicated an external, Asiatic, sun- or fire-worshipping influence (83–4). Francis Ledwich (1739–1823), on the other hand, considered them the work of the "Danes" (O'Halloran 60). What was certain was the allure of their continuing mystery, with Ledwich writing in 1781 that they "have opened to men of leisure and erudition, a spacious field for hypothesis and conjecture" (quoted in O'Halloran 60). With some round towers rising to 34 metres in height, they represented to eighteenth- and nineteenth-century antiquaries the footprint of a mysterious, forgotten culture. Whether or not they were considered symbols of Gaelic culture, their presence in the Gaelic landscapes of Ireland and Scotland enhanced the image of the mystical Gael.

CONCLUSION

The late eighteenth- and early nineteenth-century scientific travelogues examined here produced an imagined Gaelic geography grounded in physical and cultural artefacts. The interplay between Romanticism and the sciences was expressed against the intellectual background of established Enlightenment ideas about the relationship between climate (or environment) and culture. The Gaelic cultural landscape provided rich fodder for scholarly speculation and dispute, from the contested origins of the Ossian poems to the mysterious purposes of round towers. The role of mystification is important, making it at once possible for contemporaries to argue for or against Gaels' ethnological relationship to other Britons, and to align Gaels with other Northern people, such as the Sámi. Such alignments placed Gaels and other intra-European colonized peoples close to the bottom of the developmental hierarchy outlined in Enlightenment stadial theory, thereby integrating and dominating them simultaneously. It is also worth considering whether Gaelic exclusion from Roman Europe influenced Romantic perceptions of Gaels, rendering them more likely to be aligned in the literary and scientific texts of the age with northern Europe.

The misty Celtic landscape envisioned by Joseph Banks in 1772 endures in the twenty-first century as a potent cultural force. Celtic mysticism is presented today as a form of ecological spiritualism that provides an escape from modernity—just as Gaelic landscapes provided Romantic men of science with a window on the past. The commodification of "traditional" Gaelic culture (Irish culture in particular) also continues today in mass-market entertainment like *Lord of the Dance*, *Riverdance*, and *Celtic Woman*. The twentieth- and twenty-first-century fetishization of Celtic culture as ecological, traditional, and spiritual, then, has a direct lineage dating back to James Macpherson's Ossian poems and has proven to be not only a pervasive cultural force, but a means by which Britain's Gaelic fringe maintained, for outsiders at least, the vestiges of an ancient British past.

AUTHOR'S NOTE

This material was delivered under a broader title, "Imagining the North: Science and Romanticism in the Sub-Arctic, c. 1800–1830," at the International Congress of Arctic Social Sciences VII conference in Akureyri, Iceland. The author acknowledges the support of a CARA Postdoctoral Mobility Fellowship in the Humanities and Social Sciences (Irish Research Council/Marie Curie COFUND, 2010–13) held at the Department of History, National University of Ireland Maynooth, and the Institute for the History and Philosophy of Science and Technology, University of Toronto.

1. The contemporary term "men of science" is employed here to avoid anachronistic use of the word *scientist*. The term reflects the heterogeneity of the scientific community and emphasizes "the person rather than the activity undertaken...the qualities of mind and character supposedly needed for and formed by the practice of science" (Barton 81).

2. To avoid repetitive use of *sic*, note that in all quotations in this chapter, original spelling, punctuation, and capitalization have been retained. Here, *Celtic* is used as an umbrella term, as it was until the nineteenth century. *Gael(ic)* refers to the Irish-Scottish fringe of the United Kingdom, or the traditionally Gaelic-speaking regions and people of Scotland and Ireland. There was much confusion in ethnological terminology in the eighteenth and early nineteenth centuries; *Celt* and *Goth* were often conflated, and *Celt* often excluded *Gaelic* (Kidd 185–210). This is further complicated by the subsuming of Irish culture into representations of Scottish culture from the mid-eighteenth century (chiefly by Macpherson's Ossian), something later abused for political ends (Carruthers and Rawes 2).

3. Macpherson's publications were hugely popular and internationally influential, but their authenticity was the subject of controversy. See Curley; Haugen; Porter; Shields 24–54.

4. This cave came to be known as Fingal's Cave (from the Gaelic name Fionn) and attracted visits by nineteenth-century scientists, artists, composers, and architects (Allen and deRis Allen 22–47).

5. Colin Kidd has noted the nineteenth-century creation of "the familiar stereotype of...the economically hopeless Celt wrapped up in melancholy, mysticism, sentiment and the poetic" and the earlier roots of this stereotype in Thomas Percy's highlighting of the druidical influence in Gaelic society in *Northern Antiquities* (1770) (Kidd 199, 208).

6. Beinn a' Bhuird is Britain's eleventh highest mountain. Magillicuddy's Reeks mountain range does include Ireland's highest peaks.

7. The cave was long thought to have been the site of a massacre of the local Clanranalds by the MacLeods of Harris in 1577, but this is now disputed.

8. "Thule" has a long and complex history. Pytheas of Massalia reported visiting an island named Thule in the fourth century BCE, which was retained in classical geographies as the most northerly place on earth. It can also be understood as a literary, mythological, and cultural production (see Mund-Dopchie).

9. Sixty-five round towers are extant in Ireland, plus the remnants of many more. Two have been found in Scotland and one on the Isle of Man (Corlett 25).

WORKS CITED

Allen, P.M., and J. deRis Allen. *Fingal's Cave, the Poems of Ossian, and Celtic Christianity.* New York: Continuum, 1999.

Banks, J. *Journal of a Voyage up Great Britain's West Coast and to Iceland.* Manuscript, Rare Books and Special Collections, McGill University, Montreal: Blacker-Wood Collection [MS QH11 B36 1772], 1772.

Barton, R. "'Men of Science': Language, Identity and Professionalization in the Mid-Victorian Scientific Community." *History of Science* 41 (2003): 73–119.

Byrne, A. *Geographies of the Romantic North: Science, Antiquarianism, and Travel, 1790–1830.* New York: Palgrave, 2013.

Carruthers, G., and A. Rawes, eds. *English Romanticism and the Celtic World.* Cambridge: Cambridge UP, 2003.

Clarke, E.D. *Travels in Various Countries of Scandinavia; Including Denmark, Sweden, Norway, Lapland, and Finland.* 3 vols. London: T. Cadell & W. Davies, 1838.

Corlett, C. "Interpretation of Round Towers: Public Appeal or Professional Opinion?" *Archaeology Ireland* 12.2 (1998): 24–7.

Cunningham, A., and N. Jardine, eds. *Romanticism and the Sciences.* Cambridge: Cambridge UP, 1990.

Curley, T.M. *Samuel Johnson, the Ossian Fraud, and the Celtic Revival in Great Britain and Ireland.* Cambridge: Cambridge UP, 2009.

D'Alton, J. "Essay on the Ancient History, Religion, Learning, Arts, and Government of Ireland." *Transactions of the Royal Irish Academy* 16 (1830): 1–380.

Davidson, P. *The Idea of North.* London: Reaktion, 2005.

Drummond, W.H. *The Giant's Causeway, a Poem.* Belfast: Archer, 1811.

Edmondston, A. *A View of the Ancient and Present State of the Zetland Islands.* 2 vols. Edinburgh: Ballantyne, 1809.

Everest, R. *A Journey Through Norway, Lapland, and Sweden.* London: Underwood, 1829.

Fielding, P. *Scotland and the Fictions of Geography: North Britain 1760–1830.* Cambridge: Cambridge UP, 2009.

Fjågesund, P., and R.A. Symes. *The Northern Utopia: British Perceptions of Norway in the Nineteenth Century.* Amsterdam: Rodopi, 2003.

Fulford, T., D. Lee, and P.J. Kitson. *Literature, Science and Exploration in the Romantic Era: Bodies of Knowledge.* Cambridge: Cambridge UP, 2004.

Grydehøj, A. "Ethnicity and the Origins of Local Identity in Shetland, UK—Part I: Picts, Vikings, Fairies, Finns, and Aryans." *Journal of Marine and Island Cultures* 2 (2013): 39–48.

Harvey, D.C. "'National' Identities and the Politics of Ancient Heritage: Continuity and
Change at Ancient Monuments in Britain and Ireland, c.1675–1850." *Transactions
of the Institute of British Geographers*, New Series 28.4 (2003): 473–87.

Haugen, K.L. "Ossian and the Invention of Textual History." *Journal of the History of
Ideas* 59 (1998): 309–27.

Heringman, N., ed. *Romantic Science: The Literary Forms of Natural History*. Albany:
State U of New York P, 2003.

———. *Romantic Rocks, Aesthetic Geology*. Ithaca: Cornell UP, 2004.

Hibbert, S. *A Description of the Shetland Islands, Comprising an Account of their Geology,
Scenery, Antiquities, and Superstitions*. Edinburgh: Constable, 1822.

Jacques, T.C. "From Savages and Barbarians to Primitives: Africa, Social Typologies, and
History in Eighteenth-Century French Philosophy." *History and Theory* 36 (1997):
190–215.

Jameson, R. *Mineralogy of the Scottish Isles*. 2 vols. Edinburgh: Stewart, 1800.

Keightley, T. *The Fairy Mythology; Illustrative of the Romance and Superstition of Various
Countries*. 2 vols. London: Whittaker, 1833.

Kennedy, A. "In Search of the 'True Prospect': Making and Knowing the Giant's
Causeway as a Field Site in the Seventeenth Century." *British Journal for the History
of Science* 41.1 (2008): 19–41.

Kidd, C. *British Identities Before Nationalism: Ethnicity and Nationhood in the Atlantic
World, 1606–1800*. Cambridge: Cambridge UP, 1999.

Laing, S. *Journal of a Residence in Norway During the Years 1834, 1835, & 1836*. 2nd ed.
London: Longman, 1837.

Lee, J. *Tour from Holywell to Dublin and Fermoy*. Manuscript, St John's College,
Cambridge [MS U.30 (2)], 1806–7.

Leerssen, J. *Mere Irish and Fíor-Ghael: Studies in the Idea of Irish Nationality, its
Development and Literary Expression Prior to the Nineteenth Century*. Cork:
Cork UP, 1986.

Lönnroth, L. "The Nordic Sublime: The Romantic Rediscovery of Icelandic Myth and
Poetry." *Wagner's Ring and its Icelandic Sources*. Ed. Ú. Bragason. Reykjavík:
Stofnun Sigurðar Nordals, 1995. 31–41.

Mund-Dopchie, M. *Ultima Thulé: Histoire d'un lieu et genèse d'un mythe*. Geneva:
Librarie Droz, 2009.

O'Halloran, C. *Golden Ages and Barbarous Nations: Antiquarian Debate and Cultural
Politics in Ireland, c. 1750–1800*. Cork: Cork UP, 2004.

Otter, W., ed. *The Life and Remains of Edward Daniel Clarke*. 2 vols. London: G. Cowie,
1825.

Pennant, T. *A Tour in Scotland and the Hebrides*. 2 vols. 4th ed. London: White, 1776.

Porter, J. "'Bring me the Head of James Macpherson': The Execution of Ossian and the Wellsprings of Folkloristic Discourse." *Journal of American Folklore* 114 (2001): 396–435.

Shields, J. *Sentimental Literature and Anglo-Scottish Identity, 1745–1820*. Cambridge: Cambridge UP, 2010.

Silver, C. "On the Origin of Fairies: Victorians, Romantics, and Folk Belief." *Browning Institute Studies* 14 (1986): 141–56.

Wawn, A. *The Vikings and the Victorians: Inventing the Old North in Nineteenth-Century Britain*. Cambridge: Brewer, 2000.

Weld, I. *Illustrations of the Scenery of Killarney and the Surrounding Country*. London: Longman, 1807.

Wilson, E. *The Spiritual History of Ice: Romanticism, Science and the Imagination*. New York: Palgrave, 2003.

Wolloch, N. "Edward Gibbon's Cosmology." *International Journal of the Classical Tradition* 17 (2010): 165–77.

9 Mesmerism and Victorian Arctic Exploration

SHANE MCCORRISTINE

INTRODUCTION

Arctic exploration in primary and secondary sources has been cast traditionally in the military terms of heroism and struggle: as a battle between a male actor and the elements that creates a sense of transcendence and corresponding denial or victory over corporeal presence. The origins of this tension between embodiment and disembodiment can be traced back to the "classic" era of Regency and Victorian Arctic exploration in British history (c. 1818–76). During this period, the log-books and official expedition accounts of naval explorers in search of a Northwest Passage were only part of a much larger narrative field of northern discovery that could include diverse artistic, poetic, and spiritualist voyages across the Atlantic Ocean to an "otherworldly" polar environment. In this chapter I will argue that far from being ethereal and insubstantial, Arctic ghosts, dreams, visions, and spirits can be physical entities, with social histories and material consequences.

Historically, the Arctic in the western imagination has been thought of in terms of the unseen. Biblical ideas of the North as the domain of

Satan were succeeded by the ideas of Ultima Thule and the early modern hope of discovering gold in the land termed "Meta-Incognita" (Franklin). By the time of the era of state-sponsored naval exploration, the attribution of a type of nonhuman agency to the Arctic regions was extremely common and consistent. Just as there came to be a way in which Africa or the African "should look" (Neumann 1), Western representations of the Arctic appealed to Romantic ontological categories. Whether imagined as the "Genius of the North," the "Polar Spirit," or "The Powers of Frost and Air," in all Arctic exploration there was a sense of crossing an ontological boundary into a non-historical realm. Time and again, this caused the explorer to express his experiences in terms of dreams, visions, and castles in the air.

By focusing on the uncanny and the spectral aspects of imperial exploration, it is possible to challenge the traditional views of this phenomenon as a rational process involving heroic male characters. Firstly, this approach can reveal new histories that localize people and place together with the spirits that inhabit that place, thereby bringing European explorers into a more complex engagement with indigenous cosmologies. Secondly, this approach expands the concept of the explorer by including sectors of imperial society not traditionally associated with exploration, such as women, the young, colonial subjects, and the dead. This chapter deals with a particular feature of Victorian exploration history: the lost expedition led by Sir John Franklin to seek the Northwest Passage through the Arctic Archipelago in 1845. Whether through naval missions, armchair speculation, or poetry, the period from 1849–59 witnessed a remarkable series of attempts to rescue this expedition or reconstruct what happened. In this chapter I focus on the cases of people who were put into a mesmeric trance and "sent" to the Arctic to seek information on the fate of Franklin.

MESMERISM AND ARCTIC EXPLORATION

Originating in the practices of Franz Anton Mesmer's "animal magnetism" in the 1770s, mesmerism referred to the many different types of therapies, surgical practices, and entertainments that hypothesized magnetic fluid emanating from living bodies. The process of mesmerism involved making "passes," using materials such as magnets or candles, or simply engaging in suggestion and other mind-techniques to place the patient in a sleep state ranging from totally comatose to highly sensitive. There is an embarrassment of riches when it comes to the study of Victorian mesmerism and spiritualism, partly due to the contested nature of these practices and the importance in which they were held by many different sectors of society in the Western world, from scientists, royalty, and aristocrats to middle-class amateurs, plebeian socialists, and medical practitioners at both the centre and fringes of their profession. The popularity of these practices resulted in an extensive print culture, much of it highly visual. Furthermore, the principles of mesmerism were extremely relevant to the psychological and medical sciences that were developing during this period. Studies of nineteenth-century experimental knowledge have drawn attention to the importance of public sites of scientific and medical experiments as locations where authority, doctrine, and faith were hotly contested (Cooter; Desmond; Secord).

Building on how mesmeric practices travelled between colonial India and Britain (Winter), in this chapter I seek to develop the theory of how such practices structured relationships between personal and geographical identity, particularly in relation to spiritual quests associated with exploration, loss, and revelation. In other words, I will argue that such practices co-constructed notions of distance, identity, and place in both Britain and the Arctic. Furthermore, I will highlight the figure of the clairvoyant as a person capable of providing male authorities with contested information, but—connecting with recent work on emotions and embodiment—also as a site of "affectual forces." Affectivity, which can be defined as the way(s) in which feelings and emotions travel through space and time, gives us insights into how Arctic exploration could involve transferential relationships that problematized distinct binaries such as home/abroad, mind/body, and subject/object. Cultural geographers have shown how spiritual and dreamy practices can emerge within the normal routines and space of the everyday, in the very profane places that modernist religious studies posited as desanctified and secular (Holloway). Within this context, Teresa Brennan has pointed out that feeling and affectivity can change the body on a physical level, whether through pheromones, psychological trans- ference, or biological cues. Disappearance in the Arctic had somatic consequences among British audiences, as melancholy, anxiety, hope, and other affective registers guided peoples' relationship with explorers.

The British Admiralty faced a serious problem when sending out successive expeditions to search for Franklin, for traversing the long distances to the Arctic through the Atlantic or Pacific meant that author- ities back home experienced extended periods of "dead time" with little or no reliable knowledge of what was occurring in the field. At this point mesmerism was a marginal science, but one with significant support from the medical and cultural establishments and was envisaged as a new tech- nique along a spectrum of mid-Victorian discoveries about the unseen world, stretching from electricity to microscopy. While mesmerism would quickly become interwoven with variants of spiritualism in the 1850s, in 1849 it was quite rare for females in a trance to speak with the dead or visit a spirit realm. At that point, mesmeric travelling was predominantly envisaged as a form of mobility across real space and time through contact or rapport with living bodies.

Contemporary newspaper reports reveal the existence of dozens of clairvoyants (mostly young women) in Ireland, Britain, India, and Australia who, on being put into a mesmeric trance, described visiting Franklin in the Arctic. Beginning at the time of greatest anxiety regarding the fate of the expedition, these clairvoyant visionaries and their operators formed part of an incredibly vibrant field of speculations and experi- ments involving marvels ranging from flying balloons to tagged foxes. As cultural authority regarding the fate of Franklin broke down, dozens of hoaxes and false leads were taken seriously by the Admiralty, the press, and the general public from 1847 until the return of Francis Leopold McClintock's expedition with news of the fate of the expedition in 1859

(Gillies Ross). Rumours received at port towns, however bizarre, suddenly gained publicity in the national and international press. As a contemporary wrote:

> [e]very circumstance, however trifling, which could be supposed to emanate from the north, became invested with importance, and linked to the all-absorbing subject. This solicitude was felt from the shores of the Scheldt to North Cape, and from North Cape to the Strait of Behring; but joined to this noble feeling was much wildness of thought as to the probable course and position of the unfortunate Franklin and his companions; hence, however well meant, the feeling, by its very intensity, often contributed to render confusion more confounded (Brown 272).

In this context, it seemed that the clairvoyant was a highly sensitive person capable of collapsing the distance between the explorers and those searching for them through disembodied travelling during her mesmeric séances. She could name locations for audiences, bring back news, and "perform" Arctic experiences, such as cold and hardship. Clairvoyance reveals a multiplicity of overlapping spatialities: the psychic space of the clairvoyant, the Arctic space of the explorers, the medical space of the mesmeriser, and the intimate spaces linking clairvoyant, operator, and Arctic in an affectual force field. Both critics and supporters of clairvoyance tried to use the Franklin episode as a unique experiment to prove or disprove the claims of this new technique. I would argue, however, that the voice of the clairvoyant was part of a multi-vocal Arctic, an Arctic made up of bodies such as the Admiralty and other official bodies, persons on the peripheries of the Admiralty such as John Ross and Richard King, and Inuit and local informants in the Arctic. In contrast with other voices, therefore, these clairvoyants projected different kinds of presences onto the Arctic and deployed the Arctic for different ends.

The most celebrated case of Franklin-related mesmerism was that of Emma, the "Seeress of Bolton" (Hood 143). Emma was the domestic servant of a surgeon-apothecary named Dr. Joseph W. Haddock (1800–61). Haddock carried out many mesmeric experiments on his patients and was the author of a pamphlet entitled *Somnolism and Psycheism: Or the Science of the Soul and the Phenomena of Nervation as Revealed by Vital Magnetism, etc.* He frequently gave lectures on the subject and advertised his services to patients "desirous that the faculty of Clairvoyance be used as an aid in discovering the cause and nature of their complaints" (xii). Haddock referred to clairvoyance as a kind of "magnetic vision" or "internal sight, or sight of the soul" (63) in which light is projected from within "as the spark flies from the excited electric machine, so the perception seems, as it were, to seek the corresponding sensation" (66). The role of the mesmeriser was therefore analogous to a machine operator and he referred to the lucid, mesmerised subject as "a living stethoscope" that assists the judgement of the physician, "just as the astronomer uses his telescope" (53).

According to Haddock, "Emma L." was born around 1826 in Worcestershire and entered his service in Bolton in 1846. She was of a "nervous-bilious temperament" (84) and had suffered from inflammatory disease as a teenager. On a visit in early 1849, Harriet Martineau described her as "a vulgar girl, anything but handsome, and extremely ignorant" (cited in Chapman 355). In common with other medical physicians, Haddock began experimenting with ether as an anaesthetic. Emma was familiar with the substance, for her cousin had used it to mesmerise her, and upon learning this Haddock decided to observe its effects upon her. Haddock believed she had a remarkable susceptibility to the drug and began reducing the quantity he gave her until he realized that her condition was actually one of mesmeric trance. Haddock's experiments gradually began to cover the traditional spectrum of susceptibility, from the creation of illusions to the ability to mesmerise Emma at a distance. As she was illiterate, Haddock decided to test her clairvoyant ability using pictures that, upon being concealed and placed on her head, Emma was able to describe. Yet to Emma, they appeared not as pictures "but as the things represented. So that the picture of a rose would convey as vivid and real an idea to her sensorium, as the rose itself would do, to an individual in the ordinary state" (Haddock, *Somnolism...: Otherwise Vital Magnetism* 100).

Another aspect of Emma's repertoire was the ability to travel to distant parts of the globe in search of people on request, usually making a connection through a sample of their handwriting. As with the pictures, her method was to place a letter over her head and then describe the person who wrote it. On one occasion, the writing of a man from Australia was given to her, and "she was soon mentally there, described the climate and season, and expressed her surprise at finding the seasons reversed, when compared with England, having no knowledge of the effect of latitude and longitude in altering season and time" (Haddock, *Somnolism...: Or the Science of the Soul* 180). Indeed, Emma's travels were not limited to the earth: Haddock sent her on an "excursion to the moon," where she saw the inhabitants who "were very small—dwarfs—not larger than children on our earth" (Haddock, *Somnolism...: Otherwise Vital Magnetism* 58). It was in this context of mental travelling to unseen and exotic locations that Emma's clairvoyant abilities would be called upon in an attempt to solve the mystery of Franklin's fate. The knowledge she provided would be all the more marvellous because it came from such an "uneducated" and naive source.

Haddock was contacted by "a naval gentleman" in September 1849 about the possibility of using the clairvoyant to shed light on the matter. This gentleman was Captain Alexander Maconochie (1787–1860), who was a penal reformer, and both professor of geography at the University of London and secretary of the Royal Geographical Society from 1833–36. He was a friend of Franklin's and had served as his private secretary in Van Diemen's Land. Maconochie was in frequent contact with Jane Franklin throughout 1848 (Woodward 262) and had already made enquiries among clairvoyants in London and Paris regarding the lost expedition "in concert with different members of Sir John Franklin's family." After hearing about Emma, Maconochie wrote to Haddock to "enquire whether he thought

that his Clairvoyante cd [could] discover the fate of Sir J. Franklin."
Haddock replied requesting a letter in Franklin's handwriting and a
morsel of his hair, if possible. Maconochie immediately sent an old letter
of Franklin's from 1836, and wrote "to friends in London" seeking the
hair. Although pessimistic about the fortunes of the expedition, Haddock
consulted Emma on September 21 and was surprised to hear her state that
Franklin was still alive "with three or four companions." She stated that
they were "clothed in rough skins" and that many of Franklin's men were
dead (Letters 7/189).

Accordingly, Maconochie came to Bolton and was present at three
séances with Emma. He described her as "a very plain, ignorant, common
looking person" who was unassuming and mannerly. Yet in her "abnormal
state," Maconochie stated that she became "extremely familiar, almost
pert & childish in her whole demeanour." When interrogated, Emma
was frequently incoherent and voluble, and her "ejaculating manner"
caused Haddock to enlist an assistant to take notes (Letters 7/189). As
reported by Maconochie, Emma obtained information from the Arctic
through conversations with Franklin, talking "ideally" as Haddock put it
(*Somnolism...: Or the Science of the Soul* 146). She reported that Franklin
was alive "and is in good hopes of getting to England in nine months and
a half, provided no unforeseen accident occurs" ("Sir John Franklin"). At
this stage in her seership, Emma was apparently unable to take questions
while "away," although Haddock noted in a letter of December 1849 that
"I can communicate with Emma when *away*, it saves her strength and
enables me to put enquiries" (Letters 7/189). While talking with Franklin,
Emma could also communicate his state of mind to her audience. In a
séance of January 13, 1850, she reported that Franklin "Thinks much of
Lady F. and some children, *not babes*... He wonders no one has been to help
him—thinks it very strange" (Letters 7/189). This process demonstrates
that the issue of emotions, in this case Franklin's feelings of love and
melancholy, had become conjoined with the presence of the dis/embodied
female in the articulation and recreation of the lost expedition.

Emma's narratives were full of picturesque details regarding Franklin
(she correctly stated that he was bald), the ice, marvellous animals, and

"many queer looking things." On one occasion she appeared to imitate Franklin by drinking some fish oil, "wh[ich] produced a great deal of Nausea" (Letters 7/189). For Maconochie, the geographical location of Franklin was paramount, and he "very earnestly begged her to ascertain what o'clock it was where Sir J.F. was; & when it was 11.30AM with us, she said it wanted 10m to six with him, indicating a difference of long. of from 80 to 85 degrees" (Letters 7/189). In later séances Emma maintained that there was a seven-hour time difference between Bolton and the Arctic, usually ascertained by looking at clocks or timepieces while away. She believed that Franklin's watch kept the "best time," while Maconochie noted "Time in Bolton now *Greenwich* Time, from the Railways" (Letters 7/189). A later observer, the mesmerist and scientist William Gregory, thought it "quite absurd to suppose that this totally uneducated girl has any notion of the longitude to time, or of the difference between an arctic day and one in our latitude" (305).

Emma pointed out the west side of Hudson's Bay on a map provided, although it was "very inconveniently bound up in a volume of the Penny Cyclopaedia, and required by her to be rested on her head—not held to her eyes and thus reversed, no very precise indication could be obtained" (Letters 7/189). Emma's geographical strategies took Maconochie by surprise, but he thought this an unlikely, if plausible, location to seek the expedition. Eager to locate the rescue expedition led by James Clark Ross, Maconochie used an old note of Ross's and asked Emma to look for him: she "pointed to Bank's Land almost at once" (Letters 7/189).

Maconochie sent detailed memorandums on Emma to the Admiralty, and W.A.B. Hamilton, the Second Secretary of the Admiralty, independently contacted Maconochie ("Captain M." in the newspaper reports) through the *Manchester Guardian*. Hamilton maintained a correspondence with Maconochie on this matter, and through his influence Maconochie procured letters and autographs of some of the officers on the Franklin expedition for Emma's use. In October, Haddock tried Emma with a larger map of the polar regions and she "two or three times kept feeling with her fingers along Barrow's Straits and Westwards" (Letters 7/189); on another occasion she decided Franklin's party was at the Parry Islands (now Queen

Elizabeth Islands). In attempting to map out the trajectories of Emma's visions, Haddock believed her confusing references to warmer regions could be explained by Franklin's previous residence in Van Diemen's Land: "it would seem that she mentally followed him through other climes, and former scenes, to his then situation" (Letters 7/189).

The autumn and winter of 1849 was a particularly significant period in the search for Franklin. By this stage it was clear that no contact had been made with the expedition by the Canadian or Russian authorities and that the food supplies taken in 1845 must be finished. The first batch of search-and-rescue missions, in fact, had achieved little, and the expedition led by James Clark Ross, which overwintered at Port Leopold in 1848 (far from Banks Land), was actually making its way out of Baffin's Bay in October, reaching Scarborough on November 3. For Jane Franklin this failure dashed her hopes: the news that Ross's expedition had neither heard nor seen anything of Franklin and had not come into contact with any Inuit, undermined the accounts of the whalers. It was not until August 1850 that the first real traces of the Franklin expedition were found on Beechey Island, and October when these discoveries were publicized on the return of that season's ships. The period from the winter of 1849 to the autumn of 1850 was therefore dominated by rampant speculation and wonder. Jane Franklin commenced her decade-long lobbying campaign for the rescue of her husband, and this was also the point at which the myth of the Franklin expedition began to enter the popular imagination.

Emma's visions were widely reported in the British press in September and October 1849 and in the colonies in the early months of 1850. Emma's news that all was well on the expedition and that it would return in September 1850 quickly reached Lady Franklin and her niece Sophia Cracroft in the Orkney Islands. Emma's visions were reported by most newspapers as positive news about Franklin (seemingly alone with three companions), despite the communications that described seeing a sunken ship and "the shells (dead bodies) of others, in different postures under the snow" (Letters 7/189). Cracroft, however, was sceptical, and suggested to a correspondent that having several clairvoyants consulted "on the same day in different parts" would be a fruitful experiment (Sophia 248/247/15). Although they first read about Emma in the newspaper, by October 15 Jane Franklin and Cracroft had been sent a copy of Maconochie's report by John Franklin's daughter from his first marriage, Eleanor Gell. While Gell thought it "exceedingly interesting & satisfactory" (Sophia 248/247/17), Cracroft and Jane Franklin believed that there was "a diseased imagination, or over excited nerves, at work" (Sophia 248/247/21). Yet at the same time, Cracroft was struck by the second statement published about Emma, particularly due to the fact that the longitude of her uncle's position was given. In a letter to her mother and sister, Cracroft revealed that she was "very much inclined to place confidence" in this revelation. She requested that they send her her own statement about Ellen Dawson, another clairvoyant whom she and her aunt had consulted in London that May, presumably to compare with Emma's visions.

CONCLUSION

Between 1849 and 1852 there were at least a dozen clairvoyants who, under mesmeric trance, reported visiting Franklin and either gave general locations, times (whereby longitude could be calculated), or named the district in which the ships lay frozen. Typically the clairvoyant was an uneducated young woman, frequently a domestic servant with a history of illness or sensitivity. In many cases she was put into a trance by medical practitioners with a history of interest in homeopathy, phrenology, and ether experiments. On occasions, as in the case of Emma, the displays of the clairvoyant were reported extensively in the press and journalists and naval personnel attended her trances to hear the revelations. These communications aroused much interest in the newspaper press of the time and were frequently satirized in medical journals and in papers such as *Punch*.

For many audiences, Emma's published clairvoyant techniques provided an opportunity to prove or disprove the claims of the mesmeric movement. If the revelations of Emma and other contemporary clairvoyants in Britain and its colonies regarding Franklin's whereabouts were true, then surely it would just be a matter of time before everyone could be certain? As interest in the Franklin search and rescue missions died down after 1852, so too did the mesmeric visions. When verified Inuit testimony about the fate of the expedition arrived in England in 1854, visions about Franklin suddenly jumped into the spirit realm. Mediums, particularly those in the United States, began to visit Franklin in the otherworld where, in the company of other dead celebrities, he would reveal the make-up and cosmology of the next life.

Of course, Franklin had died in June 1847, and by 1850 there were certainly no survivors or ships to rescue. Yet almost all of the clairvoyants said that Franklin was alive and well, and either had hopes of returning at some point, or was within contactable distance of rescuing ships. All of the visions contained similarities. The focus was always on the person of Franklin or officers close to him. His sufferings, diet, and clothing were obviously of great concern to the audiences at these séances and the clairvoyants typically obliged by throwing in material details. At the time, the content of these visions were taken very seriously, even though the women were supposed to be uneducated and naive. Analyzing their descriptions of the North soon exposes a whole raft of clichés prevalent at the time about ice, Eskimos, and polar bears, and one avenue for exploration is seeing just how far these visions were informed by the popular culture of the Arctic, particularly the stereotypes found in panoramas and other media.

For the cultural historian, however, the accuracy or inaccuracy of the visions themselves is less important than the issues of embodiment and disembodiment that these visions raised, for the clairvoyant body was utilized as a travelling device within a web of geographical relations. When sent to the northern regions, many of them described experiencing the cold, but also appeared to shiver and shake. There are issues of performance and self-representation here, but also fundamental questions about how people imagine floating bodies or travelling souls to be. How can they feel, smell, and talk "ideally" to living bodies elsewhere?

In around 1848 there was a remarkable cultural shift in western societies in which the notion of "communities of sensation" suddenly became relevant to a variety of fields (see McCorristine). In mesmerism, the "community of sensation" refers to the unique interconnection created between the operator and his subject, whereby feelings and thoughts could be psychically transferred from one to the other. It is interesting that in the original publicity for Emma, her visions were imagined within the context of tele-technologies such as the telegraph machine and photographic process: "when we make the lightening carry our messages and the sun take our portraits, it is very difficult to draw the precise line betwixt the possible and the impossible" ("Sir John Franklin"). Emma was referred to as a telegraph machine and the whole area of clairvoyance was linked to the transport revolution occurring at the time. While Irish, Australian, and Indian mesmerisers were undoubtedly taking their lead from British investigations, the representation of the clairvoyant as a component of tele-technology opened the door to speculations independent of news being transmitted from Britain. Mesmerism therefore served as a dissenting route of information and consolation to people cut off from the northern hemisphere, adding their sensations to the network of imperial affects.

To briefly highlight another contemporary instance of clairvoyance, the case of Ludwig Leichhardt offers a colonial example of how the disappearance of a famous explorer could initiate affectual thinking. Leichhardt was a Prussian explorer who disappeared in 1848 during an attempt to cross Australia from east to west. This caught the attention of some mesmerists in Melbourne, who in 1850 sent a 'Franklin clairvoyant' in search of Leichhardt and his companions. In this case the clairvoyant "(mentally) wandered through the Australian wilderness in search of the intrepid traveller" ("Leichhardt"). She even claimed to have secured an interview with Leichhardt in which he revealed that all of the party were dead except for two men and himself. In a subsequent update he was described as having reached water "but not before having killed a horse and giving the blood to one of the party" ("Victoria"). Building upon the same kind of communication network that was showcased by British clairvoyants such as Emma, the Melbourne mesmerists demonstrated how colonial practitioners could move beyond a concern for Franklin by implicating the female body in the solution of local geographical mysteries.

Thinking about the clairvoyant in the context of the Franklin disappearance offers many avenues for further research. As a technology of travel, as a dissenting route of—and object for—geographical knowledge, or as a flashpoint in the skirmishes between mesmerism and its opponents, the clairvoyant's deployment has wider implications for our understanding of imperial exploration. In conclusion, I would argue that the cases of Emma and other clairvoyants reveal interrelated histories of affectivity and Arctic exploration. The dynamic intimacy existing between operator and the clairvoyant made tangible the affectual forces circulating around the Franklin disaster. The Arctic was imagined as a realm of spiritualized masculine endeavour and this set the stage for an encounter in popular culture in which male bodies and spectral female presences acted together.

Further examination of the psychosexual intimacies of the séance and the clairvoyant as a site of medical and mesmeric experimentation would provide an opportunity to rethink nineteenth-century exploration. For much of the twentieth century, studies of imperial exploration were dominated by geographical and biographical accounts. Cultural studies and various interdisciplinary critiques problematized the voice of the male explorer in terra incognita. Looking more closely at the séance and the clairvoyant uncovers an emergent "multi-vocal" Arctic made up of an expanded social field. This chapter has demonstrated how the disappearance of the Franklin expedition enabled some hitherto "unauthorized" or excluded voices to gain publicity and, in some cases, credence. Clairvoyance and paranormal modes of thinking were part of this process, but underlying them were the same intimacies and articulations of the Franklin disaster that haunted other diverse audiences interested in the Arctic.

AUTHOR'S NOTE

The author wishes to acknowledge the generous support of the Irish Research Council CARA Postdoctoral Mobility Fellowship in conducting this research.

WORKS CITED

Brennan, T. *The Transmission of Affect*. Ithaca: Cornell UP, 2004.

Brown, J. *The North-West Passage, and the Plans for the Search for Sir John Franklin. A Review*. London: Stanford, 1858.

Chapman, M.W. *Harriet Martineau's Autobiography: With Memorials*. Vol. 3. London: Smith, 1877.

Cooter, R. *The Cultural Meaning of Popular Science: Phrenology and the Organization of Consent in Nineteenth-Century Britain*. Cambridge: Cambridge UP, 1984.

Desmond, A. *The Politics of Evolution: Morphology, Medicine, and Reform in Radical London*. Chicago: U of Chicago P, 1989.

Franklin, C. "'An Habitation of Devils, a Domicill for Unclean Spirits, and a Den of Goblings': The Marvelous North in Early Modern English Literature." *The Mysterious and the Foreign in Early Modern England*. Eds. H. Ostovich, M.V. Silcox, and G. Roebuck. Newark: U of Delaware P, 2008. 27–38.

Gillies Ross, W. "Clairvoyants and Mediums search for Franklin." *Polar Record* 39 (2003): 1–18.

Gregory, W. *Letters to a Candid Inquirer, on Animal Magnetism*. London: Taylor, 1851.

Haddock, J.W. *Somnolism and Psycheism: Or the Science of the Soul and the Phenomena of Nervation as Revealed by Vital Magnetism, etc.* London: Hodson, 1851.

———. *Somnolism and Psycheism: Otherwise Vital Magnetism, or Mesmerism: Considered Physiologically and Philosophically*. London: Hodson, 1849.

Holloway, J. "Make-believe: Spiritual Practice, Embodiment, and Sacred Space." *Environment and Planning* A 35 (2003): 1961–74.

Hood, E.P. *Dream Land and Ghost Land: Visits and Wanderings there in the Nineteenth Century*. London: Partridge, 1852.

"Leichhardt." *Bell's Life in Sydney and Sporting Reviewer* 9 Nov. 1850.

Letters to the Admiralty. ADM/7/189. Public Record Office, Kew, London.

McCorristine, S. *Spectres of the Self: Thinking about Ghosts and Ghost-seeing in England, 1750–1920*. Cambridge: Cambridge UP, 2010.

Neumann, R.P. *Imposing Wilderness: Struggles over Livelihood and Nature Preservation in Africa*. Berkeley: U of California P, 2002.

Secord, J.A. *Victorian Sensation: The Extraordinary Publication, Reception, and Secret Authorship of Vestiges of the Natural History of Creation*. Chicago: U of Chicago P, 2000.

"Sir John Franklin." *The Morning Post* 4 Oct. 1849.

Sophia Cracroft Letters. 1849–51. MS 248/247. Scott Polar Research Institute Archives.

"Victoria." *South Australian Register* 9 Dec. 1850.

Winter, A. *Mesmerized: Powers of Mind in Victorian Britain*. Chicago: U of Chicago P, 1998.

Woodward, F.J. *Portrait of Jane: A Life of Lady Jane Franklin*. London: Hodder, 1951.

10 Myths of Iceland and Mount Hekla and their Deconstruction

Ida Pfeiffer's Journey to Iceland

JENNIFER E. MICHAELS

INTRODUCTION

At a time when few foreigners visited Iceland, the Austrian travel writer and explorer Ida Pfeiffer travelled there alone and recorded her experiences in *Reise nach dem scandinavischen Norden und der Insel Island im Jahre 1845*.[1] She was probably the first Austrian woman to visit Iceland, and her text provides a fascinating document of mid-nineteenth century life there. Pfeiffer was eager to visit Iceland because of what she perceived as its uniqueness: "Iceland was one of those regions towards which, from the earliest period of my consciousness, I had felt myself impelled. In this country, stamped as it is by Nature with features so peculiar, as probably to have no counterpart on the face of the globe." She hoped to see "things which should fill me with new and inexpressible astonishment" (*Journey* 4). From her previous reading she expected to find an Arcadia, but she was disappointed by many of the people she met. She did not find the wealthier people hospitable, and she was shocked by the primitive and dirty living conditions of the poor. She stayed two and a half months in Iceland, from 15 May to 29 July 1845, during which time she travelled extensively, and she vividly depicted the country's landscape and people. Throughout her text, she mixed discourses of Romanticism with realism to describe her reactions to both Icelandic society and scenery. The forthright Pfeiffer, who prided herself on describing what she had seen with her own eyes, and who struggled to be taken seriously as a travel writer, was generally not receptive to notions of the supernatural, to which she occasionally alludes, but always undermines. Discussing the supernatural could be dismissed as fanciful or even frivolous, criticisms often levelled against women travel writers, and she did not want to damage her credibility.

EUROPEAN FASCINATION WITH ICELAND

Pfeiffer decided to explore Iceland after she realized that her hope of visiting the North Pole was not feasible (Habinger 38). It is not surprising that Pfeiffer was eager to see Iceland. Like many European countries, German-speaking areas had a longstanding fascination with Iceland that reached an apex in the nineteenth century, especially during the years of German Romanticism. There were at that time few firsthand accounts of Iceland. In fact, in announcing the first edition of Pfeiffer's book, her publisher stressed that Iceland was a country about "which so little recent information exists" (*Journey* 2). Like the North in general, Iceland, situated on the periphery of Europe, functioned as an exotic realm in the European imagination since there were few facts to challenge such constructs. In particular "16th and 17th century sources imagined and constructed the north as a mythical place, full of marvels and magic, bestowed with unique spiritual qualities that could be considered beneficial, yet were most often perceived as threatening and diabolic" (Donecker 2). Europeans, especially those from northern countries, gradually came to see Iceland not only as an exotic, mythical realm, but also, as they discovered more about Icelandic culture, perceived connections with their own cultures. In the 1750s, Paul-Henri Mallet, a Swiss professor of French who lived in Copenhagen, fostered a Nordic renaissance, "inspired by Norse myth and eddic poetry" (Clunies Ross and Lönnroth 3).[2] Among many others, the German philosopher and poet Johann Gottfried Herder became fascinated by Norse legends and was influential in German Romanticism in the late eighteenth and early nineteenth centuries "when the obscure myths and enigmatic imagery of Old Norse poetry were admired for their sublime and spiritual qualities" (7). In the period of national Romanticism, Old Norse poetry and myth "took on a special ethnic significance." Northern countries, including (vicariously) German-speaking ones, viewed them as important parts of their heritage (18).[3] Later in the nineteenth century, this fascination with Norse mythology, encouraged by both German Romanticism and ideas of nation building, extended to middle-class culture in German-speaking countries. Readers found the heroic tales of Norse gods and heroes gripping, and Iceland became for many a mysterious (and threatening) realm of the supernatural. Clunies Ross and Lönnroth point out, however, that as Old Norse mythology grew in popularity in German-speaking areas, some artists became contemptuous of "the Viking kitsch promoted by overenthusiastic admirers of Old Norse culture. Thus 'Viking culture' in its romantic and nationalistic guise became an integral part of bourgeois culture or even of mass culture, while it declined as an intellectual movement and as an innovative force in art and literature" (23). The Nordic Renaissance, however, shaped European aesthetic notions. For the German Romantics, for instance, who were rebelling against classical aesthetics, sublime art was no longer the classical ideal of harmony, but rather "terrible, violent, and awe-inspiring, like thunderstorms, enormous threatening mountains, endless deserts, nightmares, madness, divine revelations, and visions of hell" (15). This change in aesthetics turned what had been seen as barren, desolate landscapes in Iceland into potentially "majestic and awesome" ones (Oslund 318). Beginning in the eighteenth century, travel accounts depicted Iceland as a wilderness "of exotic and unusual natural extremes" (314).

Another focus on Iceland at this time was scientific. On his journey to Iceland in 1772, for example, Joseph Banks had brought back specimens, and in the nineteenth century naturalists increasingly came to Iceland to follow his example. Especially after the catastrophic 1783 eruptions, Icelandic volcanism inspired growing interest among European geologists (Oslund 318). Pfeiffer, who was an avid reader throughout her life and devoured all travel accounts she could find, was aware of the interest in volcanism and familiar with previous descriptions of an imagined Iceland, which she acerbically dismissed as the over-active imaginations of their authors.[4]

IDA PFEIFFER'S LIFE OF TRAVEL WRITING

Surmounting many difficulties, Pfeiffer became a widely read and highly respected travel writer; in Europe, she was one of the most celebrated travel writers of her time. She was one of the first German-language female explorers, and her travel books were translated into seven languages.[5] Once she began travelling she led a life of adventure and accomplishment. Pfeiffer was born in Vienna in 1797 as Ida Reyer, the only girl in a large family of boys. Her father raised and educated her like her brothers, allowed her to wear boys' clothes, and fostered her interest in active, outdoor pursuits. When she was nine, her father died and her mother took over her education and tried, despite Ida's vehement protests, to prepare her to be a "lady." She had to discard her boys' clothes, wear dresses, and take piano lessons. Since she was young, she had dreamed of travelling, and the travelogues she eagerly read helped her escape for a while from the confines of her upbringing. When she was 17, she fell in love with her tutor, a feeling that he reciprocated, but her mother, who wanted a better match for her daughter, opposed the relationship. At the age of 22, she married the middle-aged lawyer Dr. Mark Anton Pfeiffer, a widower who held an important position in the Austrian government. They had two sons. Dr. Pfeiffer later lost his position, and the family found itself impoverished. Ida Pfeiffer gave music and drawing lessons to earn some money, but finances were very tight. When her mother died in 1831, she left her daughter a small inheritance that just covered living expenses and her sons' education. Pfeiffer separated from her husband in 1835. By 1842, when both sons had their own homes, she had decided to follow her dream of travelling. Thus, she did not begin travelling until the age of 45, after she had raised her family, and she continued to travel for the remainder of her life. She made five major journeys between 1842 and 1858. For Pfeiffer, this new life was exciting and fulfilling. Her first visit was to the Holy Land.[6] To counter protests from her family, horrified not only by her plans to travel, but also to do so alone, she disguised this journey as a pilgrimage, which was considered more "respectable." She had no intention, however, of simply visiting the Holy Land and included present-day Turkey, Syria, Jordan, Lebanon, Egypt, and Italy in her itinerary. Her second journey took her to Denmark, Norway, Sweden, and Iceland.[7]

CONTESTING GENDER EXPECTATIONS

One difficulty Pfeiffer had to surmount was widespread nineteenth-century notions of the proper role for women. Nineteenth-century bourgeois society viewed women as "unfit for the rigours of travel" and feared travel could make them "discontented, assertive, and so unfit to fulfil their proper role as wives" (Howe 326). At this time, most women who travelled either accompanied their husbands or other family members to overseas postings or were missionaries. It was most unusual for a bourgeois woman to travel alone for the love of travelling. If she did, it was viewed as a radical break with her previous "respectable" life. As Helga Watt points out, Pfeiffer dared "to imagine and pursue the virtually impossible: a mid-nineteenth century middle-class older woman exploring the remotest corners of the world—and doing it alone" (Watt 339). In her preface to her *Journey to Iceland* Pfeiffer felt obliged to defend herself, to ask her readers not to judge her too harshly, and to justify her love of travelling: "It is only because this love of travelling does not, according to established notions, seem proper for one of my sex, that I have allowed my feelings to speak in my defence." She stressed that, despite what her critics claimed, she did not travel to gain attention:

"When I was but a little child, I had already a strong desire to see the world," and as she grew older nothing gave her "so much pleasure as the perusal of voyages and travels." She chose Iceland as her destination because "I hoped there to find Nature in a garb such as she wears nowhere else. I feel so completely happy, so brought into communion with my Maker, when I contemplate sublime natural phenomena, that in my eyes no degree of toil or difficulty is too great a price at which to purchase such perfect enjoyment" (*Journey* 3–4). Pfeiffer often used references to God as a way of making her travels appear respectable.

Like other women travel writers of her time, Pfeiffer was forced to adopt strategies to conform to nineteenth-century "accepted notions of womanhood" and to retain "feminine" perspectives (Howe 326). As her conclusion to *A Visit to the Holy Land, Egypt, and Italy* and her preface to *A Lady's Voyage Around the World* suggest, Pfeiffer affected a voice of humble simplicity and self-effacement. Through this persona, she succeeded in the world of men because she was perceived as unpretentious and non-threatening. In his preface to *A Visit to the Holy Land, Egypt, and Italy*, Pfeiffer's Viennese publisher, for example, called her "a delicate lady." In his opinion, "strict truth shines forth from every page, and no one can doubt but that so pure and noble a mind must see things in a right point of view" (*Visit* preface n.pag.). One of her admiring readers, the famous explorer Alexander von Humboldt, stressed her "womanly virtues and delicacy" (Watt 349). Even at the end of her life, the editor of her last travel work, which includes her experiences in Madagascar, stressed in his remarks that Pfeiffer did not give the impression of being an unusual woman, an emancipated woman, or a masculine woman, all derogatory terms at the time (Felden 52). Yet a careful reading of her preface to *A Lady's Voyage Around the World* reveals that she was affecting a character. For example, she wrote that the memories of her travels were the comfort of her old age, thereby conjuring up an image of an old and rather feeble woman (*Eine Frauenfahrt* preface n.pag.). In spite of her posturing, her actions made clear that the real Pfeiffer was very different from the modest, self-effacing woman she pretended to be. Readers taken in by her literary persona would be surprised to learn that this "old" woman had the stamina and will power to ride through miles of desert, and despite the difficulties of some of her travels, which would have made the faint-hearted give up, she was determined to continue exploring. For Pfeiffer and other nineteenth-century women, travel was liberating because it freed them from stifling bourgeois conventions and gave them a self-determination they could rarely achieve at home. As Pfeiffer noted in the first chapter of her Iceland book, "I had found by experience, that a woman of an energetic mind can find her way through the world as well as a man" (*Journey* 4). Though her lack of patronage presented financial problems, it also gave her the independence to write as she saw fit, since she was not under obligation to sponsors.

Yet another difficulty she had to overcome were attitudes in the nine-teenth century toward travel literature, much of which was looked down upon as light entertainment. As Helga Watt observes, it is only since the 1970s and 1980s, encouraged by feminist and post-colonial studies, that "we have gained an appreciation for travelogues as largely nonfic-tional prose works of importance to our culture and literature" (339). In the nineteenth century, women travel writers, who had appropriated a genre that had previously been considered typically masculine, encoun-tered more difficulties than men in being taken seriously, and their travel works were frequently dismissed as frivolous. Ravina Aggarwal points out that women travel writers "were caught in a 'double-bind situation,' unfa-vorably judged and trivialized if their texts were construed as feminine, and questioned for the legitimacy and truth value of their work if they chose masculine adventure-hero forms" (554). Generally, women were not considered capable or qualified to discuss "serious" issues such as politics, economy, art, and science (Felden 2).

In her preface to *A Lady's Voyage Around the World,* Pfeiffer noted modestly that she was neither talented enough to write entertainingly nor knowledgeable enough to make appropriate judgments about what she experienced. Despite such avowals, intended to underscore her literary persona as a simple woman, Pfeiffer was determined that her travel writing should be taken seriously. Although in all her texts she engaged in Romantic discourses of the sublime, she also presented detailed accounts of the lives and customs of the people in the different cultures she visited, and she commented extensively on geological features, agriculture, and vegetation. In Iceland, for example, she described the different colours and textures of the lava flows she observed, distinguishing between older and more recent ones, and depicted in detail features of the many hot springs she visited. When she was in Iceland she began collecting specimens such as plants, insects, and shells. The sale of these specimens, some to museums, together with the profits from her Iceland book, helped finance her future travels. Over the years, she studied methods of preserving specimens and she later became well respected for her collections.[8] Thus, being taken seriously as a woman travel writer was not only important to her because she wanted to contribute to knowledge about the countries she visited, but it was also crucial for her finances. For this reason, she largely avoided anything that could be dismissed as fanciful, such as the supernatural.

INVOKING THE SUPERNATURAL

Yet on several occasions during her stay in Iceland, Pfeiffer invoked the supernatural to reinforce and then to deconstruct the persona she had created or to enhance atmosphere. On one occasion during her travels, she had to sleep in a church because there were no inns in the countryside. She wrote of the incident: "A certain feeling of discomfort always attaches to the fact of sleeping in a church alone, in the midst of a graveyard" (*Journey* 47), a comment that was likely included to conform to notions of women being fearful and superstitious. Later, however, she resolutely overcame "any superstitious fears derived from the proximity of my silent neighbours in the churchyard" (52). She also drew from texts that, although they did not focus on Iceland, gave Romantic depictions of the supernatural and hell. When she travelled to Þingvellir, the site of Iceland's first parliament, she and her guide had to ride into a deep chasm with overhanging blocks of lava. This chasm, which made her shudder, reminded her of Carl Maria von Weber's Romantic opera *Der Freischütz* ("The Marksman," 1821), specifically of the "Wolf's Hollow," often called the "Wolf's Glen," scene in the second act (*Journey* 51). Readers familiar with this popular opera would know this famous scene of the supernatural and the diabolical. It is peopled with demonic figures, spirits appear, and magic bullets are made. Later, while waiting for the geyser to erupt,[9] Pfeiffer explored nearby hot springs, impressed with the transparency of the water that enabled her to see into the depths of the caves. This called to mind Friedrich Schiller's ballad "Der Taucher" ("The Diver"), written in 1797 during his Sturm und Drang period, the precursor of German Romanticism. In this ballad Schiller described wide-open jaws of a whirlpool that seemed to lead into the depths of hell, filled with fearsome monsters. As she looked into the hot springs, Pfeiffer could "fancy I saw the monsters rise from the bottom" (*Journey* 70). By relying on these famous Romantic texts by men to express her own impressions of the supernatural in the Icelandic landscape, she avoided potential accusations that her reactions were fanciful.

At other times, however, the normally down-to-earth Pfeiffer had little sympathy with what she saw as over-vivid imaginations and she dismissed the Icelandic legends she encountered. As Karen Oslund remarks, "Icelandic legends about outlaws and supernatural creatures such as trolls living among the lava rocks" are quite widespread (Oslund 332). Pfeiffer did not comment on legends about trolls, but she did hear of legends about robbers and she remained sceptical about such tales. When a priest told her that a cave used to be "the resort of a mighty band of robbers," Pfeiffer viewed this "as a legend or a fable." She could not imagine "what robbers had to do in Iceland," certainly not in a cavern so far from the sea (*Journey* 59). Pfeiffer reported that many Icelanders believed that in the interior there was "a peculiar race of men" whose only contact with their fellow countrymen was one day a year when they bought necessities: "They then vanish suddenly, and no one knows in which direction they are gone." One man she talked to wanted to command a group of well-armed soldiers to search for "these wild men." People who claimed to have seen them said they were "taller and stronger than other Icelanders" and that they had a lot of money "acquired by pillage." Pfeiffer was sceptical: "When I inquired what respectable inhabitants of Iceland had been robbed by these savages, and when and where, no one could give me an answer. For my part, I scarcely think that one man, certainly not a whole race, could live by pillage in Iceland" (86). These tales, some of which had a historical basis, belong to Icelandic folklore. The perception that the robbers were taller and stronger than other Icelanders and that they could mysteriously and suddenly vanish, make them appear like supernatural beings.

PFEIFFER'S FOCUS ON AUTHENTICITY

Intent on being taken seriously, Pfeiffer wanted to give "a faithful account" of everything she saw (*Journey* 19), thereby underscoring that, as an eyewitness, her work had authenticity. Kamakshi Murti notes Pfeiffer's "refreshing candor" and argues that "her natural aversion to sensationalism combined with her common sense and lack of literary pretensions create rare vignettes of reality." Through her "matter-of-fact description" the reader "receives an almost photographic likeness of the other cultures" (Murti 85–7). In her book, Pfeiffer tried to give objective insights into the reality of Iceland, but she acknowledged that she might not always be right. Her book reveals that her gaze was shaped at least to some extent by her bourgeois values and mannerisms, as, for example, her aversion to dirt demonstrates.

Pfeiffer criticized previous depictions of Iceland, which she considered fanciful. When she attended a religious ceremony in Reykjavík she thought of "the poetical descriptions of the northern romancers, who grow enthusiastic in praise of ideal 'angels' heads with golden tresses." In her opinion, "the beautiful faces which are said to beam forth from among those golden locks exist only in the poet's vivid imagination" (*Journey* 37). Previous descriptions of the geysers, such as that by Joseph Banks on his visit to Iceland in 1772, reported noises like the firing of a distant cannon, followed by ever louder sounds and the shaking of the ground before the eruption (Banks 47). This did not match Pfeiffer's experience. Although she heard "some hollow sounds, as if a cannon were being fired at a great distance, and its echoing sounds were borne by the breeze" (*Journey* 68), she assured her readers that she did not find "every thing as I had anticipated it according to the descriptions and accounts I had read. I never heard a greater noise than I have mentioned, and never felt any trembling of the earth, although I paid the greatest attention to every little circumstance, and held my head to the ground during an eruption" (71). From her previous reading, she expected "subterranean noises, violent cracking and trembling of the earth" (68). In her opinion: "It is singular how many people repeat every thing they hear from others—how some, with an over-excited imagination, seem to see, hear, and feel things which do not exist; and how others, again, tell the most unblushing falsehoods" (71). Even if her view might not be right, she conceded, she at least possessed "the virtue of describing facts as I see them, and do not repeat them from the accounts of others" (83).

When Pfeiffer set out from Copenhagen to Iceland, her sailing ship encountered storms and she suffered from seasickness during the eleven-day voyage, a detail that underscores her resolve not to let hardships deter her from travel. Before depicting her own impressions of Iceland, Pfeiffer drew on the Scottish mineralogist George Mackenzie and Henry Holland's *Travels in the Island of Iceland 1810*, first published in 1810 and reprinted in 1841. Referencing male authors was a strategy that women travel writers often used to authenticate their own observations. The book included a short history of Iceland from its earliest settlement. She was impressed with the Alþing and noted that people possessed an excellent code of laws. Pfeiffer also admired the medieval culture of Iceland, calling it a golden age when education, literature, and refined poetry flourished, and she praised the sagas and Eddas (*Journey* 25). She also mentioned that Iceland's climate was once warmer: corn was said to have grown there, and trees and shrubs were larger than at the present, an observation with which others concur (Rauschenberg 191).

She drew attention to Iceland's colonization by Norway and then Denmark. She then highlighted a series of disasters such as the plague in 1402, when two thirds of the population died; the smallpox epidemic in the early eighteenth century, in which more than 16,000 people died; and the famine of 1757, which killed 10,000. In 1783, she reported, severe volcanic eruptions reshaped the Icelandic landscape, killed livestock, led to crop failure, and caused famine and disease. As a result of these catastrophes, 11,000 people, a quarter of the population, died. At the time of her visit, Iceland's population was estimated at 48,000. Her overview of Icelandic history suggests that although her views were shaped in part by Romantic aesthetics of the awe-inspiring and the sublime, hers would not be primarily a Romantic view of Iceland, since she sympathized with the many problems the people faced in trying to exist in the country's harsh climate and she unflinchingly depicted their poverty.

PFEIFFER'S DEPICTIONS OF ICELANDIC PEOPLE

As in all her travel works, Pfeiffer was interested in the people she encountered. Some people in Iceland were kind to her, but she was less than enthusiastic about others. From her previous reading she had expected to find an Eden, peopled with noble inhabitants who lived cut off from civilization and in harmony with nature. This was a common Romantic trope derived from Rousseau. Instead, she encountered either wealthy snobs or extreme poverty. The "high society" of Reykjavík snubbed her because she was not wealthy and treated her with a "dignified coldness" (*Journey* 30). Pfeiffer thought that many of their houses differed little from houses she had seen in other countries. They had rich furnishings, including grand pianos, which amazed her since they had to be shipped from Denmark. In contrast, poorer houses, which looked like small mounds, were built of lava and covered with turf, and she found them squalid and filthy on account of their lack of windows and smoky atmosphere. She recognized, however, that these houses were adapted to the harsh climate. Their low passageways were designed "as an additional defence against the cold"

(27).[10] The people themselves, not just in Reykjavík, but also farming families in the countryside, had in her view virtues as well as faults. Except for priests and other individuals who helped her, she tended to make generalizations about the Icelanders. Among their virtues were absolute honesty and lack of crime, and she was impressed that nearly all the people she met were literate and had books in their cottages. Many had religious books, and one wealthy farmer owned a copy of Homer's *Odyssey*. On the negative side, she did not find them very hospitable and saw as their faults drunkenness, a lack of cleanliness, and especially indolence. She confessed that she "found the character of the Icelanders in every respect below the estimate I had previously formed of it, and still further below the standard given in books" (40).

Despite her criticisms, Pfeiffer was sensitive to the hard lives many Icelanders led. Fishing, one of Iceland's main occupations, she reported, was dangerous, and many fishermen drowned in fierce storms. To prevent entire families being destroyed, when members of one family went fishing, the father and the sons went in different boats so that some might survive. When they were unable to fish, families had to subsist on dried fish heads. People in the countryside lived isolated from each other and tried to eke a living from the unproductive soil. Priests were also poor, and those in the countryside had to conduct services in several different, far-distant churches. Likewise, the few doctors, who were ill paid, had to undertake long and dangerous journeys to reach their patients.

While Pfeiffer was observing and judging the Icelanders, they were, however, also gazing at and judging her. She related, often with annoyance, but sometimes with humour, that when she had to spend a night in churches, the local people gathered to observe her: "As usual, all the inhabitants of the place ranged themselves in and before the church, probably to increase their knowledge of the human race by studying my peculiarities" (*Journey* 73). They were just as curious about her as she was about them, but she did not reflect that the Icelanders might have found her gaze equally intrusive.

LANDSCAPE DEPICTIONS

Throughout her account, Pfeiffer was overwhelmed by both the bleakness and the majesty of the landscape. She was fascinated by Iceland's natural wonders. Before going ashore she was eager to "tread the shores of Iceland, the longed-for, and bask as it were in the wonders of this island, so poor in the creations of art, so rich in the phenomena of Nature" (*Journey* 24). On her arrival she wrote, for example, that she could not "tire of gazing and wondering at this terribly beautiful picture of destruction" (28), caused by volcanic eruptions and subsequent lava flows. In addition she admired the beautiful sunsets and was impressed with "the profound silence and solitude" (54). In the interior of the country everything "seemed dead, all round was barren and desert, so that the effect was truly Icelandic" (58). Although she was unimpressed with the sounds she had heard prior to the geyser's eruption, when she actually saw it she wrote: "Words fail me when I try to describe it: such a magnificent and overpowering sight can only be seen once in a lifetime" (69). Her landscape depictions vary between such Romantic expressions of the sublime and detailed and exact descriptions of lava, swamps, and geological features. On occasions she undermined notions of the sublime by focusing on the mundane. For example, the townspeople used the hot springs she visited near Reykjavík for bathing, cooking, and washing clothes (44). Pfeiffer realized that from the Icelanders' point of view, the hot springs were utilitarian rather than exotically Romantic. As Karen Oslund remarks, for Icelanders the hot springs "were about as remarkable and interesting as a laundromat might be to us" (Oslund 330).

PFEIFFER'S ASCENT OF MOUNT HEKLA

The literal high point of Pfeiffer's stay in Iceland was climbing Mount Hekla, which made her the first foreigner to do so in nine years, and perhaps the first foreign woman ever. Pfeiffer was not deterred by Hekla's longstanding connection to the supernatural, and perhaps Hekla's notoriety encouraged her to see it for herself. After its first documented eruption in 1104, stories arose that Hekla was the gateway to Hell, and later eruptions only reinforced this legend. Some people thought that one could "hear the wails of tormented sinners in the vicinity of the fiery mountain" (Donecker 6). Hekla continued to be viewed as a particularly evil and demonic place, an opening into hell or purgatory (see Oslund 319) and as a site where witches gathered (see, for example, Grimm 1002). Grimm points out that the Danish expression "gaa du dig til Häkkenfeldt" ("go to the devil") refers to Mount Hekla (Grimm 1001).[11] As the writer Kristof Magnusson told me, one Swedish expression for "go to the devil" or "go to hell" is "dra åt Häcklefjäll" ("go to Hekla").[12] Hekla's reputation offended the Icelandic humanist Arngrímur Jónsson (1568–1648), who tried to refute such myths, which he attributed to "the intolerable errors of foreigners" (Morgan n.pag.). He considered "the Hekla legend as derogatory, almost insulting, to his native country" (Donecker 6–7).

Pfeiffer did not engage with such myths of the supernatural. Instead, she vividly recorded her climb and the surrounding area, and accurately described Hekla's situation in a volcanic ridge. With her two guides she rode part way and then attained the summit on foot, a challenging and strenuous ascent. She called the volcano "fearful" (*Journey* 73), not, however, because of its supernatural reputation, but because of the "death and destruction" its eruptions had caused (74). She was impressed by the great contrasts between the grass in the valley and the hills of black, shining lava, and she noted that Hekla had "the blackest lava and the blackest sand" (74). Before her ascent she spent the night in a small village at the foot of Mount Hekla and observed: "Nowhere, not even on Mount Vesuvius, had I heard such hollow, droning sounds as here—the echoes of the heavy footsteps of the peasants. These sounds made a very awful impression on me" (75). These sounds could have been an early indication of the eruption that occurred in September of that year. Pfeiffer described the difficult ascent over hills of lava and chasms filled with snow. After three and a half hours, they had to leave the horses and continue on foot. It was a fearful journey during which she fell many times and cut her hands on the sharp lava: "After two hours' more labour we reached the summit of the mountain. I stood now on Mount Hecla, and eagerly sought the crater on the snowless top, but did not find it. I was the more surprised, as I had read detailed accounts of it in several descriptions of travel" (77). Since Hekla's crater had long been viewed as an entrance to hell, by pointing out that the crater did not exist Pfeiffer indirectly undermined such previous superstitions. She traversed the whole summit and saw no sign of a fissure or crater but did observe a fissure lower down, from which she accurately assumed that lava erupted. When it began to snow she hoped she would be able to determine hot places on Hekla by the snow melting. In this she was disappointed, since the snow did not melt. From the summit she could see far into the uninhabited country. It seemed like "a petrified creation, dead and motionless, and yet magnificent,—a picture which once seen can never again fade from the memory, and which alone amply compensates for all the previous troubles and dangers. A whole world of glaciers, lava-mountains, snow and ice-fields, rivers and lakes." She reflected that nature "must have laboured and raged till these forms were created" (78). Pfeiffer wondered whether it was over now: "Has the destroying element exhausted itself; or does it only rest, like the hundred-headed Hydra, to break forth with renewed strength?" (78). Shortly after she left Iceland, Hekla erupted on 2 September 1845.

PFEIFFER'S DECONSTRUCTION OF ASSUMPTIONS ABOUT GENDER

As Pfeiffer's ascent of Hekla demonstrates, and in contrast to the conventional feminine role she often assumed, she occasionally took on the voice of the heroic traveller common to much travel literature written by men. She mentioned her fatigue, for example, after a three-day trip during which she rode 114 miles over rough terrain and through storms and was benumbed with cold. On another occasion, on which she rode nearly 255 miles in six days, she noted that she was blessed with a nature for travelling: "No rain or wind was powerful enough to give me even a cold." In these six days she had no warm food and had eaten only bread and cheese, but despite the hardships she arrived back in Reykjavík "in good health and spirits" (*Journey* 63). She often included humorous comments such as her description of riding. She remarked that riding is supposedly "most beneficial to those who suffer from liver-complaints," but in her opinion those "who rode upon an Icelandic horse, with an Icelandic side-saddle, every day for the space of four weeks, would find, at the expiration of that time, her liver shaken to a pulp, and no part of it remaining" (41). Her travels were a major accomplishment, since such journeys on horseback were strenuous and there was at that time no tourist infrastructure. For Pfeiffer, riding long distances on horseback was challenging, as the first time she had ever sat on a horse was a few years previously during her journey to the Holy Land.

CONCLUSION

Throughout her text, Pfeiffer's sheer enthusiasm for travelling shines through, and she vividly communicates to her readers this excitement and the awe she experienced in Iceland. She dismissed the fatigues of her journey: "What were they in comparison to the unutterably beautiful and marvellous phenomena of the north, which will remain ever present to my imagination so long as memory shall be spared me?" (*Journey* 49). Although shaped by Romantic discourses of the sublime, she also showed the reality of Iceland as she experienced it. Not only did she give insights into the beauty of the Icelandic landscape, but also into the volcanism that shaped it. Even though she found fault with Icelanders, she nevertheless accurately and sympathetically depicted the harsh lives they had to lead. In her book, Pfeiffer contests and subtly undermines not only nineteenth-century views of women, but also of Iceland. As her ascent of Mount Hekla and her strenuous travels through the countryside demonstrate, she subverts notions of gender by showing that women could effectively pursue such "masculine" activities. Similarly, by often focusing on the mundane and the harsh reality of everyday life, she subverts notions of Iceland as a mythic and exotic realm of the supernatural.

1. *Journey to Iceland and Travels in Sweden and Norway, 1852.* Quotations in the text are from *Journey to Iceland,* 2nd ed., no trans., Project Gutenberg. Included as an appendix in the English edition is a translation of the famous poem "Völuspá" from the *Poetic Edda* that tells the story of the world's creation, its coming end, and subsequent rebirth, related by a *völva* ("seeress") to Odin.

2. Mallet's work was translated into English and German and shaped many readers' views of Old Norse poetry and myth.

3. I discuss here only views that Pfeiffer was likely to have encountered. I do not include the later misrepresentation of Norse myths by the Nazis.

4. In her travel texts Pfeiffer typically referred by name only to authors she admired, such as Alexander von Humboldt, or, in the case of Iceland, George Mackenzie and Henry Holland, whose book she thought was "of sterling value" (*Journey* 25). She did not name those authors whom she criticized for their inaccuracy or their overly fertile imaginations. Although she left no list of books she had read prior to her visit to Iceland, one can surmise that she was familiar with the German Romantics such as Herder and Mallet. In her travel account she mentioned Friedrich Schiller's ballad "Der Taucher" and Carl Maria von Weber's Romantic opera *Der Freischütz.*

5. For many years, Pfeiffer was almost forgotten. The reissue of her texts in German and English, in both paperback and Kindle, has renewed and fostered interest in her work.

6. See *Reise einer Wienerin ins Heilige Land* (1844, *A Visit to the Holy Land, Egypt, and Italy,* 1852).

7. Pfeiffer then journeyed around the world twice, trips that were represented in her works *Eine Frauenfahrt um die Welt* (1850, *A Lady's Voyage Round the World: a Selected Translation,* 1851) and *Meine zweite Weltreise* (1856, *A Lady's Second Journey round the World; from...,* 1855). The English translation appeared before the German original. Her final journey was to Madagascar: *Reise nach Madagaskar: Nebst einer Biographie der Verfasserin, nach ihren eigenen Aufzeichnungen* (1861, *The Last Travels of Ida Pfeiffer,* 1861).

8. See, for example, Kollar (1–7).

9. Pfeiffer does not specify which geyser, but it would likely have been Geysir, sometimes called the Great Geysir, which at that time was Iceland's most powerful geyser.

10. Others also stressed the unhealthy living conditions in the smoky, badly ventilated houses. See Magnus Olafsson, quoted in Rauschenberg (193).

11. The first edition of Jacob Grimm's *Deutsche Mythologie* appeared in 1835 and was influential in shaping views of the North. It was reprinted several times and appeared also in English.

12. Discussion with Kristof Magnusson in May 2011 at Grinnell College.

WORKS CITED

Aggarwal, R. "Point of Departure: Feminist Locations and the Politics of Travel in India." *Feminist Studies* 26.3 (2000): 535–62.

Banks, J. *The Letters of Sir Joseph Banks: A Selection 1768–1820.* Ed. N. Chambers. London: Imperial College P, 2000.

Clunies Ross, M., and L. Lönnroth. "The Norse Muse: Report from an International Research Project." *Alvíssmál* 9 (1999): 3–28.

Donecker, S. "The Lion, the Witch and the Walrus: Images of the Sorcerous North in the 16th and 17th Centuries." *TRANS. Internet-Zeitschrift für Kulturwissenschaften* 17. 2010. <http://www.inst.at/trans/17Nr/4-5/4-5_donecker.htm> 24 Nov 2012.

Felden, T. *Frauen Reisen: Zur literarischen Repräsentation weiblicher Geschlechterrollenerfahrung im 19. Jahrhundert.* New York: Lang, 1993.

Grimm, J. *Teutonic Mythology.* 4th ed. Vol. 3. Trans. J.S. Stallybrass. London: Bell, 1883.

Habinger, G., ed. *Ida Pfeiffer— "Wir leben nach Matrosenweise": Briefe einer Weltreisenden des 19. Jahrhunderts.* Vienna: Promedia, 2008.

Howe, P. "Die Wirklichkeit ist anders: Ida Pfeiffer's Visit to China 1847." *German Life and Letters* 52 (1999): 325–42.

Kollar, V. *Über Ida Pfeiffer's Sendungen von Naturalien aus Mauritius und Madagascar.* Vienna: Hof-und Staatsdruckerei, 1858.

Morgan, H. "The Island Defenders: Humanist Patriots in Early-Modern Iceland and Ireland." *Nations and Nationalities in Historical Perspective.* Eds. G. Hálfdanarson and A.K. Isaacs. Pisa: Ed. Plus, 2001. 223–45. Clioh's Workshop 3.

Murti, K.P. *India: The Seductive and Seduced "Other" of German Orientalism.* Westport: Greenwood, 2001.

Oslund, K. "Imagining Iceland: Narratives of Nature and History in the North Atlantic." *The British Journal for the History of Science* 35 (2002): 313–34.

Pfeiffer, I. *Eine Frauenfahrt um die Welt.* Vienna: Gerold, 1850.

———. *Journey to Iceland.* 2nd ed. London: Cooke, 1853.

———. *A Lady's Second Journey round the World; from London to the Cape of Good Hope, Borneo, Java, Sumatra, Celebes, Ceram, the Moluccas, etc., California, Panama, Peru, Ecuador and the United States.* Trans. Mrs. Percy Sinnett. London: Longman, 1855.

———. *A Lady's Voyage Round the World: a Selected Translation.* Trans. Mrs. Percy Sinnett. London: Longman, 1851.

———. *The Last Travels of Ida Pfeiffer Inclusive of a Visit to Madagascar, with a Biographical Memoir of the Author.* Trans. H.W. Dulcken. London: Routledge, 1861.

———. *Meine zweite Weltreise.* Vienna: Gerold, 1856.

———. *Reise einer Wienerin ins Heilige Land.* Vienna: Dirnböck, 1844.

———. *Reise nach dem scandinavischen Norden und der Insel Island im Jahre 1845.* Pest: Heckenast, 1846.

———. *Reise nach Madagaskar: Nebst einer Biographie der Verfasserin, nach ihren eigenen Aufzeichnungen.* Vienna: Gerold 1861.

———. *A Visit to the Holy Land, Egypt, and Italy.* Trans. H.W. Dulcken. London: Ingram Cooke, 1852.

Rauschenberg, R. "The Journals of Joseph Banks's Voyage up Great Britain's West Coast to Iceland and to the Orkney Isles July to October, 1772." *Proceedings of the American Philosophical Society* 117 (1973): 186–226.

Schiller, F. "Der Taucher." 1797. <http://meister.igl.uni-freiburg.de/gedichte/sch_fv06.html> 1 June 2013.

Watt, H.S. "Ida Pfeiffer: A Nineteenth-Century Woman Travel Writer." *The German Quarterly* 64 (1991): 339–52.

11 Moon Men and Inland Dwellers

The Dissemination of Greenlandic Legends and Myths in the
Writings of Hinrich Rink and Knud Rasmussen

SILVIJE HABULINEC

A brother and a sister once lived together, and were very much
attached to each other. The sister, who was very desirous of going off
for the salmon-fishing, asked her brother to take her up to a salmon
river. Not being able to deny her, he put the boat into the sea and went
with her to the fishing place; but when they had landed and discharged
the boat, putting all their things on the beach, she climbed a little way
up the rocks, and went across a smooth level to the brook. All at once
she saw an inorusek...close behind her. Stupefied with terror, she tried
to escape; but he caught hold of her and carried her further and further
inland. The others plainly heard her shrieks for help, and hurried off
to rescue her; but she was already gone, and her cries soon died away
among the mountains. (Rink 265–6)

FOR CENTURIES, Europeans have regarded the Far North as an abode of
the supernatural, as numerous examples in this present volume testify. In
many instances, the otherworldly North was perceived as uncanny,

threatening, or even downright monstrous. However, if we as observers broaden our perspective, we soon realize that the topography of the supernatural is not as straightforward as it might seem at first glance. The indigenous Greenlandic Inuit—who, from a European perspective, dwell in one of the most remote and wondrous parts of the North—developed their very own tales of otherness. In Inuit lore, the inaccessible, remote, and thoroughly inhospitable Greenlandic interior and the ice cap serve as the foil to the coastal regions, which provided the familiar surroundings of a society whose subsistence economy, social organization, material culture, and spirituality were oriented toward the sea (Grønnow 192; cf. Gulløv). In the interior, strange and dreadful things could happen. A girl abducted by the inland dwellers might be forced to wear boots full of spiders and vermin that devour flesh and leave only bare bones (Rink 266). Worse, she might find herself married to a giant worm (Rink 186–8; cf. Grønnow 198). Broadly speaking, this contrast between the familiar littoral landscape and the supernatural interior is not unlike the opposition between Europe and its northern peripheries in the ancient, medieval, and early modern imagination.

Like many other researchers, I first became acquainted with the rich oral tradition of Greenland through two books by Knud Rasmussen, the famous explorer and anthropologist of Greenland and Arctic Canada. The first, *The People of Polar North*, was edited by G. Herring and published in London in 1908. The second, *Eskimo Folk-Tales*, was edited by William Worster and published in London in 1921. Both volumes were translations based on Rasmussen's notes, containing various stories of the indigenous Greenlandic people. By the early 1920s, Rasmussen was already well known as the preeminent expert on Greenland and its inhabitants. This was a reputation duly emphasized by his translator and editor, who wrote the following of him:

> No man is better qualified to tell the story of Greenland, or the stories of its people. Knud Rasmussen is himself partly of Eskimo origin; his childhood was spent in Greenland, and to Greenland he returned again

and again, studying, exploring, crossing the desert of the inland ice,
making unique collections of material, tangible and otherwise, from all
parts of that vast and little-known land. (Rasmussen, Eskimo 5)

I later came across an older volume, *The Tales and Traditions of the Eskimo* by Hinrich Rink, which was published in 1875, also in London. The introduction states that

[t]he author of this work has partly resided, partly been travelling
about, on the shores of Davis Strait, from the southernmost point of
Greenland up to 73° north latitude, for sixteen winters and twenty-two
summers; first as a scientific explorer, afterwards as Royal Inspector or
Governor of the Southern Danish establishments in Greenland. (Rink v)

During his tenure as Royal Inspector, Rink issued a circular in which he appealed to the locals to write down their oral stories and send them to him. In response to Rink's initiative, approximately five hundred stories were submitted. Many of these tales were contributed by the famous indigenous narrators and artists Aron of Kangeq (1822–69) and Jens Kreutzmann of Kangaamiut (1828–99) (Thisted, *Jens*; Thisted, *Således*). Together with the efforts of Norwegian and Danish missionaries, such as the Egede family, during the eighteenth century, the collections of Rink and Rasmussen form the foundation of anthropological research on indigenous Greenlandic lore (Høiris; cf. Grønnow 192).

Near the beginning of my research into these stories, I presented my preliminary findings at the Seventh International Congress of Arctic Social Sciences in June 2011. At the time, the title of my presentation was "Greenlandic Legends and Myths." Between then and now, I have altered the title to reflect the fact that, as an ethnologist and historian, my research is based primarily on the written evidence for the oral tales. This chapter is divided into three parts. In the first part I will try to explain the terms *myth, legend,* and *folktale* and explore the problems associated with such definitions. In the second part I will focus on the stories presented in

Rasmussen and Rink's books, while in the third part I will compare and contrast these myths and legends with those that originate in cultures far away from Greenland. Particular emphasis is placed on the accounts of the "inland dwellers" and the notions of otherness associated with these enigmatic beings. My hope is that this analysis will form the foundations for further investigations into Greenlandic legends and myths.

MYTH, LEGEND, AND FOLKTALE

Attempts to define terms such as *myth*, *legend*, and *folktale* present us with many problems. According to the American folklorist and anthropologist William Bascom,

> [m]yths are prose narratives which, in the society in which they are told, are considered to be truthful accounts of what happened in the remote past. They are accepted on faith; they are taught to be believed; and they can be cited as authority in answer to ignorance, doubt, or disbelief. Myths are the embodiment of dogma; they are usually sacred; and they are often associated with theology and ritual. Their main characters are not usually human beings, but they often have human attributes; they are animals, deities, or culture heroes, whose actions are set in an earlier world, when the earth was different from what it is today, or in another world such as the sky or underworld. Myths account for the origin of the world, of mankind, of death, or for characteristics of birds, animals, geographical features, and the phenomena of nature. They may recount the activities of the deities, their love affairs, their family relationships, their friendships and enmities, their victories and defeats. They may purport to "explain" details of ceremonial paraphernalia or ritual, or why taboos must be observed, but such etiological elements are not confined to myths. (4)

Bascom also provides similar definitions for the words *legend* and *folktale*:

Legends are prose narratives which, like myths, are regarded as true by the narrator and his audience, but they are set in a period considered less remote, when the world was much as it is today. Legends are more often secular than sacred, and their principal characters are human. They tell of migrations, wars and victories, deeds of past heroes, chiefs, and kings, and succession in ruling dynasties. In this they are often the counterpart in verbal tradition of written history, but they also include local tales of buried treasure, ghosts, fairies, and saints. (4–5)

Folktales are prose narratives which are regarded as fiction. They are not considered as dogma or history, they may or may not have happened, and they are not to be taken seriously. Nevertheless, although it is often said that they are told only for amusement, they have other important functions, as the class of moral folktales should have suggested. Folktales may-be set in any time and any place, and in this sense they are almost timeless and placeless. They have been called "nursery tales" but in many societies they are not restricted to children. They have also been known as "fairy tales" but this is inappropriate both because narratives about fairies are usually regarded as true, and because fairies do not appear in most folktales. Fairies, ogres, and even deities may appear, but folktales usually recount the adventures of animal or human characters. (4)

Though these definitions are detailed and precise, I am not sure that they can be suitably transferred and applied to an analysis of the Greenlandic stories. On a more general scale they serve their purpose, but if a researcher wants to apply them to the sources, then he or she is soon confronted with some difficulties. The problem is that these three definitions assume that such myths are always oral prose narratives, preserved in written forms like the Greenlandic stories that are the focus of this analysis. Yet the question that we must ask is this: If only the written form of a myth is available to us, is the narrative in question still to be considered a myth?[1] One might debate whether Bascom's definition implied a general exclusion of every written form of a story, but as the classicist Eric Csapo notes, "any definition of myth that excludes the contents of the *Iliad*, the Mesopotamian *Epic of Gilgamesh*, the Hittite *Song of Ullikummi*, or the Vedic scriptures of India to me seems unpersuasive" (5).

Hinrich Rink also provides some definitions that were, apparently, based on the indigenous storytellers' own terminology. For the purposes of this chapter, Rink's terminology seems more precise and appropriate, since it was created with the corpus of Greenlandic lore in mind:

> *Firstly, it must be observed that the natives themselves divide their tales into two classes—the ancient tales, called* окalugtuat *(plural of* окalugtuaк), *and the more recent ones, called* окalualârutit *(plural of* окalualârut). *The first kind may be more or less considered the property of the whole nation, at least of the greater part of its tribes; while the tales included under the second are, on the other hand, limited to certain parts of the country, or even to certain people related to each other, thus presenting the character of family records. (83)*

Rink even dates these stories. For the ancient ones, he presumes that they are older than one thousand years, while the recent ones are not older than two hundred years (84). If we combine Bascom's and Rink's definitions, we reach the conclusion that the ancient Greenlandic stories would fall into the category of myths, while more recent ones would be classified legends or even folktales, since Rink does not provide a sharp delineation between truth or fiction. It might be tempting to employ Bascom's definitions to explore the differences between various Greenlandic tales and to establish which ones are "myths," which are "legends," and which are "folktales." To avoid conceptual confusion, however, I have decided to use the simple, straightforward term *stories* instead, thus enabling me to focus on the content rather than on the nuances of terminology.

RASMUSSEN'S AND RINK'S COLLECTIONS

Even with a quick glance at the stories in the two collections, the difference between Rasmussen and Rink become apparent. In general, the stories in Rink's book are much easier to understand. Rasmussen's collection tends to present shorter stories, but they are usually more difficult to comprehend. It seems that, in Rink's case, the stories have been more assertively revised to be accessible to a European audience. Therefore the distinction between the content of the indigenous oral tradition and the published text is greater than in Rasmussen. As Rink himself noted, "the materials upon which the author has founded this collection have been written down partly by natives, partly by Europeans, from the verbal recital of the natives, and in the latter case to a large extent by the author himself" (90). Rink collected many previously written stories, but he was aware of this flaw: "To be properly appreciated, even the tales must be heard in Greenland, related by a native raconteur in his own language" (65).

Rasmussen, on the other hand, collected his stories directly from the native storytellers from different parts of Greenland—from the west, the east,[2] and the north[3]—and exerted less editorial influence on the composition of the stories. One major problem, however, occurs in all three books. It might seem self-evident that Rink's and Rasmussen's publications were intended for European readers, but this point must be emphasized, since we must bear in mind that authors, editors, and publishers were well aware of their readerships' tastes and expectations. The prefaces (Rink vi; Rasmussen, *People* x; Rasmussen, *Eskimo* 5–6) state that the editors chose those stories that were believed to be interesting for the readers; and if a story turned out to be too long, they shortened it to a reasonable length in order to make it more readable for European audiences.

COMMON THEMES AND MOTIFS

According to Rasmussen (*Eskimo* 6), Greenlandic stories have one specific purpose. They were told during long nights in winter, when there was little work to do but it was impossible to sleep the whole night. The aim of a storyteller was to send his listeners to sleep. When he did not have to finish the story because everybody was already sleeping, he had succeeded in his intention. Although some stories begin with the phrase "Once upon a time," on many other occasions the narrative begins with: "No one has ever heard this story till the end." With this opening, the acts of telling and listening become a kind of struggle between the storyteller's creativity and his audience's endurance. Because of that, stories were very easy to expand during telling.

An experienced Greenlandic storyteller had various options to expand a story in his repertoire. For example, a story must always have a hero. In the course of the tale, our hero can travel through unfamiliar lands and face various trials and adventures. These types of Greenlandic stories can be easy to expand because after seven rivers, seven mountains, seven valleys, and seven seas our hero needs to cross the eighth river, mountain, valley, and sea. Another example is that the protagonist needs to fulfil different tasks before reaching the goal. In Rasmussen's 1921 collection, the foster father of the hero Qujâvârssuk is singled out as an example for this narrative technique (*Eskimo* 8): To prepare for Qujâvârssuk's birth, he has to find not only "the carrion of a cormorant, with only the skeleton remaining," but also "a soft stone, which has never felt the sun, a stone good to make a lamp of."

Although it seems that only the storyteller knows the whole story— after all, "no one has ever heard this story till the end"—this is not the case. As Rasmussen states, "The legends are known to all; it is the grandmother's business to teach them to her grandchildren" (*People* 159). Similarly, Rink notes that "[g]enerally, even the smallest deviation from the original version will be taken notice of and corrected, if any intelligent person happens to be present" (85). Apparently, the act of telling the story and the way in which it was told was more important than the content, which was usually known to most of the audience. The end of a story— if an end was reached—may be equivalent to the classical "happily ever after," or a blunter and more direct statement along the lines of "here ends the story," or "I have no more to tell."

Use of magic is a common motif, especially in situations where the hero is confronted with a seemingly insurmountable problem. In such cases, previously unmentioned magical abilities are often presented as a *deus ex machina* solution. For example, just at the end of story "How the Narwhal came," we find out that our hero is a magician capable of reviving his dead sister: "Then he collected his sister's bones, put them in a bag and carried them away. He was a great magician, and as he carried his sister thus on his back, she began gradually to come to life again, and at last she began to talk" (Rasmussen, *People* 170).

Some stories express ideas that seem quite in line with modern scientific knowledge. In the story "The Coming of Men, a long, long while ago," the existence of a great flood is evidenced by shells that can be found high in the mountains (Rasmussen, *Eskimo* 17). "The Two Friends who set off to Travel round the World" presupposes the concept of a spherical Earth, evidenced not only in the story's title, but more explicitly in the course of the narrative: "And they set out, each going away from the other, that they might go by different ways and meet again some day...and at last one day, they met" (15). "The Very Obstinate Man" explains the influence of the moon, personified by the Moon Man, on the tides. Defeated by his opponent in a wrestling match, the Moon Man tries to explain why it would be unwise to kill him: "'There will be no more ebb-tide or flood if you strangle me', said the Moon Man" (57).

The struggle between the Obstinate Man and the Moon Man is certainly not the only violent episode in Rink's and Rasmussen's collections. Violence is common, particularly among family members, and explanations are rarely provided. For instance, "The Boy from the Bottom of the Sea, who Frightened the People of the House to Death" does not only have a rather gruesome title and plot, it also provides an opening that seems very disturbing to European readers: "Well, you see, it was the usual thing: 'The Obstinate One' had taken a wife, and of course he beat her, and when he wanted to make it an extra special beating, he took a box, and banged her about with that" (Rasmussen, *Eskimo* 64). The story "The Inhabitants of the Moon" begins with a similar statement: "There was once upon a time a woman who ran away to the hills; she could not walk, but had to crawl, for her husband had stabbed the soles of her feet with his knife" (Rasmussen, *People* 174). Again, no explanation is provided for the husband's abusive behaviour.[4]

MOON MEN AND INLAND DWELLERS

The protagonists in the stories collected by Rink and Rasmussen are usually human men, women, and children, but they share the world of Greenlandic lore with various supernatural beings. In some tales, the main characters are animals; such stories tend to resemble fables. There are also some examples in which humans and animals talk with each other or even found a family together, such as "The Man who took a Wife from among the Wild Geese" or "The Man who took a Fox for Wife" (Rasmussen, *People* 165–8).

A recurring feature in many tales are beings associated with the moon. The Moon Man, as personification of the moon, has already been mentioned as the loser in a wrestling bout with the Obstinate Man. His role in the story (Rasmussen, *Eskimo* 56–9), however, is much more important than that. He confronts the Obstinate Man when the latter forces his mourning wife to work for him. Although he loses in combat, the Moon Man teaches the Obstinate Man to respect his wife's mourning. In one of the stories collected by Rink (441–2), the Moon Man appears in a similar role, as an enforcer of taboos who challenges those who disregard them (cf. Kleivan and Sonne 30). The Moon Man is also known to assist the heroes when they have to face another being associated with the moon: the entrail-seizer, an old hag who dwells in the vicinity of the Moon Man and rips out the entrails of every person whom she can tempt to laugh (Rink 48, 440–2).

One of the most persistent and popular set of characters in Greenlandic lore are the inland dwellers, whom are regularly featured in stories from all parts of the country. In the imagination of the maritime Inuit, the desolate and inhospitable interior of Greenland was envisioned as a strange and dangerous liminal zone, where humans were abducted and transformed and where they had to face deadly supernatural challenges (Grønnow 200). Rink (72–3) surmised that the tales of the inland dwellers were inspired by hostile encounters between Inuit and Native Americans on the continent and remained part of Inuit folklore even after they migrated to Greenland (see Kleivan).

In 2009, Bjarne Grønnow compiled a list of various entities associated with the inland, ranging from human outcasts to ghosts, undead and non-human monstrous races.[5] Most of these beings are already documented in the collections of Rink and Rasmussen.

Among the inland dwellers, the *qivittut* were the most mundane beings. In several stories (e.g., Rink 260–2, 302–8, 410–3), ordinary humans— often women—might leave society behind and disappear into the interior. These loners usually did not possess supernatural powers and were driven by "normal" human emotions like disappointment and jealousy, which caused them to "go *qivittoq*." Nevertheless, the familiarity of these loners with the dreaded interior of Greenland was often reason enough to fear them (Grønnow 193, 199–200). Kaassassuk, one of the most well-known characters of Greenlandic folklore, grows from an abused orphan boy to an invincible strongman when a spirit (*inua*) of the inland country gives him superhuman strength (see Sonne 111). Again, it is implied that contact with the forces of the interior profoundly changes a person.

Other beings of the inland, however, were clearly imagined to be non-human: "The majority of the dangerous and lethal beings of their [the Inuit's] cosmology lived inland. Roughly, the further inland people ventured, the more dreadful and deadly were the beings they would encounter" (Grønnow 99). Giant-like races such as the *tornit* (cf. Kleivan) and the *inorusit* still shared some common features with humans and regularly interacted with them, often by abducting human women (e.g., Rink 265–7). Yet even the animal-shaped monsters of the interior, such as the giant worm or caterpillar known as *kullugiaq* or *aassik*, were believed to be capable of sexual and even marital relationships with human girls. Rink (186–8) provides an interesting example of these creatures in a story of a girl married to such a giant "vermin," and the efforts of her brothers to get rid of the monstrous "brother-in-law."

The vicious *eqqillit*, creatures with a human head and torso and a dog's body, were among the most notorious of the inland dwellers. They were believed to be thoroughly monstrous, in their behaviour as well as their appearance, and were feared as dangerous raiders who attacked and killed humans without hesitation (although, in the recorded stories, they usually receive their well-deserved punishment at the hands of the hero).

A tale in Rink's collection, the story of Inuarutligak, ascribes extraordinary supernatural abilities to the monstrous *eqqillit*:

> It is told that they once met with some singular people, whose upper limbs were those of human beings, but below the waist they were shaped like dogs. These creatures were armed with bows, and dreadful to behold, and could catch the scent of man and beast against the wind like animals.... They also knew how to diminish the distance from one place to another, by drawing the various parts of the country closer, and performed this by merely kneeling down together and spreading their arms out towards the mountain-tops. (Rink 401–2)

This remarkable ability—"to draw parts of the country closer"—is, most likely, to be understood as an expression of the close ties between the *eqqillit* and the landscape of interior Greenland that allows them to control and master space. Interior Greenland is, so to speak, the spatial expression of the supernatural and the monstrous, and it is only appropriate that the most monstrous among the inland dwellers master this space.

SIMILARITIES OF GREENLANDIC STORIES WITH TALES FROM THE OTHER CULTURES

Although the primary aim of this chapter is not a comparative mythology, it is worth pointing out some similarities between the Greenlandic stories compiled by Rasmussen and Rink and the folklore of other cultures.

Upon close reading, many similarities become apparent. In the following, I would like to draw attention to some remarkable concurrences, which allow us to reflect on the relationship between the Rasmussen and Rink collections and European mythological knowledge.

The previously mentioned story "The Coming of Men, a long, long time ago" features the motif of the great flood, which exists in many cultures around the world—the deluge and Noah's Ark mentioned in the Bible and the Qur'an being the most famous examples. The tale of Kúnigseq (Rasmussen, *Eskimo* 38–9) tells of a visit to the underworld, which bears a certain resemblance to the ancient Greek myth of Orpheus and Eurydice. In the well-known Greek myth, Orpheus has to descend to the underworld to retrieve his wife Eurydice. Hades, the god of the underworld, agrees on one condition: Orpheus must walk in front of his wife without looking back until both had reached the upper world. The wizard Kúngiseq, the hero of the Greenlandic tale, visits the underworld and encounters his mother there, but his helping spirits tell him that she must not kiss him, nor can he eat any berries that were gathered by his mother. If he does so, he will stay in the underworld forever.

Another famous Greek myth, the story of Odysseus and his adventure with the cyclops Polyphemus, also has a Greenlandic equivalent, although in the Inuit tale the giant is duped but not harmed. The story, simply labelled with the title "Giant" in Rasmussen's first collection (*People* 178–9) tells of a giant who, one day, spotted five kayaks and decided to take the men in them home, to use them as amulets. So he caught them, brought them to his oversized house, and put them on a shelf. While the giant was sleeping, the men managed to escape. The story's conclusion almost seems to be an ironic reference to the Polyphemus myth and the blinding of the cyclops, only with roles reversed: "When the giant awoke and discovered that the men had escaped, he cried, annoyed with himself: 'Oh, why did I not tear the eyes out of their heads'" (179).

"Ímarasugssuaq, who ate his Wives" (Rasmussen, *Eskimo* 44–5) is yet another Greenlandic story with close parallels in European folk-lore—in this case, Charles Perrault's fairy tale "Bluebeard." Both stories centre on a powerful man who murders his wives. In the Greenlandic version, Ímarasugssuaq's cannibalistic habits are described in the beginning,[6] while in Perrault's tale, Bluebeard's present wife discovers her husband's murderous nature in the course of the story. Both stories also have a similar outcome, in that each wife is saved by her brothers. In the Greenlandic version of the story, Ímarasugssuaq is overcome by the wife's brothers, who hold him down so that his wife can stab him. In Perrault's fairy tale, the brothers themselves administer justice and slay the villain.

CONCLUSION

The entwined fates of Bluebeard and Ímarasugssuaq, the shared experiences of Orpheus and Kúngiseq, and numerous other similarities between Greenlandic stories and European folklore and mythology are undoubtedly intriguing. At the same time, they pose a certain problem for researchers working on Greenlandic lore: One might be tempted to assume that certain narrative patterns are "universal themes" that were developed into similar stories in Europe and Greenland, independently of each other. Yet we need to bear in mind the particularities of recording and dissemination in mind. The tales were collected by Europeans—or by Greenlanders with a European background, like Knud Rasmussen—and addressed to a European audience. Collectors or editors might have altered the stories they had heard, to bring them in line with well-known topoi to which their readers could relate. Likewise, the narrators themselves might have been influenced by European lore, either consciously or unconsciously. After all, Europeans and Greenlandic Inuit had been in contact for centuries when Rink and Rasmussen collected these tales.

We might be tempted to denounce such emendations as an inappropriate meddling with authentic indigenous lore. However, such a judgement may well be misleading. As Kirsten Thisted has shown, Knud Rasmussen acted as a cultural translator who negotiated the transfer of knowledge between Europeans and Inuit, but also among the Inuit themselves:

Due to his roots in the European culture and the inspiration from his scholarly father, Rasmussen was at the same time able to see the Inuit culture from the outside and to collect and represent it in a way that would make it comprehensible not only to the Europeans, but also to the future generation of urbanised Inuit with no roots in the hunting culture and its old belief systems. (Thisted, "Voicing" 78)

In his role as an intermediary between different spheres of knowledge, Rasmussen could not refrain from influencing the stories and the way they were understood by the addressees: "Rasmussen's framing of what he learns from the Inuit unavoidably directs our understanding in certain directions, eliminating other possible interpretations. The cultural translator grants himself great privileges in terms of the power to represent and define" (74).

In the case of the "inland dwellers," this act of cultural translation entails a transition from the mundane to the supernatural. When Inuit and Europeans met in eighteenth-century Greenland, the former apparently perceived the *tornit*, the *eqqillit*, and all the other wondrous races of the interior as unusual, but by no means "otherworldly" or "supernatural" beings (Kleivan 221). With regard to the Alaskan Inuit, Ernest S. Burch, Jr., observed that "[t]he distinction between empirical and nonempirical phenomena may be meaningless to the members of a given society, the one realm merging imperceptibly into the other in the world view that constitutes the fundamental reality of their existence" (163). The same holds true for the indigenous inhabitants of Greenland: The dichotomy of the "natural" vis-à-vis the "supernatural"—a thoroughly modern European pattern of thought—made little sense to them. It was European missionaries like Hans Egede who first labelled the "inland dwellers" as supernatural and likened them to mountain trolls and other mythological entities (Kleivan 221–2).

This process—re-casting the wondrous as supernatural—was continuing and intensifying when Rink and Rasmussen compiled and published their collections of Greenlandic stories. "Cultural translation" implied that these "translated" stories could no longer be told, collected, or understood independently of European traditions—and these traditions included the venerable, long-lived topos of the Supernatural North. In the nineteenth and early twentieth centuries, any "northern" narrative required a liminal sphere of supernatural phenomena. In Rink's and Rasmussen's collections, the interior of Greenland and the monstrous "inland dwellers" answer the need for an Arctic Other.

NOTES

1. The word *legend* derives from Latin *legenda*, "something that should be read." However if we want something to read, first it must be written. In ancient times, only important information was deemed worthy to be written down; therefore, the claim that "something should be read" meant that it was truly important. The word *myth*, on the other hand, derives from the ancient Greek μῦθος—"word," "speech," or "(hi)story." Thus, it refers only to something that is told. According to this etymology, an oral narrative cannot be considered a legend. Bascom's definitions point out one important aspect: myths are older than legends, since one first needs to hear something that is told before one is able to write it down.

2. Actually, neither Rasmussen nor Rink collected Eastern Greenlandic stories in situ on the east coast of Greenland. Instead, they relied on East Greenlanders who had moved to the south and west.

3. In the end of the nineteenth century and the beginning of the twentiethth century, the geographical north of Greenland was unexplored, but the term *North Greenland* was used in an administrative context to refer to the geographical west of Greenland. That is the reason why Rasmussen used terms like "polar people" and "people of the Polar North."

4. One might assume that the indigenous narrator—or the European collectors and editors—believed domestic violence to be common among the Greenlandic Inuit, and took it for granted. However, it is equally possible that the narrators, in these cases, deliberately wanted to provoke their listeners with cynical, laconic remarks on domestic abuse.

5. Burch (152–8) provides a similar overview of monstrous beings from Alaskan folklore.

6. Cannibalism is a recurrent topic in Greenlandic stories, and the story of Ímarasugssuaq is by no means the only account of a man-eater.

WORKS CITED

Bascom, W. "The Forms of Folklore: Prose Narratives." *Journal of American Folklore* 78 (1965): 3–20.

Burch, E.S. "The Nonempirical Environment of the Arctic Alaskan Eskimos." *Southwestern Journal of Anthropology* 27 (1971): 148–65.

Csapo, E. *Theories of Mythology.* Oxford: Blackwell, 2005.

Grønnow, B. "Blessings and Horrors of the Interior: Ethno-Historical Studies of Inuit Perceptions Concerning the Inland Region of West Greenland." *Arctic Anthropology* 46 (2009): 191–201.

Gulløv, H.C. *From Middle Ages to Colonial Times: Archaeological and Ethnohistorical Studies of the Thule Culture in South West Greenland 1300–1800 AD.* Copenhagen: The Commission for Scientific Research in Greenland, 1997. Meddeleser om Grønland / Man & Society 23.

Høiris, O. "Grønlænderne i dansk antropologi før 2.verdenskrig." *Grønland* 1983.1: 30–46.

Kleivan, I. "Inuit Oral Tradition about Tunit in Greenland." *The Paleo-Eskimo Cultures of Greenland: New Perspectives in Greenlandic Archaeology.* Eds. B. Grønnow and J. Pind. Copenhagen: Danish Polar Center, 1996. 215–36. Danish Polar Center Publications 1.

Kleivan, I., and B. Sonne. *Eskimos: Greenland and Canada.* Leiden: Brill, 1985. Iconography of Religions 8/2.

Rasmussen, K. *Eskimo Folk-tales.* London: Gyldendal, 1921.

———. *The People of the Polar North: A Record.* London: Kegan Paul, 1908.

Rink, H. *Tales and Traditions of the Eskimo, with a Sketch of their Habits, Religion, Language and other Peculiarities.* Edinburgh: Blackwood, 1875.

Sonne, B. "Who's afraid of Kaassassuk? Writing as a tool in coping with changing cosmology." *Études/Inuit/Studies* 34.2 (2010): 107–27.

Thisted, K. *Jens Kreutzmann. Fortællinger og akvareller.* Nuuk: Atuakkiorfik, 1997.

———. *"Således skriver jeg, Aron": Samlede fortællinger og illustrationer af Aron fra Kangeq.* Nuuk: Atuakkiorfik, 1999.

———. "Voicing the Arctic: Knud Rasmussen and the Ambivalence of Cultural Translation." *Arctic Discourses.* Eds. A. Ryall, J. Schimanski, and H.H. Wærp. Newcastle: Cambridge Scholars, 2010. 59–81.

IV Contemporary Perspectives

The Desire for a Supernatural North

12   A Distant Northern Land

Nabokov's Zembla *and Aesthetic Bliss*

BRIAN WALTER

VLADIMIR NABOKOV'S 1962 novel *Pale Fire* ends with an obscure sentence: "Zembla, a distant northern land." The final entry in a bizarre index, this last sentence, according to Nabokov (*Strong Opinions* 74), signals that the author of the index, the insane annotator Charles Kinbote, has committed suicide after invoking, for the last time, the beloved polar country from which he claims to have been exiled. The final reference to Zembla thus makes the narrative end simultaneously with the protagonist's life, a striking coincidence in several of Nabokov's novels. In *Invitation to a Beheading*, *Bend Sinister*, and *Lolita*, for example, this carefully orchestrated correspondence suggests that the worlds their protagonists inhabit—to at least some degree—are created and exist only within the imagination of those protagonists. For *Pale Fire*'s Kinbote and his improbably obscure and romanticized homeland of Zembla, reality seems even more tenuous. If Kinbote dies before he can even list any page references for his distant northern land, does Zembla exist everywhere or nowhere in the text?

Or maybe Zembla exists *both* everywhere and nowhere in *Pale Fire*— a paradox that the incorrigible puzzle-maker in Nabokov clearly built carefully into its structure. The book comprises four distinct texts by two fictional authors. Theoretically, the primary text is the 999-line autobiographical poem, also named "Pale Fire," written by the avuncular New England poet John Shade just before his death. The other three texts are Kinbote's preface, commentary, and index, which occupy far more of the book than does Shade's poem. Complicating matters further, these scholarly supplements continually forsake the poem that supposedly prompted them to tell, in considerable detail, the story of Charles Xavier, the exiled king of Zembla and Kinbote's real identity (or so he hints). Moreover, Kinbote's notes to Shade's poem constantly direct the reader to jump around to other notes throughout the commentary, turning the whole reading experience into a dizzying tour through an endless hall of mirrors.

The challenges hardly end there. Among other puzzles and mysteries, Nabokov plants clues throughout Kinbote's supposed scholia that point to a more elusive truth: Kinbote is not Kinbote or even Charles Xavier, but rather Charles Botkin, a delusional professor of Russian and a colleague of Shade's at Wordsmith University. As Nabokov scholar Brian Boyd has convincingly argued, Botkin contrives the entire story of the deposed king of Zembla apparently to cope with his loosening grip on reality (709). Layer upon layer and mask upon mask, Nabokov uses *Pale Fire* to masterfully shroud the fictive "reality" of the narrative in endlessly elusive possibilities.

Pale Fire's remarkably intricate narrative structure combines with Zembla's status as the distant and possibly imaginary northern land to further Nabokov's long campaign for the primacy of subjective perception over objective reality. Reality, Nabokov once wrote, is "one of the few words that mean nothing without quotes" (*Annotated Lolita* 312), an idea he elaborated on numerous occasions, once declaring that the "reality perceived by all of us...is not the true reality," for this "[a]verage reality begins to rot and stink as soon as the act of individual creation ceases to animate a subjectively perceived texture" (*Strong Opinions* 118). Objective reality, in other words, waits upon the subjective imagination, the creative artist "plung[ing]...into chaos and drag[ging] out of it, with all its wet stars, his cosmos" (*Pale Fire* 151). For Nabokov, objective reality only matters—in fact, really only exists—in its subjective realization. The artist literally creates worlds, treating reality as the means to an end, but never as an end in itself (see Nabokov, "Good Readers" 1–2).

Within Nabokov's campaign for subjective reality, *Pale Fire*'s key contribution is Kinbote's distant northern land of Zembla. Critics of *Pale Fire* have long characterized the book as a remarkable manifestation of Nabokov's resolutely solitary, exquisitely imbalanced, and rigorously self-marginalized artistic imagination. In the extraordinarily complex and ingeniously dialectical relationship it musters between Shade the poet and Kinbote the annotator, *Pale Fire* galvanizes psychological desperation with artistic exuberance. And the key to this characterization is Kinbote's inspired fantasy of Zembla. What I will argue is that Zembla can exemplify supernatural Northernness by allowing—in its geographical remoteness—the author to moralize the implacable forces of history and, finally, both to redeem and enshrine the besieged imagination. If the "supernatural" refers to that which the accepted laws of nature cannot explain or contain,[1] then Zembla serves as a medium of the supernatural in *Pale Fire* by elusively but crucially connecting the natural world that Botkin and Shade inhabit to a realm of tantalizing spiritual possibility.

In making this argument, I am both drawing on and significantly departing from the work of Priscilla Meyer and Brian Boyd, two of *Pale Fire*'s best-known critics and scholars. Meyer locates *Pale Fire*'s use of the supernatural within the dialectical relationship between the religious, myth-minded Kinbote and the rationalist, atheist Shade (*Find What the Sailor* 190–2); for Meyer, in fact, Zembla primarily constitutes a complex updating of northern mythologies and legends. As she puts it, Nabokov in *Pale Fire* "sketches the evolution of Anglo-American culture from its beginnings, discerning a thematic unity that adumbrates his personal fate [and] parodies this endeavor in Kinbote's superimposition of his imaginative universe on Shade's poem" ("Pale Fire" 61). Of particular interest to Meyer is Nabokov and Kinbote's borrowing and updating of "[r]egicide, murder and revenge [as] recurring themes in Scandinavian lore [which] in the Eddas are shown to be transcended through poetry" ("Pale Fire" 62). Boyd, for his part, emphasizes the subtle, complex connections between Zembla and the apparent attempts of Hazel Shade, the daughter of John Shade, to communicate with her parents after her death by suicide. As Boyd puts it, a "breath from beyond pervades the Zembla scenes," so that Zembla becomes an "escape, an indulgent dream...underneath [which] we can glimpse a new depth of human truth" (154).

What I would like to add to these findings is the important sense in which Zembla's simple location in the remote, mythical polar climes combine with its very topography to thwart mundane "reality" and connect the physical to the metaphysical. If the supernatural has (since the nineteenth century) largely been associated with danger and evil (and therefore, to some degree, a critique of Enlightenment views of ratio- nalized nature), then Zembla helps *Pale Fire* envisage a different kind of supernaturalism, in which rational history is the source of danger, and the persistence of the irrational and inexplicable validates the fantastically imaginative view—or even distortion—of nature.

Zembla was hardly the first polar setting that Nabokov carefully constructed to reify, pressurize, liberate, or otherwise inspire the artistic sensibilities of a character, but it is arguably the most fully and exuber- antly realized. Veterans of Nabokov's work can rely on his artist and proto-artist characters to share several defining traits, including obsession to the point of mania and an associated inability to function effectively in everyday reality. A third defining trait is no less crucial but more subtle: the Nabokovian artist's obsession consistently grounds itself in a tangible object, person, or some other materially experienced phenom- enon, finding forms or patterns in nature to stoke the obsession, a physical means to metaphysical transports. In the case of *Pale Fire*, Zembla serves as Kinbote's counterpart to Humbert Humbert's eponymous nymphet in *Lolita*, the obsession to which the mentally and emotionally besieged writer must somehow give life before death overtakes him. It is, therefore, in its extreme qualities—which are enabled particularly by its polar loca- tion—that Zembla underwrites the achievement of Nabokov's "aesthetic bliss," a "sense of being somehow, somewhere connected with other states of being where art (curiosity, tenderness, kindness, ecstasy) is the norm" (Nabokov, *Annotated Lolita* 314). It is precisely in its isolation and possible ephemerality that Zembla enables Kinbote to bask in compassionate possibility and imaginative freedom.

Zembla emerges from Kinbote's disjointed commentary as a realm barely of this world. Like the historical Nova Zembla, it is a vaguely defined territory situated to the northwest of Russia, its gigantic neighbour, as Kinbote refers to it (Nabokov, *Pale Fire* 57). Politically, Zembla functions as a benign feudal aristocracy. In fact, as Meyer has suggested, Zembla could even serve as a fancified vision of Russia if the Tsars had not been deposed, retaining a sturdy peasant population topped by an aristocracy that enjoys lives of gentlemanly leisure, even of concerted whimsy (Meyer, "Pale Fire" 65). Charles Xavier's father, for example, is an amateur pilot who routinely crashes his bi-plane at various points around the country, whereupon he finds himself forced to give impromptu speeches to the confused peasants who have witnessed the crash. Xavier himself has two favourite hobbies: the teaching of literature, and the soldiers in his regiment, whom he openly and vigorously prefers sexually to the daughters of the various schemers and foreign nobles who present themselves as candidates for marriage. The nemesis of this gentleman's monarchy is the historical and political extremism of the Soviet Union, which eventually helps to initiate the Zemblan Revolution that imprisons and then exiles the king. However, this does not occur until 1958, some four decades after the Bolshevik Revolution, suggesting that history arrives only slowly in Zembla.

In its elusive kinship to the Soviet Union, Zembla manifests one of the central themes in Nabokov's autobiography, *Speak, Memory*: "objective" history opposes, undermines, and works to thwart the creators of innately and enduringly subjective art. This theme is clear in the description of the village schoolmaster whom his father hired to tutor the young Nabokov in Russian: "To him, in a way, I owe the ability to continue for another stretch along my private footpath which runs parallel to the road of that troubled decade" (Nabokov, *Novels and Memoirs* 377). Where Orwell sees the writer's life written into the margins of history,[2] Nabokov decisively inverts the image. The ruptures and tumults of the Russian Revolution and Soviet Socialism that transform Zembla's sprawling neighbour into a future scourge reduce to little more than a footnote in Kinbote's account of Charles Xavier, serenely pursuing his life of leisure in his distant northern land.

So, even when the Zemblan Revolution succeeds in handing his idyllic kingdom over to historical imperative, Kinbote takes his fight for old Zembla into the realm of literature. Kinbote shamelessly uses his notes to Shade's poem to preserve the "blue, inenubilable Zembla" that burns so fervently in his imagination (Nabokov, *Pale Fire* 167), embedding his derivative, even parasitical homeland as deeply as possible into Shade's artistic creation. He thus manages to embody Zembla within the structure and even within the very compositional materials of the poem. Like Nabokov (especially in *Speak, Memory*), Kinbote conjures figures that blend time and space, wedding the abstract and the material in ways that anchor the former and exalt the latter. The cards on which Shade drafts his poem, for example, become Zembla itself for the artistically deluded annotator: "Solemnly I weighed in my hand what I was carrying under my left armpit, and for a moment, I found myself enriched with an indescribable amazement.... I was holding all Zembla pressed to my heart" (Nabokov, *Pale Fire* 168). After Shade's death, Kinbote binds Shade's text still more literally to his Zembla, not only zealously guarding the precious manuscript cards, but also making them a part of his very person:

> Some of my readers may laugh when they learn that I fussily removed
> [the manuscript cards] from my black valise...and for several days wore
> [them], as it were, having distributed the ninety-two index cards about
> my person, twenty in the right-hand pocket of my coat, as many in the
> left-hand one, a batch of forty against my right nipple and the twelve
> precious ones with variants in my innermost left-breast pocket.... Thus

with cautious steps, among deceived enemies, I circulated, plated with
poetry, armored with rhymes, stout with another man's song, stiff with
cardboard, bullet-proof at long last. (173)

To secure Zembla's and his own survival, Kinbote secures Shade's
poem, his obsession with it fuelled by his paranoid fear that history—
the record of time's inexorable passing and triumph over matter—will
somehow prove his nemesis. This terror of time takes form particularly in
the figure of Gradus, the Extremist Zemblan assassin who stalks Kinbote
throughout the text. Kinbote calls Gradus a "clockwork man" (*Pale Fire*,
152), a clear reference to the "clockwork toy" that triggers Shade's first
seizure (38). Just as the clockwork toy of Shade's poem triggers his transition into another state of consciousness, Gradus's arrival signals the end
of the poem, the end of Kinbote's commentary, and—if he had not (in
Kinbote's characterization) bungled the job by killing Shade instead of the
exiled king—Kinbote's life. In Gradus, the human embodiment of mind-
less but implacable and lethal history, Kinbote acknowledges the fateful
serpent that is all too native in his Edenic Zembla:

> *We shall accompany Gradus in constant thought, as he makes his way*
> *from distant dim Zembla to green Appalachia, through the entire*
> *length of the poem, following the road of its rhythm, riding past in a*
> *rhyme, skidding around the corner of a run-on, breathing with the*
> *caesura, swinging down to the foot of the page from line to line as from*
> *branch to branch, hiding between two words (see note to line 596),*
> *reappearing on the horizon of a new canto, steadily marching nearer*
> *in iambic motion, crossing streets, moving up with his valise on the*
> *escalator of the pentameter, stepping off, boarding a new train of*
> *thought, entering the hall of a hotel, putting out the bedlight, while*
> *Shade blots out a word, and falling asleep as the poet lays down his*
> *pen for the night. (58)*

Gradus, one might say, *is* time, the engine of history, embedding Zembla still more deeply within the very structure and process of Shade's artistic creation in his carefully synchronized pursuit of Kinbote.

Yet if Gradus injects deadly time into *Pale Fire*, the process of combination and blending works in the opposite direction as well, with Zembla subtly thwarting and, thereby, moralizing the experience of time and history. This magical quality resides within the very geography and topography of the distant northern land:

> *The Bera Range, a two-hundred-mile-long chain of rugged mountains, not quite reaching the northern end of the Zemblan peninsula (cut off basally by an impassable canal from the mainland of madness), divides it into two parts, the flourishing eastern region of Onhava and other townships, such as Aros and Grindelwod, and the much narrower western strip with its quaint fishing hamlets and pleasant beach resorts. The two coasts are connected by two asphalted highways; the older one shirks difficulties by running first along the eastern slopes northward to Odevalla, Yeslove and Embla, and only then turning west at the northmost point of the peninsula; the newer one, an elaborate, twisting, marvelously graded road, traverses the range westward from just north of Onhava to Bregberg, and is termed in tourist booklets a "scenic drive." Several trails cross the mountains at various points and lead to passes none of which exceeds an altitude of five thousand feet; a few peaks rise some two thousand feet higher and retain their snow in midsummer; and from one of them, the highest and hardest, Mt. Glitterntin, one can distinguish on clear days, far out to the east, beyond the Gulf of Surprise, a dim iridescence which some say is Russia. (89)*

This description abounds with symbolic and emblematic implications, from the dialectical qualities enforced by the mountain range to the remarkably humane geography of this distant northern land, with quite manageable peaks, welcoming seaside resorts, and a "scenic route" devised to provide the leisurely traveller with an endearingly convoluted tour of Zembla. However, perhaps the most telling aspect is, once again, the antagonism with Nabokov's former homeland. It is only from the "highest and hardest" peak in Zembla that one can glimpse Russia, which implacable, clockwork history turned into the Soviet Union, exiling Nabokov some four decades before he wrote *Pale Fire*. Zembla thus renders Russia as a beatific optical effect, an "iridescence" all the more lovely for its remoteness—so remote, in fact, that one cannot be sure where material nature stops and immaterial imagination starts in forming the beloved image. This perspective comprises Zembla's supernatural power, to hold history and the natural world of mundane experience at bay. In fact, what the highest peak in Zembla allows is precisely what Nabokov describes in *Speak, Memory* as the goal of autobiography, the use of writing to explore and determine one's identity:

> It is certainly not then—not in dreams—but when one is wide awake, at moments of robust joy and achievement, on the highest terrace of consciousness, that mortality has a chance to peer beyond its own limits, from the mast, from the past and its castle tower. And although nothing much can be seen through the mist, there is somehow the blissful feeling that one is looking in the right direction. (Novels and Memoirs 395–6)

This distant northern land in Kinbote's head affords the same kind of expansive visions—the heightened consciousness—that Nabokov seeks in making memory his muse: a past that is not simply idealized, but left as intact as it is irrecoverable. Not surprisingly, then, Kinbote could be speaking for Nabokov when he closes his commentary by bravely speculating on future plans: "Oh, I may do many things! History permitting, I may sail back to my recovered kingdom, and with a great sob greet the gray coastline and the gleam of a roof in the rain" (*Pale Fire* 173). Nabokov departed Russia at the age of 20 and never returned, except in his work, through superb imaginative vehicles such as Kinbote and his Zembla.

This subtle but many-layered correspondence between character and author is what allows Zembla to realize a version of Nabokov's aesthetic bliss, the fairy tale northern land poignantly isolating the obsessive artistic imagination from the compulsions of history. Alienation for Kinbote (as for Nabokov) rises to the status of an ethic. Zembla in fact serves as Kinbote's "unreal estate," Nabokov's term in *Speak, Memory* for what his mother taught him to preserve in memory and imagination no matter what history would literally deprive him of:

> *As if feeling that in a few years the tangible part of her world would perish, she cultivated an extraordinary consciousness of the various time marks distributed throughout our country place. She cherished her own past with the same retrospective fervor that I now do her image and my past. Thus, in a way, I inherited an exquisite simulacrum—the beauty of intangible property, unreal estate—and this proved a splendid training for the endurance of later losses.* (Novels and Memoirs *387*)

The exquisite simulacrum of Zembla that Kinbote constructs and attaches to Shade's poem once again realizes the dialectic of artistic creation: nature presents the thesis of the actual place that passes through the antithesis of the exiled imagination to produce the synthesis of the literary text and its life-giving image of a homeland. Hence, when Kinbote reaches the end of his work, the final entry of his index, he knows that the Zembla he has constructed must also end, a realm bound less by space than by time. The omission of any page references from Zembla's index entry (the only entry not to include specific references for the reader's convenience) suggests that Zembla exists both nowhere and everywhere, that it suffuses the book, reifying the combination of psychological need and exuberance that informs not just Kinbote's aesthetic bliss, but also Nabokov's and even the reader's. As a figure of the supernatural North, then, the distant northern land of Zembla requires that the North remain forever distant, less a region to be charted and catalogued for history than a blissfully cloudy realm of tantalizing possibility, a home for the literally exiled but incorrigibly exuberant artistic imagination.

NOTES

1. In this brief and somewhat simplified distinction, I am drawing particularly on Benson Saler's article, "Supernatural as a Western Category," in which he traces the development of the complicated relationship between the "natural" and the "supernatural" through various Western philosophical and theological traditions. In particular, he emphasizes the "well-considered antithesis between immanence and transcendence," which depends on our belief that "nature operates in accordance with certain principles or laws that are immanent in it." This understanding leads us to see "any posited interference with [those laws] or departure from them [to] suggest the operation of principles or forces that transcend nature" (51). In effect, I am arguing that Kinbote works to make Zembla transcend nature and its immanent principles.

2. See Orwell's "Why I Write," where he claims that a writer's "subject matter will be determined by the age he lives in—at least this is true in tumultuous, revolutionary ages like our own," and declares it "nonsense, in a period like our own, to think that one can avoid writing of [political] subjects" (n.pag.).

WORKS CITED

Boyd, B. *Vladimir Nabokov: The American Years.* Princeton: Princeton UP, 1991.

Meyer, P. *Find What the Sailor Has Hidden: Vladimir Nabokov's Pale Fire.* Middletown: Wesleyan UP, 1988.

———. "Pale Fire as Cultural Astrolabe: The Sagas of the North." *Russian Review* 47.1 (1988): 61–74.

Nabokov, V. *The Annotated Lolita.* New York: Vintage, 1991.

———. "Good Readers and Good Writers." *Lectures on Literature.* Ed. F. Bowers. New York: Harcourt, 1980. 1–6.

———. *Novels and Memoirs 1941–1951.* New York: Library of America, 1996.

———. *Pale Fire.* 1962. Berkley: Berkley Publishing, 1968.

———. *Strong Opinions.* 1973. New York: Vintage, 1990.

Orwell, G. "Why I Write." 1946. *George Orwell.* 24 Aug. 2015. <http://orwell.ru/library/essays/wiw/english/e_wiw>

Saler, B. "Supernatural as a Western Category." *Ethos* 5.1 (1977): 31–5.

13 The Idea of North

Intertextuality and Environmentalism in Philip Pullman's
The Golden Compass

DANIELLE MARIE CUDMORE

IN PHILIP PULLMAN'S 1995 novel *The Golden Compass*,[1] the eponymous device responds to the truth just as "a compass responds to the idea
of North" (173) as one character puts it. However, it is not only compass
needles that find the idea of North magnetic, for over the centuries adven-
turers, explorers, entrepreneurs, aesthetes, poets, and not least, fiction
writers, have been drawn northwards. But what exactly is North? Anyone
familiar with literary studies will know that a cardinal direction is never
just a cardinal direction and that North, South, East, and West are created
by discourses as much as they are latitudinal lines and meridians. Like
the magnetic pole, which constantly shifts its position, these ideas are
not always the same, nor do these terms always refer to the same ideas.
As Peter Davidson says, "Everyone carries their own idea of north within
them....'true north' goes beyond the idea of the prodigious (or malign
north) and suggests that, for each individual, there exists somewhere the
place that is the absolute of the north, the north in essence, northness in
concentration and purity" (11).[2]

On a cultural level, such ideas create what Edward Said termed "imaginative geographies" formed and bounded by the stereotypes and common conceptions of outsiders.[3] Imaginative geographies most often express difference, what separates "us" from "them." Though Said refers to the relation of a monumentalized East to an equally monumentalized West, the term "imaginative geography" is particularly relevant to the Arctic North, which Robert McGhee has called the "last imaginary place" (10).[4] This chapter examines how Philip Pullman engages with a dominant imaginative geography of the North by reproducing and then subverting stereotypes, conventions, and expectations present in other literary works, particularly folk and fairy tales of Northern Europe and English fantasy writing, especially that of C.S. Lewis. In subverting the tropes and expectations of his literary forebears, Pullman examines the consequences, particularly environmental, of imagining the "North" along conventional lines.

THE SAME NORTH IN DIFFERENT UNIVERSES

Throughout his novel Pullman destabilizes the reader by taking the familiar and making it strange, not only through intertextuality, but also through the more basic aspects of plot and setting. The novel begins in the semi-familiar setting of Oxford in Victorian or Edwardian England, but in an alternate—or, more appropriately, parallel—universe.[5] The protagonist Lyra Belacqua, the supposedly orphaned child of an aristocratic family, spends the first eleven years of her life in Oxford. She was entrusted to the masters of a college by her uncle, who is in reality her father, a scientist and explorer named Lord Asriel. The idea of North broods over Lyra's childhood England. In the approximate time period in which the novel is set, England was experiencing something of a renaissance of interest in the North—which encompassed Scandinavia and the Arctic—both in terms of past culture and current exploration.[6] It is unsurprising this increased interest in the cultural relationship between England and the North should coincide with its most active period of

Arctic exploration.[7] Pullman draws heavily from both Scandinavian history and literature and the culture of nineteenth-century Arctic exploration, each of which has left its mark on English identity (the former in the form of fantasy literature, for example). Superstition and tales of strange creatures, ghosts,[8] and barbarous tribes[9] form a backdrop to Lyra's early idea of North, as do tales of Arctic exploration. Lyra, who longs to follow her uncle northwards, visits the Royal Arctic Institute,[10] and at one point even tells a dinner guest a tall tale about how her parents died in the North. All her life, Lyra feels a "deep thrill...on hearing the word *North*" (*GC* 133). Lyra inhabits a world that, in this regard, is very much like our own.

One of the unique features of Lyra's world is that people's souls are externalized and made flesh in the form of animal companions called dæmons that can never stray too far from their human counterparts. A child's dæmon can change form at will, but when the child reaches puberty, the dæmon begins to settle on a fixed form reflective of its human counterpart. It is at this time that Dust settles on people. This Dust, which Lyra learns about while spying on a meeting between her uncle and the college heads, is a metaphysical particle attracted to self-conscious and self-aware beings; consequently it is attracted to adults and not children. Dust seems to be flowing into Lyra's world from many billions of parallel worlds, occasionally visible through the veils of the aurora borealis, or Northern Lights, the phantasmagoric result of magnetically charged particles interacting with the earth's atmosphere. Dust is hated and feared as the effect and evidence of Original Sin by the Magisterium, a powerful and oppressive religious authority that exerts absolute control over both institutions and behaviours in Lyra's world.

The members of the Magisterium, like Lyra's uncle, are keenly interested in Dust and the North. Around the time Lyra learns about Dust, children throughout England are disappearing, abducted by a secret sect of the Magisterium called the Oblation Board. The Oblation Board operates under the innocuous name Northern Progress Exploration Company, a title that may equate the experimentation of the Oblation board with the also insidious exploitation of Arctic resources. The abducted children are sent to a place called Bolvanger (a word Pullman created from Norwegian for "fields of evil") in northern Norway. Here they undergo an experimental process called "intercision" in which the children are "severed" from their dæmons. The intention is to protect the pre-pubescent children from Original Sin by "cutting off" their sexual impulses before they begin. To Pullman and to the protagonists of the book, this is tantamount to castration and spiritual murder. Heading this group and responsible for single-handedly abducting many of the children is the beautiful, ambitious, and ruthless Mrs. Coulter, who also happens to be Lyra's estranged mother. Among those abducted is Lyra's best friend Roger, whom she vows to rescue. Before Lyra leaves Oxford, the Master of Jordan College entrusts her with the "Golden Compass," also known as an alethiometer, or "truth measurer." This is a prophetic device that responds to Dust, and eventually Lyra becomes adept at reading its symbols and swinging needles.

Having briefly been in the thrall of Mrs. Coulter, Lyra escapes and takes up with a group of "gyptians," embarking on a Northward journey to rescue the abducted children, and her friend in particular. Lyra and the gyptians begin their expedition from a port called Trollesund in northern Norway. Her first physical experience with the North, as she sails into Trollesund, is particularly telling:

> Directly ahead of the ship a mountain rose, green flanked and snow-capped and a little town and harbor lay below it: wooden houses with steep roofs, an oratory spire, cranes in the harbor and the clouds of gulls wheeling and crying. The smell was of fish but mixed with it came land smells too: pine resin and earth and something animal and musky and something else that was cold and blank and wild: it might have been snow. It was the smell of North (GC 168).

The North that Lyra encounters here is a mix of familiar sights, sounds and smells, things she can recognize and identify with, but also things that are unfamiliar and mysterious. Pristine nature dominates the scene and looms over the small settlement. While Trollesund turns out to be a fairly prosaic place, the name of this gateway town to the North suggests enchantment and liminality.[11] This idea of North as both "Self" and "Other" is central to Pullman's engagement with "imaginative geography" of the North, which encompasses both Scandinavia and the Arctic regions beyond it. Pullman's North is like his narrative: it is something with which we can identify, but it is also unfamiliar, destabilizing, and new.

In Trollesund, Lyra and the gyptians employ Lee Scoresby (a Texan aeronaut named for Western actor Lee Van Cleef and Arctic explorer William Scoresby) and Iorek Byrnison, an exiled armoured polar bear from the bear Kingdom of Svalbard (a wildlife refuge for polar bears), and ally themselves with Serafina Pekkala, a Lapland witch. While the bears have Germanic sounding names, the exclusively female witches tend to have Finnic names[12] and are able to send their dæmons much further from their bodies than normal humans.[13] They believe in a goddess of death called Yambe Akka, based on an actual figure from Sámi folklore,[14] and practice a shamanic religion that often aligns well with scientific precepts.

After an arduous journey, Lyra succeeds in rescuing the children at Bolvanger, restoring Iorek Byrnison to his rightful position as king of Svalbard and freeing Lord Asriel from imprisonment (by order of the Magisterium) on the same island. However, Lyra's newly rescued friend Roger becomes Asriel's sacrifice to create a bridge to the other worlds visible in the aurora. As the novel closes, Lyra gathers her courage and walks into the Northern Lights. The remaining two books in the trilogy are a spirited romp through Pullman's multiverse culminating with nothing less than a war on Heaven in which the new order overthrows the Authority. This Authority is not a Creator but a weak and petty demiurge who mediates between the denizens of the multiverse and, apparently, nothing. Following the Death of "God," the spiritually liberated Republic of Heaven emerges, the new republic's inception being simultaneous with the onset of Lyra's sexual maturation. It is, not unintentionally, a science fiction *Götterdämmerung* of pubescent proportions.

Much has been made of Pullman's theological views and his broad array of literary sources, including William Blake, John Milton, and Heinrich von Kleist.[15] However, my interest is in the folk and fairy tale elements fused with this higher literature, and how they contribute to Pullman's treatment of North. These particular elements create an intertextual matrix with not only some of the popular tales that many of Pullman's readers have likely heard or read as children, but also with other well-known works of fantasy literature, particularly C.S. Lewis's *Chronicles of Narnia*,[16] for which Pullman has a particular loathing ("Dark Side").[17] In reference to *Narnia*, Lewis writes that "I wrote fairy stories because the Fairy Tale seemed the ideal Form for the stuff I had to say" ("Sometimes" 527).[18] According to Pullman this "stuff" amounts to: "Death is better than life; boys are better than girls; light-coloured people are better than dark-coloured people; and so on" (Pullman, "Dark Side"). Pullman also suggests that Lewis "didn't like women in general, or sexuality at all, at least at the stage in his life when he wrote the Narnia books. He was frightened and appalled at the notion of wanting to grow up" ("Dark Side"). Jennifer Miller has noted that while Pullman "does not explicitly use the world of Narnia[,] his explicit criticism of Lewis's series positions *His Dark Materials* as an alternative to the *Chronicles of Narnia* that rewrites desire for the divine as sexual desire" (127).

Some of Pullman's most savvy destabilizing moves in *The Golden Compass* involve his dialogue with *The Lion, The Witch and the Wardrobe*, in which he re-imagines certain plot elements and motifs, as well literary influences upon which Lewis also relied. A brief and non-exhaustive inventory includes the narrative beginning with a young girl hiding in a wardrobe, talking animals, a boreal (if not directionally northern) setting, a betrayal, and witches. Two particular elements deserve our attention: the "Northern" setting, which will be addressed later on in more detail, and the White Witch. In *The Lion, the Witch and the Wardrobe*, Narnia is under the sway of the White Witch, Jadis, who is beautiful but thoroughly wicked. After destroying her own (parallel) world, she usurps the throne of Narnia and turns it into a boreal wasteland of eternal winter to which Christmas never comes. This reduces Narnia to a state of despair by depriving it of the hope of salvation implied by Christmas. She hates and fears "sons of Adam and daughters of Eve." With promises of Turkish delight and hot chocolate, she seduces Edmund, the third child of the four Pevensie children who are the protagonists of the novel, so that he betrays his siblings and their ally, the Christ-lion Aslan, whose return to Narnia signifies the end of winter and, with it, the Witch's reign.

The White Witch is at least in part based on the titular character in Hans Christian Andersen's "The Snow Queen" ("Snedronningen"). The Snow Queen seduces and abducts a little boy named Kay, who already suffers from rogue splinters of a shattered troll-mirror lodged in his eye and heart. Kay's friend Gerda, an innocent little girl, embarks on a quest Northward to free him. With the help of a troupe of robbers,[19] Finnish and Sámi witches, and talking reindeer, Gerda makes her way to the palace in the Far North. There, Kay sits by the Snow Queen's throne and puzzles over ice shards, trying to make them spell the word "eternity," which will release him from the Snow Queen's thrall. The Snow Queen's sexuality is cold and dead, perhaps reflecting to a degree how uncomfortable Andersen himself was with the idea of children developing sexually. The Snow Queen's implied sexual hold over Kay makes it impossible for him to spell "eternity" because he can't conceive of it, in the sense that eternity means salvation, which is unattainable for Kay in his corrupted and despairing state.[20] Kay is rescued when Gerda's tears melt his heart and dislodge the shard in his eye. Though the children find they have "grown up" during their travels, the two return home and the tale concludes with Gerda's grandmother reading Matthew 18:3, which states that "unless you are converted and become as little children, you will by no means enter the kingdom of heaven."

The Golden Compass follows a basic "Snow Queen" narrative: a young girl travels Northward to save her male best friend from the clutches of a beautiful but evil woman, aided along the way by animals, socially marginal groups, and Finnish/Sámi witches. Mrs. Coulter seems to be a response to the White Witch and her literary progenitor the Snow Queen. Like the White Witch and Snow Queen, she is extremely beautiful and clad in fur when she enters the narrative.[21] Both Mrs. Coulter and the Witch lull children into a sense of security with the promise of hot chocolate. Mrs. Coulter, like the Snow Queen, brings children to the North,[22] but therein lies the important difference, which illustrates how Pullman subverts familiar tales. While the Snow Queen's allure is spiritually devoid, and succumbing to her cuts off children from entry to the Kingdom of Heaven, Mrs. Coulter's crime is that she works to "cut off" children from adulthood and sexual maturation, an act that keeps them ever docile and without the free thought and experience to participate in a Republic of Heaven. Andersen and Pullman conceive of opposite ideal states for humanity against which the antagonists work: for Andersen it is one of childhood and innocence, but for Pullman it is one of maturity and freedom, of which sexuality is a natural part. Given Lewis's prudishness, sexualization of the White Witch is kept to a minimum, but, as Miller says, "by invoking various outside images in his texts, including that of the Snow Queen, Lewis brings not only those images into his world, but the themes and histories of those images as well" (128). This also applies to Pullman.

Like the White Witch, Mrs. Coulter is an alien presence who has usurped and altered the landscape for her own purposes, but in both cases their attempts at control fail.[23] Thus, the presence of a demonic and powerful female figure associated with the North is central to both narratives. We can see this paralleling of the "femininization" of the Arctic landscape as either a deadly temptress or a bride to be conquered. Nineteenth- and twentieth-century depictions of the Arctic, fiction and non-fiction, present the Arctic as locus for masculine heroic action corresponding to the feminized landscape and "construct the North...as a space for virile, white male adventure in a harsh but magnificent, unspoiled landscape" (Grace 174). While the White Witch embodies the icy femme fatale, who has turned Narnia into a boreal desert, Mrs. Coulter is not a natural inhabitant of the North, but has come from the South and usurped the landscape in an exploitative manner.[24] Pullman's use of a female child protagonist also defies the gendering of the Arctic experience, yet Lyra is no Lucy Pevensie or Gerda, whose innocent good-naturedness seems to be the key to survival in a hostile land. Lyra is stubborn, resourceful, and not above expedient fabrication.

With its female protagonist and far-flung journeying, *The Golden Compass* also calls to mind "Østenfor Sol og Vestenfor Måne" ("East of the Sun and West of the Moon"), a Norwegian "Eros and Psyche" tale from Asbjørnsen and Moe's seminal folklore collection. Though a part of a widespread and international folktale-type, 425A, "The Animal as Bridegroom,"[25] "East of the Sun and West of the Moon" is particularly well known and contains some imagery that seems to have bearing on *The Golden Compass*. In the tale, a poor couple gives their daughter to a white bear, who is really a cursed prince, and who can only join her in his human form in the darkness. The young woman's desire to see her human lover eventually dooms their relationship. The Prince is whisked off to a land "East of the Sun and West of the Moon," where he will be forced to marry the hideous daughter of the troll woman who cursed him. If the young woman had restrained herself for just a year the curse would have been broken. The young woman then embarks on a quest to find this paradoxical land, a place so remote only the North Wind can transport her there. The young woman's purity as a good Christian saves her husband from his lascivious would-be bride, and of course they live happily ever after. As he is bestial when visible, and invisible when he lies with his bride at night, the "Animal Groom" can be read as representative of a young woman's aversion to and fear of sexuality (Bettelheim 277–310).

In *The Golden Compass*, Lyra and Iorek the polar bear form a deep bond and Lyra helps restore him to his rightful kingship.[26] However, their bond is one of empathy and respect, and the bear's exile is less the result of a curse than dishonest bear-politics. The bear is decidedly not human under his white fur,[27] and the one bear that tries to be human (the usurping king of Svalbard) does so to his ruin. That the bears can speak gives them a literal say in their own destiny. The polar bear kingdom ultimately reclaims itself from human influence and tears down the artifices of human construction, creating a clear environmental commentary. Indeed, Pullman's own environmentalism is well documented. In one interview with *The Telegraph* he says,

> *The armoured bears in my trilogy survive. Just. I've got a soft spot for them.... Now, they're all going to be extinct if there's no ice left, unless they put them all in zoos or round them up and put a fence round them and throw them a seal or two from time to time. But that's no life. If the polar bears leapt from the pages of my fiction into reality and saw what was happening, they'd eat us. Eat as many of us as quickly as they possibly could. And good luck to them. (Simms, n.pag.)*

NATURE AND NARRATIVES

Pullman sees environmentalism as a sort of storytelling,[28] and one that requires a better methodology:

> *I suppose the real story, the basic story, the story I would like to hear, see, read, is the story about how connected we are, not only with one another but also with the place we live in. And how it's almost infi-nitely rich, but it's in some danger; and that despite the danger, we can do something to overcome it. (Simms, n.pag.)*

Through setting the plot of the novel so much in the Arctic North and through the use of Northern folklore and literary tropes, Pullman creates an environmental narrative. The North, while used as a fantastic setting, never quite becomes an "otherworld" and on some levels even seems to reject the supernatural associations. It is also worth noting that *Once Upon a Time in the North*, Pullman's short prequel to *The Golden Compass*, is tellingly devoid of the supernatural or magical. The bears are present in this tale, but they are dealing with social issues of discrimination and exclusion (and, in *The Golden Compass*, alcoholism), not unlike issues associated with disenfranchised indigenous peoples. The full-length book, which features Lee Scoresby, is less of a science fiction novel and more of a boreal Western, with an underlying commentary on the evils of big business capitalism and the exploitation of oil in the Arctic.

Pullman's North is a land of the imagination.[29] Indeed, Pullman instrumentalizes the North for the purpose of narrative, much like his predecessors in folklore and fiction. *The Golden Compass* is a young protagonist's voyage of self-discovery and maturity in a Northern landscape populated by talking animals, witches, and deviant social groups. Yet, ultimately, the North is not the allegorical otherworld of Narnia, but a part of our sphere. As with the witches and bears, whose wildly different cultures Lyra comes to accept and appreciate (if not entirely understand), Pullman allows for equally valid differences, not only in appearance but in beliefs, ideas, and even experiences of the same landscape. While the Magisterium requires the "darkness and obscurity" (*GC*, 374) of the North to perform the hideous process of intercision, to Lyra the North is alive with light and energy and "so beautiful it [is] almost holy" (184). For the bears, it is the only place in which they can survive.

Perhaps a clue to how Pullman's North works can be found in Glenn Gould's sound documentary *The Idea of North*, to which Pullman may be alluding in the identically titled second chapter of *The Golden Compass*. *The Idea of North* weaves together the voices of five Canadians (though none of them indigenous inhabitants) recounting their different experiences in northern Canada, resisting the reduction of North to one single idea and illustrating the inherently polysemous and interpretive nature of landscape. Pullman's treatment of the North reveals a multivalent landscape, open to a variety of interpretations but resisting the imposition of a single one. As with his engagement with theology and literature, he "encourages the reader to move forward, confront previously held expectations, and consider new possibilities...and the consequences of human behavior in general" (Smith 150). Pullman suggests that unless we do confront these things, there may eventually be little real North left to imagine.

NOTES

1. Published originally as *Northern Lights* in the United Kingdom. Citations throughout will be from the 1996 American edition. Cited hereafter as GC.

2. Cf. Sherrill Grace: "North is multiple, shifting and elastic; it is a process, not an eternal fixed goal or condition" (16). While Grace focuses on North in Canadian culture, her book contains cogent discussion of discursive formations of North in European and North American cultures.

3. See Said, ch. 2.

4. McGhee writes, "stories, true and false, have gradually accumulated to form the vision of a distant and fantastic Arctic as seen through the window of Western culture. The image of the Arctic as a world apart, where the laws of science and society may be in abeyance, is informed not only by what we hear from present day observers or what we see when we visit the area ourselves. It is also moulded by a view of the Arctic that comes down to us from the distant past, when the region was as alien and as impossible for most people to reach as another planet. For millennia this Arctic vision has successfully absorbed the hearsay evidence of travellers' tales, the accelerating flow of scientific information, and in recent years even the tedium of government reports, while retaining its aura of wonder. This Arctic is not so much a region as a dream: the dream of a unique unattainable and compellingly attractive world" (10). See also Barry Lopez's *Arctic Dreams*, for an extended, in-depth discussion of imagination and desire.

5. Lenz offers a thorough examination of Pullman's world(s).

6. See, for example, Wawm on the increased interest during the nineteenth century in England's "Viking" past.

7. Spufford discusses cultural imagination and Arctic exploration in Victorian England. See also Shane McCorristine's contribution to this volume.

8. See Davidson (44–58) on North as the territory of ghosts and revenants.

9. Lord Asriel exploits this particular stereotype to convince the Oxford scholars to fund an expedition to the North by presenting the head of a colleague, supposedly mutilated by Tatars. As it turns out, the head has been trepanned, which is, in fact, a "great privilege" (GC 228) and an honour that the Tatars bestow on their dead.

10. See GC (76–7) for a nutshell collection of alternate Arctic exploits: "After lunch Mrs. Coulter showed her some of the precious arctic relics in the institute library— the harpoon with which the great whale Grimssdur had been killed; the stone carved with an inscription in an unknown language which was found in the hand of the explorer Lord Rukh, frozen to death in his lonely tent; a fire-striker used by

Captain Hudson on his famous voyage to Van Tieren's Land...Lyra felt her heart stir with admiration for these great, brave, distant heroes."

11. Trollesund can be translated from Norwegian as "Enchanted" or "Magic Sound."

12. Lapp, or more appropriately Sámi, and Finnish have been collapsed in Pullman's world.

13. See Karsten (57–8) on the supposed ability of Sámi shamans to send their souls from their bodies, and Holmberg (80–96) for more general information on shamanism.

14. On this figure, also spelled *Jabmeakka*, see Holmberg (27–8).

15. See Scott 2005 on how Pullman uses "his three major literary sources—Milton, Blake, and the Bible—to reinterpret the ontology of humankind's moral and ethical universe" (93).

16. See Hatlen for a reading of how Pullman challenges the fantasy literature of Lewis and Tolkien. According to Hatlen, Pullman offers an alternative to Tolkien's "attitudes toward the contemporary world, toward hierarchical power structures, and toward the relationship of good and evil," and, above all to "Tolkien's metaphysical dualism" (79) and Lewis's "orthodox" reading of Milton.

17. Of *The Chronicles of Narnia*, Pullman says "there is no doubt in my mind that it is one of the most ugly and poisonous things I've ever read" ("Dark Side").

18. Lewis describes what this "stuff" is in the following way: "I thought I saw how stories of this kind could steal past a certain inhibition which had paralyzed much of my own religion in childhood. Why did one find it so hard to feel as one was told one ought to feel about God or about the sufferings of Christ? I thought the chief reason was that one was told one ought to... But supposing that by casting all these things into an imaginary world, striping them of their stained-glass and Sunday school associations, one could make them for the first time appear in their real potency?" ("Sometimes" 527–8).

19. Compare this socially marginal group to Pullman's "gyptians."

20. Weitzman's compelling argument about Kiergekaardian despair and "The Snow Queen" suggests that Kay's desire, in spelling the word eternity, is as follows: "the world, shattered into shards, must be put together in its entirety, all at once" (1112). Fragmentation of the world, illustrated by the fragmented demon mirror and the mathematically fragmented lake in "The Snow Queen," is cause for despair. The Snow Queen's realm is one of "frigid mathematical perfection," where Kay pursues a sort of absolute knowledge that—ironically—isolates the subject. For Andersen, the only solution is communion with other humans and with God. In *The Golden Compass*, we may hear echoes of this fragmentation and despair in the practice

of intercision, which severs two parts of a previous whole. This leaves the subject fragmented and incomplete with no hope of reunification, and as the plight of the "severed" children reveals, for following the intercision they usually sicken and die (213–9).

21. Compare the following descriptions of the Snow Queen, The White Witch, and Mrs. Coulter: Anderson says that the Snow Queen "was beautiful but all made of ice: cold, blindingly glittering ice; and yet she was alive, for her eyes stared at Kai like two stars..." (237), and "The fur hat and the coat were made of snow; the driver was a woman: how tall and straight she stood! She was the Snow Queen" (239). In *The Lion, the Witch and the Wardrobe*, Lewis describes the White Witch as "a great lady, taller than any woman Edmund had ever seen. She also was covered in white fur up to her throat and held a long straight golden wand in her right hand and wore a golden crown on her head. Her face was white—not merely pale, but white like snow or paper or icing sugar, except for her very red mouth. It was a beautiful face in other respects, but proud and cold and stern" (27). In *The Golden Compass*, Mrs. Coulter is depicted as "A lady in a long yellow-red fox-fur coat, a beautiful young lady whose dark hair falls, shining delicately.... The young lady's dæmon...is in the form of a monkey, but no ordinary monkey: his fur is long and silky and of the most deep and lustrous gold" (41).

22. In *The Lion, the Witch and the Wardrobe*, Edmund journeys himself to the Witch's palace. We might consider the stone figures populating the White Witch's palace in some way akin to the placid workers and severed children at Bolvanger who have undergone the intercision process.

23. Serafina Pekkala's dæmon describes Bolvanger thus: "They burn coal spirit, which they bring in at great expense. We don't know what they do, but there is an air of hatred and fear over the place for miles around.... Animals keep away too. No birds fly there; lemmings and foxes have fled" (GC, 187).

24. In another typical subversion, Mrs. Coulter is not a witch or supernatural being (indeed, the witches in *The Golden Compass* are portrayed in a positive light), but fully human. She is a scientist of sorts and an ostensible religious fanatic (in that she works with the Magisterium to further her own power, though the depths of her own piety is questionable). Where religious—specifically Christian—forces and symbols are associated with the protagonists in both "The Snow Queen" and *The Lion, the Witch and the Wardrobe*, they are associated with the oppressive antagonists of *The Golden Compass*.

25. 425A, sub-group of 425 "The Search for the Lost Husband," includes the tale of Cupid and Psyche as its most well known variant, as well as "The Brown Bear of Norway" and "White-Bear-King Valemon." For variants see Uther (48–50).

26. Compare the image of the young girl riding the polar bear toward domestic confinement in "East of the Sun West of the Moon" with Lyra's own polar bear ride: "...she felt a wild exhilaration. She was riding a bear! And the Aurora was swaying above them in golden arcs and loops, and all around was the bitter arctic cold and the immense silence of the North" (GC 208). Like the young woman in "East of the Sun West of the Moon," this journey also marks an initiation of a new stage of life. While the young woman moves physically from one phase to the next, Lyra's transition is internal, and she wonders what she must seem like to the polar bear. In regard to this, "she had seldom considered herself before, and found the experience interesting but uncomfortable, very like riding the bear, in fact" (208–9).

27. This is illustrated beautifully in a scene, drawn directly from Kleist's "On the Marionette Theater," in which Lyra tries to duel with the bear, but he anticipates and deflects each of her blows. He explains that he is able to do this "by not being human" (GC, 226).

28. "Environmentalists also tell a story about us and ourselves and our place in the universe. In a sense it's a religious story, because that's the big question of religion. Why are we here? What is here, what does it consist of? What have we got to do now we are here? What responsibilities does being conscious place on us?" (Simms, n.pag.)

29. Mackey discusses the discrepancies between Pullman's imaginative North and her own experience as a Northern reader.

WORKS CITED

Andersen, H.C. *The Complete Fairy Tales and Stories.* Trans. E.C. Haugaard. New York: Doubleday, 1974.

Asbjørnsen, P.C., and J. Moe. *Norwegian Folk Tales.* Trans. Pat S. Iversen and C. Norman. New York: Pantheon, 1982.

Bettelheim, B. *The Uses of Enchantment: The Meaning and Importance of Fairy Tales.* New York: Knopf, 1976.

Davidson, P. *The Idea of North.* London: Reaktion, 2005.

Gould, G. *Glenn Gould's Solitude Trilogy: Three Sound Documentaries.* CBC, PSCD 2003-3. 1992.

Grace, S. *Canada and the Idea of North*. Montreal: McGill-Queen's UP, 2001.

Hatlen, B. "Pullman's *His Dark Materials*, a Challenge to the Fantasies of J.R.R. Tolkien and C.S. Lewis, with an Epilogue on Pullman's Neo-Romantic Reading of *Paradise Lost*." Lenz and Scott, 75–94.

Holmberg, U. *Lapparnas Religion*. Uppsala: Centre for Multiethnic Research, 1989.

Karsten, R. *The Religion of the Samek: Ancient Beliefs and Cults of the Scandinavian and Finnish Lapps*. Leiden: Brill, 1955.

Lenz, M. "Philip Pullman." *Alternative Worlds in Fantasy Fiction*. Eds. P. Hunt and M. Lenz. London: Continuum, 2001. 122–69.

Lenz, M., and C. Scott, eds. *His Dark Materials Illuminated: Critical Essays on Philip Pullman's Trilogy*. Detroit: Wayne State UP, 2005.

Lewis, C.S. *The Lion, the Witch and the Wardrobe*. New York: Collier, 1950.

———. "Sometimes Fairy Stories May Say Best What's To Be Said." 1956. *C.S. Lewis: Essay Collection and Other Short Pieces*. Ed. L. Walmsley. London: Harper Collins, 2000. 526–8.

Lopez, B. *Arctic Dreams*. 1986. New York: Vintage, 2001.

Mackey, M. "Northern Lights and Northern Readers: Background Knowledge, Affect Linking, and Literary Understanding." Lenz and Scott 57–67.

McGhee, R. *The Last Imaginary Place: A Human History of the Arctic*. Oxford: Oxford UP, 2005.

Miller, J.L. "No Sex in Narnia? How Hans Christian Andersen's 'Snow Queen' problematizes C.S. Lewis's *The Chronicles of Narnia*." *Mythlore* 28 (2009): 113–30.

Pullman, P. "The Dark Side of Narnia." 1998. <http://www.crlamppost.org/darkside.htm> 25 June 2012.

———. *The Golden Compass*. New York: Knopf, 1996.

———. *Once Upon a Time in the North*. New York: Knopf, 2008.

Said, E. *Orientalism*. New York: Pantheon, 1978.

Scott, C. "Pullman's Enigmatic Ontology: Revamping Old Tradition in *His Dark Materials*." Lenz and Scott 95–105.

Simms, A. "Philip Pullman: A New Brand of Environmentalism." *The Telegraph* 4 Jan. 2008. <http://www.telegraph.co.uk/earth/3322329/Philip-Pullman-new-brand-of-environmentalism.html> 25 June 2012.

Smith, K.P. "Tradition, Transformation, and the Bold Emergence: Fantastic Legacy and Pullman's *His Dark Materials*." Lenz and Scott 135–51.

Spufford, F. *I May Be Some Time: Ice and the English Imagination*. New York: Saint Martin's, 1997.

Uther, H.-J. *The Types of International Folktales: A Classification and Bibliography, Based on the System of Antti Aarne and Stith Thompson.* 3 vols. Helsinki: Suomalainen Tiedeakatemia, 2004.

Wawn, A. *The Vikings and the Victorians: Inventing the Old North in 19th-century Britain.* Cambridge: Brewer, 2000.

Weitzman, E. "The World in Pieces: Concepts of Anxiety in H.C. Andersen's 'The Snow Queen.'" *MLN* 122.5 (2007): 1105–23.

14 The Elf in Self

The Influence of Northern Mythology and Fauna on Contemporary Spiritual Subcultures

JAY JOHNSTON

THIS ARTICLE considers the use of Northern mythology and symbolic beliefs associated with Arctic fauna in Otherkin subcultures. Although encompassing a vast diversity of beliefs, individuals who identify as Otherkin are united by the belief that they are not fully human, but rather are comprised of different species at an ontological level (that is, at the most fundamental level of their being). There is a vast range of "other" species with which Otherkin identify, from animals and elves to machines and cartoon characters (Johnston, "Vampirism"). This chapter is primarily concerned with constructions of identity that reflect an engagement with Norse traditions. It will demonstrate that the widespread, long-standing perception of the North as an exotic "other" finds a new articulation in Otherkin subculture, in which its myths, traditions, and lore are adopted by individuals in order to express their contemporary identity. The first half will provide an overview of the subculture, beginning with an explanation of how Otherkin conceive of themselves, followed by an examination of how they feel their Otherkin identity affects their daily lives. The second half will examine metaphysical Norse elements in selected Otherkin discourses in more detail.

This consideration of the Norse legacy in the contemporary spiritual subculture of the Otherkin is not a straightforward linear tracing of influence, for example drawing direct correlations between motifs and ideas found in Old Norse-Icelandic literature[1] and Otherkin concepts of identity. Rather, the filtering of Norse traditions through literary and popular culture—well-known examples being J.R.R. Tolkien's fictional works and Philip Pullman's *His Dark Materials* series—and through broader western esoteric and contemporary pagan beliefs and practices have exerted strong influences on Otherkin use of this mythology. However, the influence of the metaphysical North is no less discernible because it has been filtered across time and through many different genres of literature and types of spiritual practice. In particular, it is those Norse gods and spiritual beings that cross metaphysical and ontological boundaries that feature most strongly in Otherkin identity, such as those with the capacity for shape-shifting between human and animal forms, or those that cross between human and metaphysical realms, such as elves.

OTHERKIN: THE DIFFICULTY OF DEFINITION

"Otherkin" is a general term employed to signify individuals that are something "other" than entirely human. That is, they understand themselves to be made up of more than one species of being. It should be noted that not all individuals who hold such beliefs identify with the label "Otherkin" or use the label themselves. However, the term now has a currency in both popular and academic discourse to signal the type of multi-species identity that the individuals embrace, and for this reason will be used in this discussion.[2] Examples of Otherkin discourse used in this chapter are drawn from Lupa's *A Field Guide to Otherkin*, a text written by a once highly active member of the community (who has subsequently renounced their affiliation) and based upon survey and interview data. According to Lupa, who previously identified as a Therianthrope (animal–human Otherkin), an Otherkin is

a person who believes that, through either a nonphysical or (much
more rarely) physical means, s/he is not entirely human. This means...
anyone who relates internally to a nonhuman species either through
soul, mind, body, or energetic resonance, or who believes s/he hosts
such a being in hir body/mind. (26)

As this quotation demonstrates, the "other" species inherent in
Otherkin concepts of being disrupt many prescriptions of normative
human identity, including the attribution of dimorphic concepts of gender
to the individual (Johnston, "On Having"; Johnston, "Vampirism"). Many
accounts recorded by Lupa explained that individuals felt, at a core level
of their being, different from, or "other" than, human. Further, they only
felt "whole" or "authentic" when understanding themselves as comprising
two or more species and that this often (as illustrated in Lupa's definition
above) involved incorporating or exhibiting this "otherness" in a spirit,
energetic, or soul form. For example, an eagle Therian (animal–human)
may understand their eagle anatomy, talons, wings, feathers, or beak to
exist in energetic, subtle material. Although not visible to everyday forms
of sight, nonetheless its existence is felt by the individual who may undertake various meditation and ritual practices to increase their perception
and use of their "eagle" anatomy.

The understanding of the body in Otherkin communities has been
very strongly influenced by western esoteric ideas, especially those popu-
larized in "New Age" (another problematic umbrella term) spiritual
practices (Johnston, "The Body"). This includes understanding the body–
mind–self to be made up of a type of subtle, energetic material that is both
internal and extends beyond the visible skin. This material is often
considered a link between the physical and the spiritual realms (Johnston,
Angels) as well as enabling shape-shifting across species boundaries in
contemporary shamanic practice (Greenwood). Without digressing into
the complexities of these ontological ideas, what is necessary for a basic
sense of Otherkin subjectivity is the understanding that the very concept
of self that they employ challenges (materially and immaterially) modern
concepts of the separate, ontologically stable individual self (including the

already well-contested Cartesian ideas of mind–body dualism). Indeed, Otherkin identities challenge numerous dualisms readily found in dominant discourse including those between fact and fiction (Johnston, "Vampirism"). This blurring of the boundaries also provides the foundation upon which their relation to mythological traditions is built. That is, any sharp distinction between "history" and "mythology," as those terms are generally understood, is not necessarily a feature of a subculture that challenges not only the boundaries between the human and non-human, but also the boundaries between fantasy and reality.

Before turning to examine this relation to Norse traditions directly, further examples of the range of Otherkin identities and the space in which the community operates will be outlined. As Lupa's data evidences, Otherkin communities are dominated by the age range 16–30 and are especially found in North America, Australia, Japan, the United Kingdom, and Europe (285). However, as it appears English was the only language in which the survey was administered, these geographic results reflect that bias.[3] It is largely an Internet-mediated subculture with a number of forums that have developed since the 1980s.[4] However, its emergence in cyberspace has been strongly influenced by counter-culture groups, New Age religious practices, and New Age shamanic practices. The latter two are based upon the work of Michael Harner, who proposed shamanic practice as a universal technique that any individual could learn and practice. Albeit very popular, Harner's form of "white shamanism," with its eliding of cultural difference and appropriation of indigenous knowledge, has drawn sharp criticism from many quarters (see, for example, Donaldson). In addition, the popularization of the western esoteric tradition (see von Stuckrad, *Western*) and the development of contemporary occult groups (see Partridge, *The Re-Enchantment*, 2 vols.) such as *The Werewolf Cathedral* and contemporary pagan groups have brought traditions of magic, energetic anatomy, inter-species identity, and Norse mythology and belief into the conceptual mix from which Otherkin identity is constructed (Johnston, "On Having"; Johnston, "Vampirism"). While it is impossible to trace this heady brew in detail within the confines of one chapter, special note should be made of the contemporary shamanic influence.

Lupa (2007) claimed for the subculture a heritage that predates Internet usage, which can be traced back to the 1960s. This is the time period identified by Kocku von Stuckrad (*Schamanismus*) during which contemporary shamanism emerged. These "western" renderings of shamanism often explicitly promote the association of particular animal species with an individual's "spirit" or "authentic" self (Harner). The intertwining of human and animal aspects in the self is directly reflected in Lupa's self-definition: "I look, sound, and smell human, and I cannot change that. But the spirit of Wolf still resides within me" (27).

In addition to Harner's popularization of shamanic techniques of journeying to the lower world and connections with a particular "totem" animal, Otherkin uses of the animal in individual identity construction include the influence of publications such as Ted Andrew's *Animal Speak*, in which a range of animals are presented, behaviours described, and symbolic associations detailed. Such "dictionaries" run along the lines of either offering ways to decode the meaning of a particular animal appearing in one's life (being either physically present or appearing in the imagination) and/or as describing the characteristics of a human individual for whom the animal is a "totem" (Johnston, "Vampirism").

In Scott Alexander King's *Animal Messenger: Interpreting the Symbolic Language of the World's Animals*, the Australian author presents a different style of manual, wherein animal messengers are not primarily categorized by species, but rather presented according to their geographical region. Those found in the Arctic section embody concepts like Robustness (Arctic Wolf), Brotherhood (Polar Bear), and Know-how (Walrus). Such associations are born of the roles attributed to such animals in mythology, folk tales, and stereotypes of regional identity.

These "animal spirit" guides propose two types of relationship between the human and the animal. On the one hand, the animal is a sign that the individual reads and interprets in relation to their personal biography. On the other hand, the animal is understood as archetypal, in the sense that the (largely psychologized) qualities attributed to the particular animal are also those of the individual who identifies with them. For example, someone in contemporary western culture may claim not to be *like* an otter but to *be* an otter, that is, to have an otter ontology (including spirit). In all cases, the animals are generic and universal. Indeed, shape-shifting— as presented in contemporary western forms of shamanism—is often employed by Therian Otherkin to explain their relationship to their animal "other." Unsurprisingly, accompanying these discussions are claims for specific epistemological practices and knowledge, especially those associated with the creative imagination and ritual and/or magical practice (Johnston, "Vampirism"). Shape-shifting, often employed by Therians as a way of understanding the dual elements of self, is developed and experienced via such alternate epistemologies. As Otherkin Fox Blackman explains: "Once I remembered...a dream shift in which I was a white fox...and then I saw some people and shifted back to human" (Lupa 126). In addition, numerous accounts from various traditions of gods and goddesses moving from human to animal state provide exemplars of the way in which shape shifting is conceptualized by Otherkin.

In sum, Otherkin identity and practice result from an eclectic take-up of a vast array of spiritual and mythological traditions from diverse cultures that are also influenced and expressed via contemporary media and consumer cultures.[5] At their core sits a critique of the modern, "normal" human subject with a simultaneous valorizing of the exotic, deviant, and "other."

As already indicated, animal–human Otherkin are known as Therianthropes. An individual may identify with one or more animals: wolves, bears, big cats, and birds of prey are the most popular. This is one of the largest types of Otherkin, the other large groups are Elves/Fey and Vampires (Lupa 2007). Lupa notes that the Norse and Celtic traditions and their reuse in fantasy literature of the twentieth century have had a significant influence on Otherkin concepts of elf and fairie. This is in contradistinction to the more usually benign Victorian flower fairies or their depiction in Disney films (153–71).

Mythological beasts also feature in Otherkin identity, as do angels and demons, although Angelkin and Demonkin are not necessarily influenced by Judaeo-Christian traditions (Lupa 189–96). There are also distinct groupings associated with Japanese, Korean, and Chinese cultures including Kitsune Otherkin that feature a shape-shifting fox spirit based on mythological traditions and contemporary anime productions (197–202). This listing is highly reductive, and not only are there many other "types" of Otherkin, there are also individuals who identify as "multiples." This term designates an understanding that their Otherkin identity comprises numerous parts of different species. Often it is a concept of the soul that is employed to explain multiple species identity: "one fragment [of soul] may have been part of an elf in another life, while another was part of a tiger" (62). Here the self is understood as a momentary coalescence of soul fragments and that the fragments have had many previous lives as a variety of different species.

The Otherkin community—largely generated and developed online—is a dynamic one, and there are ongoing debates within the community regarding self-definition. It seems no accident that the age demographics represented in the community are highest for teens and those in their twenties, for issues of identity and community, as well as online literacy, feature strongly in youth cultures. Searching for an adequate framework through which to present the self and understand a lived, felt difference from the "normal" human is a foundation of Otherkin identity for many (Johnston, "Vampirism"). "Otherkin," writes Lupa (30), "is a safe haven for us to express the aspects of ourselves that don't fit into the everyday world but that need to have a place nonetheless."

THE NORTHERN AFFECT: SHARDS OF THE METAPHYSICAL NORTH IN OTHERKIN IDENTITY

The complex melding of identity, mythology, and spirituality embraced in Otherkin identity is exemplified in the self-description of "Anton":

In the context of Otherkin, my primary association would be as a theri-
anthrope, with specific relation to the felidae-family, particularly...
Panthera leo spelaea [extinct since 2000–1000 years ago]. Also with
additional tendencies towards the Northern European Alfar...or Sidhe.
The soul-lore of the Northern Cultures was rather complex and convo-
luted but the animal part of the soul, similar to the totem concept of
other circum-polar cultures was called the fylgja or "fetch", which
meant "follower". Berserkers ("Bear-Shirts") would have bear fetches,
ulfhedinn (wolf men) would have had wolf fetches...These cults were
especially tied to the worship of Odin, who coincidentally has ruled my
head *for as long as I can remember. (Anton, in Lupa 98)*

There are several layers to Anton's Otherkin identification. Firstly, his
primary Therian nature is noted with a specific reference to an extinct
form of large feline; however, this is tempered with other "tendencies"
toward metaphysical beings found in Northern mythological traditions,
namely the Norse Alfar and Irish Sidhe. Indeed, Anton is very clear that
beliefs of the "North," and in particular Odin, who has "ruled [his] head"
directly inform his identity, including spirituality. As well as identifying
as Otherkin, Anton is also a member of a contemporary Nordic recon-
structionist Heathen group, Ásatrú, whose members are faithful to the
Æsir.[6] According to the data collected by Lupa's survey of the community, the majority of Otherkin also identify as contemporary pagans, for
example as Wiccan, Druid, or Ásatrú (although it should also be noted
that some identify as other faiths, including small numbers of Buddhist
and Christian participants).

As evidenced by Anton's description, Otherkin as a spiritual path
is a highly individualized and often solitary practice (this is a feature
of New Age Religion in general). Publications like Eoghan Odinsson's
Northern Lore: A Field Guide to the Northern Mind, Body and Spirit (2010)
and Krasskova and Kaldera's *Northern Tradition for the Solitary Practice*
(2009) present forms of Norse paganism packaged specifically for individual practice in the contemporary world. Both texts also emphasize the

formative nature of geography and location on their tradition. That is, the landscape of the North, its geology, fauna, and flora are implicit aspects of the belief framework. Nationality, location, region, and specific folklore and literary traditions are brought together to create identity. For example Kira, who identifies as Elvenkin, claims that her Elven nature was inherited from her Celtic and Norwegian roots with their rich traditions of Hidden People (known as *huldrefolk*), such as elves in Norwegian and Icelandic traditions, and as fairies and pixies, in Celtic traditions (Lupa).[7] This is a link made to Northern mythological and religious traditions by reference to ancestral relation. In Otherkin discourse, genetic inheritance is also given as a "reason" for one's Otherkin nature: "Thorinn, a bear therianthrope, also says that his therianthropy is genetic. Interestingly he links it to the berserkers of Germanic lore, he himself is primarily of Germanic stock" (Lupa 69).

Similar to the use of Scandinavian traditions (specifically Icelandic and Norwegian) in the construction of Otherkin identity are the nineteenth-century national identity debates that took place in Orkney, Shetland, and mainland Scotland (Seibert; Wawn). The construction of Otherkin identity intersects with contemporary debates regarding national and cultural identity. It also participates in the same quest for origins that fuelled the nineteenth-century constructions of the "Norse" (and particularly Viking) heritage of the British Isles. For both, the concept of the "North" carried desirable attributes. In Otherkin and contemporary pagan groups, the shamanic and magical attributes of the Norse gods and goddesses are often emphasised.

Other causes given for Otherkin ontology include physical or genetic heritage traced to an ancestor who had interspecies sexual relations. Lupa recounts a story that she/he attributes to Inuit mythology in which Wolverine and Muskrat mated five times and created the various races of humans. She/he presents this narrative alongside references to tales of human and bear generative relations from North America and Siberia (69). This form of origination is also found in contemporary Elven beliefs. As contemporary Heathen (Germanic pagan) Kveldulf Gundarsson notes in his overview of Hidden People traditions, *Elves, Wights and Trolls,* "Alfs, like trolls, etins and goddesses can mate with humans." He gives the example of Högni in *Þiðreks* saga, noting that, "According to the saga, he was the son of an alf and Queen Grímhildr...easily mistaken for a troll in dim light" (65–6). Such transformations, of course, were also linked to the practice of *seiðr,* a type of Old Norse "magic" (the reconstructed practice of which is also a feature of contemporary Northern paganism [Blain]).

As these references to contemporary paganism and shamanism illustrate, it is clear that elements of the metaphysical North taken into Otherkin concepts of the self are drawn from many sources. The term employed by John Chute, "taproot texts," for the influence of myths and fairytales on modern fantasy literature, is also relevant in this context (Jobling 6). However, in the case of Otherkin, fantasy literature itself has also become a "taproot" for the construction of Otherkin identity.

As Heather O'Donoghue (8) points out succinctly, "Norse mythology as it has come down to us cannot be confined to a single society or a single time." Otherkin identity construction reflects this mixed and indeterminate heritage. O' Donoghue, amongst others, has traced the Northern influence in the arts and contemporary spiritual practices in particular, from the compositions of Richard Wagner to contemporary metal music and much more besides. Therefore, it is not at all surprising to find diverse Northern traditions and their re-presentations in artistic creations and contemporary Pagan and shamanic belief systems being called upon to explain Otherkin subjectivity. Indeed, Otherkin practice re-animates Northern traditions, especially the metaphysical beings, in the daily lives of its adherents. Not only, as in the case of Anton, do individuals hold reverence for specific Norse deities, but for those that identify as Elven it also provides both their ontology and ancestry.

The positioning of the Northern world, and especially the Arctic as Other—as alien and hostile while simultaneously alluring and mysterious—has a rich and complex history that has already been (and continues to be) detailed by historians. To give one example, Robert G. David in *The Arctic in British Imagination* argues that the Arctic was an equally powerful marker of the exotic "other" as Africa was during the Victorian period (Jobling 151). This Arctic "orientalism"—perhaps more suitably termed "borealism"—was accompanied by a Norse "orientalism," strongly exemplified by the construction of Northern realms and nations in the British Isles during the Victorian period. The Norse became both a valorized and castigated "other," depending upon political and social ambition and affiliation (Wawn). This deference to the "other" that, during the Victorian period, embraced the Scandinavian genetic inheritance in the English population, lives on in a different way in Otherkin communities. The "other" is within them, implicit in their being: it is not only an ancestral relation but is also a lived aspect of their daily lives. At the deepest level of self-authenticity and identity, it directs how Otherkin understand themselves and the world around them. For many the metaphysical North plays a central part in this process.

As Anton's self-description (quoted above) and Lupa's data illustrate, a feature of Otherkin discourse—especially regarding origins—is a tendency to reference what are understood to be "ancient" or foundational myths. The association with such material provides an authenticating source for validating the individual's identity and claimed heritage. In the case of Therian and Elven identity, examples from Northern belief traditions are not hard to find. For example, as O'Donoghue recounts, in the story of Siward (in Jocelin of Furness's *Vita Waldevi*), his father Beorn Bear's ancestry was partly "other," and evident to all on account of his furry white ears. Elven and Feykin communities have adopted renderings found in Norse myths, including the division of elves as "light" and "dark." Additionally, however, it should be noted that J.R.R. Tolkien's own re-working of Norse and Teutonic traditions, especially his representations of elves and dwarves, is also evident.

Central to Anton's understanding of his Therian identity is the concept of the *fylgja* or "fetch," which he links directly to Norse traditions. As detailed by Lotte Hedeager in her discussion of Scandinavian concepts of "otherness," the *fylgja* is a type of spirit that she argues is etymologically "translated as *fylgur*, 'followers', or related to *fulga*, that is 'skin'," 'cloak' or 'animal clothing,' or a third as *fylgja*—afterbirth" (82). Such multiple meanings, and the ambiguous nature of the type of spirit represented, make analogies with the contemporary idea of a spirit guide—as suggested by Odinsson—seem quite reductive. The appeal of the *fylgjur* to Otherkin—especially Therians—is understandable, given that it is something "other" than human that is proposed as being intimately attached to an individual human being. Further, the relation to animals (i.e., "animal clothing") makes it particularly suitable to Therians, like Anton, who claim a mix of animal and figures of the metaphysical North as central to their being.

It is possible that other Therian narratives develop a similar idea but are drawn from Philip Pullman's rendering of animal dæmons in the *His Dark Materials* series. In this fiction, the "cutting away" of the "animal" aspect of self resulted in the diminishment of the individual's spirit, creativity, and capacity of individualism. Such an animal aspect also features in Odinsson's guide to Northern spirituality, wherein he provides a guided meditation to help practitioners of contemporary paganism get in touch with their "fetch." Like the universalism found in contemporary shamanism, Odinsson's guide advocates a form of contemporary spiritual universalism. That is to say, no matter what one's specific cultural background, potentially everyone may have a "fetch." Odinsson achieves this by equating the complex concept of the "fetch" with the (New Age) concept of Spirit Guide. However, as the above discussion demonstrates, this corollary is far from straightforward.

CONCLUSION

In commenting on the influence of fantasy literature on the religious imagination, J'annine Jobling writes, "with postmodern enthusiasm for bricolage, Loki can rub shoulders quite happily with Spider Woman" (1). For Otherkin adherents, this rubbing of shoulders is not only something that is implicit in their metaphysical and cosmological belief systems, but something that is also a central constituent of their physical, psychological, and spiritual selves: it is ontological. At a philosophical level, a series of important questions are being asked regarding what constitutes a human subject, how it can relate to an "other" in an ethical and harmonious way, and how this "other" is to be defined.

In order to present their own lived understanding of being "other" to the perceived "normal," Otherkin have turned to various religious and metaphysical traditions that offer them examples of a renegotiation of dualisms that sit at the heart of modern concepts of identity and epistemology. It is no surprise that this turn includes an embrace of a wide diversity of Northern traditions, from Inuit animal lore to Norse gods and goddesses. These are traditions in which spirit and matter are not separated by a harsh dualism, but rather provide examples of the metaphysical world as part of, and implicit in, the physical world, as well as traditions in which nature is revered and respected.

In addition to embracing the representation and adaptations of Western esoteric discourses, Otherkin absorb Northern mythological traditions, especially regarding the rich animism, shamanic and shape-shifting relations with animals, and with the belief and powerful agency of the Hidden People. The ethics of claiming such ontological constituents is beyond the scope of this chapter, but it is at least superficially clear that the subculture enacts yet another melding of the North as "other" in Western culture. In this practice, syncretic relations between vastly different religions are not only part of a lived belief system, but also part of how an individual actually understands their existence on a very day-to-day level. The metaphysical North embraced by Otherkin is simultaneously exotic and ordinary. For many members of the community it is most certainly a significant element in their worldview and interpersonal ethics. Thus, the metaphysical is also physical, for it is integrated in their everyday lives. In a bizarre twist, with this troubling of the physical–metaphysical binary, Otherkin belief frameworks on the nature of reality and identity are much closer to those of Scandinavian folk belief, indigenous beliefs systems of the Arctic regions, and medieval Norse mythology. It is the very framework and logic that enables Otherkin Tygermoon Fox to remark, "I love my religion and my beliefs are put into practice even for everyday mundane tasks like cleaning house. When I do ritual, I almost always officiate as cat and woman. My primary goddesses, Bast and Freyja, both have strong connections to cats" (Lupa 213).

The metaphysical and the mundane interpenetrate in such a worldview. This type of attitude is strongly evidenced in Northern traditions, in which the magical, shape-shifting, "other" realms and beings are understood to permeate reality. Indeed, it is perhaps just this troubling of the modern epistemological boundaries placed between fantasy and reality evidenced in Northern lore that appeals to contemporary Otherkin individuals. The metaphysical North can be considered to be a source of valiant deities, magical races, and shape-shifting exemplars for this contemporary subculture to revere and emulate. Further, the beliefs and myths of the various Northern traditions—with their inherent blending of the metaphysical and the physical—furnishes Otherkin's daily worldview. Northern traditions are employed to legitimate their use of fantasy and imagination in the very real world of identity politics.

NOTES

1. Specifically, the Old Norse-Icelandic sagas, Snorri Sturluson's *Prose Edda* (c. 1220) and the anonymous *Poetic Edda*, also known as the "Elder Edda" (preserved in a manuscript that dates from the 1270s).

2. For a recent academic study, see Kirby (*Fantasy*).

3. Several scholars and doctoral students are working on compiling more demographic data on this topic.

4. On the role of text in the community's formation and identity, see Kirby 2009.

5. For further discussion of conceptual heritage and types see Johnston ("Vampirism").

6. For more details of such groups, see Strimska.

7. It should be noted that this is Kira's (or Lupa's) interpretation of *huldrefolk*, rather than a scholarly assessment of the term.

WORKS CITED

Andrews, T. *Animal-Speak: The Spiritual and Magical Powers of Creatures Great & Small.* 1993. St. Paul: Llewellyn, 1998.

Blain, J. *Nine Worlds of Seid-Magic: Ecstasy and Neo-Shamanism in North European Paganism.* London: Routledge, 2002.

Donaldson, L.E. "On Medicine Women and White Shame-ans: New Age Native Americanism and Commodity Fetishism as Pop Cultural Feminism." *Journal of Women in Culture and Society* 24 (1999): 677–96.

Greenwood, S. "On Becoming an Owl: Magical Consciousness." *Religion and the Subtle Body in Asia and the West: Between Mind and Body.* Eds. G. Samuel and J. Johnston. London: Routledge, 2013. 211–23. Routledge Studies in Asian Religion and Philosophy 8.

Gundarsson, K. *Elves, Wights and Trolls.* New York: iUniverse, 2007.

Harner, M. *The Way of the Shaman.* New York: Harper, 1980.

Hedeager, L. *Iron Age Myth and Materiality: An Archaeology of Scandinavia* AD 400–1000. London: Routledge, 2011.

Jobling, J. *Fantastic Spiritualities: Monsters, Heroes, and the Contemporary Religious Imagination.* London: Clark, 2010.

Johnston, J. *Angels of Desire: Esoteric Bodies, Aesthetics and Ethics.* London: Equinox, 2008.

———. "The Body in Occult Thought." Partridge, *Occult World* 659–71.

———. "On Having a Furry Soul: Transpecies Identity and Ontological Indeterminacy in Otherkin Subcultures." *Animal Death.* Eds. J. Johnston and F. Probyn-Rapsey. Sydney: Sydney UP, 2013. 293–306.

———. "Vampirism, Lycanthropy and Otherkin." Partridge, *Occult World* 412–26.

King, S.A. *Animal Messenger: Interpreting the Symbolic Language of the World's Animals.* Sydney: New Holland, 2006.

Kirby, D. *Fantasy and Belief: Alternative Religions, Popular Narratives, and Digital Cultures.* London: Equinox, 2013.

———. "From Pulp Fiction to Revealed Text: A Study of the Role of the Text in the Otherkin Community." *Exploring Religion and the Sacred in a Media Age.* Eds. C. Deacy and E. Arwick. Farnham: Ashgate, 2009. 141–54.

Krasskova, G., and R. Kaldera. *Northern Tradition for the Solitary Practice: A Book of Prayer, Devotional Practice, and the Nine Worlds of the Spirit.* Franklin Lakes: New Page, 2009.

Lupa. *A Field Guide to Otherkin.* Stafford: Megalithica, 2007.

Odinsson, E. *Northern Lore: A Field Guide to the Northern Mind, Body and Spirit.* n.p: self-published, 2010.

O'Donoghue, H. *From Asgard to Valhalla: The Remarkable History of the Norse Myths.* London: Tauris, 2008.

Partridge, C. *New Religions—A Guide: New Religious Movements, Sects and Alternative Spiritualities.* Oxford: Oxford UP, 2004.

―――, ed. *The Occult World.* London: Routledge, 2015.

―――. *The Re-Enchantment of the West.* 2 vols. London: Clark, 2014–15.

Seibert, S. *Reception and Construction of the Norse Past in Orkney.* Oxford: Lang, 2008.

Strmiska, M.F., ed. *Modern Pagans in World Cultures: Comparative Perspectives.* Santa Barbara: ABC-CLIO, 2005.

von Stuckrad, K. *Schamanismus und Esoterik: Kultur-und wissenschaftsgeschichtliche Betrachtungen.* Leuven: Peeters, 2003. *Gnostica* 4.

―――. *Western Esotericism: A Brief History of Secret Knowledge.* London: Equinox, 2005.

Wawn, A. *The Vikings and Victorians: Inventing the Old North in Nineteenth Century Britain.* Cambridge: Brewer, 2000.

15 A Blaze in the Northern Sky

Semiotic Strategies of Constructing the Supernatural North in Music Subcultures

JAN LEICHSENRING

INTRODUCTION

Images of a supernatural North certainly have their place in popular culture, particularly in fantasy movies, books, and games.[1] In comparison, some music subcultures that incorporate such images are far less visible. This is especially true for the black and pagan metal and neofolk genres, and in the following pages, I would like to discuss the constructions of a supernatural North in these styles. The term *supernatural* will be used conventionally. The supernatural transcends the borders of sensory perception and natural science; it encompasses gods and spirits, magic and clairvoyance. I will focus on the Nordic countries, that is, the Germanic and Finno-Ugric speaking nations of Northern Europe and the North Atlantic. Here, "Nordic" refers to all things imagined to be traditional for these regions, including their characteristic landscapes and cultural heritage, ranging from folk tales to Viking Age woodcarvings.

Before delving further into the mysteries of underground music, some remarks on the notion of subculture and on the genres in question are necessary. "Subculture" refers here to groups of people sharing interests (and, to a certain extent, attitudes) important to their self-perception, through which they distance themselves significantly from mainstream culture. The social difference of subcultures is expressed in their characteristic semiotics, namely "their unorthodox, even oppositional or illegitimate, use of cultural signs" (Gelder 12). Subcultures take liminal positions between familiarity and strangeness, and research on subcultures sheds new light on potentials and functions of cultural resources.[2] Therefore social difference and deviance have been the foci of research in the social sciences and cultural studies since the days of the Chicago School in the 1920s and 1930s (see Gelder 19–24).

Metal is the superordinate concept designating music genres that emerged largely from heavy metal, the style that originated in the 1970s with bands like Judas Priest, Iron Maiden, and Black Sabbath. After the diversification of metal music beginning in the 1980s, the musical differences between metal bands have become so large that music magazines and fans usually distinguish between sub-genres such as heavy, black, death, folk, pagan, gothic, doom, and thrash metal, to name only a few that, moreover, can be differentiated still further. Though all metal styles are sometimes still referred to as "heavy metal," a closer look at them demands the aforementioned subordinate concepts, because many musical and non-musical features are specific to certain sub-genres. Black and pagan metal in particular have developed strong overall identifying characteristics in which a supernatural Northernness is constructed cross-referentially by means of music, lyrics, and artwork (i.e., the pictures and other layout elements used for sleeve covers and booklets).[3]

This latter development is also true for neofolk, a music style also known as "apocalyptic folk," which was initiated in the 1980s by the English bands Death in June, Sol Invictus, and Current 93. It has since developed into a subculture with a variety of bands and sub-genres rooted in both Europe and North America. Musically, neofolk often employs acoustic guitar and clean voice, but also includes instruments such as violins, flutes, drums, and synthesizers, as well as electronic and experimental elements. As its name suggests, neofolk draws musical inspiration from traditional folk music, but also from numerous other styles such as British and US folk movements of the 1960s, as well as from pop and post-punk bands, such as Cocteau Twins and Joy Division. Its topics range from a humanistic or Romantic emphasis on emotion and experience of nature to martial motifs and fascist ideology. The latter, more controversial features might be included for provocation or for propaganda purposes.[4] In recent years, some metal bands have taken up musical influences from neofolk, and some musicians are active in metal as well as in neofolk bands. Several neofolk bands engage with religious, neo-pagan ideas that are clearly drawn from Scandinavian mythology. Aspects of Northernness portrayed in neofolk are regularly marked as supernatural, and dealings with the supernatural are often marked as specifically Nordic, even by non-Nordic groups.

FIST OF THE NORTHERN DESTROYER: MARTIAL, SUPERNATURAL, AND NORDIC SIGNATURES IN METAL

I will treat as characteristic of black metal the Norwegian band Darkthrone's iconic album *A Blaze in the Northern Sky*, which was formative for black metal as a musically distinguishable genre. The most obvious thing about black metal is perhaps the sheer amount of "satanic" imagery in artwork and lyrics.[5] Though not every black metal band emphasizes this, a certain musical language is necessary to call a group or recording "black metal." There does not seem to be one single criterion that distinguishes black metal from other metal genres, but there are a number of attributes that black metal bands often combine in a unique way. Generally, black metal is more musically radical and less accessible than classic heavy metal. The chirring and clanging guitar sound introduced on *A Blaze...* is now widely used in black metal. Other characteristics are croaking or shrieking vocals, tremolo riffing, fast and constant double bass drumming and a tendency towards repetitive song structures. The genre's use of atonality, dissonance, and often a raw, blurry production evokes a cold and harsh atmosphere. As a kind of onomatopoetic musical language, this character-istic sound may recall the howling of storms and the breaking of ice, and this quality links it to the overall artistic concepts of black metal bands.

Album artwork and self-presentation enhance the atmosphere of the music. These non-musical elements serve as vehicles for artistic expres-sion that foreground the supernatural, martial, and environmental sides of Norse mythology, envisioning it particularly through the lens of a "sword & sorcery" fantasy, including images of an imagined archaic, pagan Northland. Such contents cohere with a musical language that promotes the combination of savage, eerie, and ominous motifs. In the case of Darkthrone, the album layout consists of blurred black-and-white photos showing nighttime scenes, and images of the band members wearing "corpse paint," a usually black and white makeup that covers the face, making it unrecognizable and spectral. While not every black metal band uses such stage makeup, its occurrence is limited almost exclusively to this genre. In some cases, corpse paint corresponds to the images of winter, forests, and wilderness used for artwork, videos, and promotional photos. The person melts into the landscape, thus becoming indistinct and ghastly.

The black metal band Immortal, also hailing from Norway, makes the Nordic winter the backdrop of their entire oeuvre. Their lyrics repeatedly connect winter and the supernatural, for example, with the character Blashyrkh, a winter spirit or god invented by the band. In the video clips for their songs "Blashyrkh, Mighty Ravendark" and "Grim and Frostbitten Kingdoms," Scandinavian nature serves as the stage and means to support the rough and obscure, but also epic, atmosphere of their music and lyrics. As they perform, the musicians in corpse paint stand on a mountaintop overlooking vast forested areas, or they are filmed surrounded by ice and snow, wearing only leather waistcoats over their bare chests. The band members thus create and act as artificial figures. Sequences cross-fading from the band into images of ravens and reptile eyes hint at animal totemism. In this way, the band embodies the image of a male warrior amidst the hostile environment of the Nordic winter (see Richard and Grünwald). The narrative method of characterizing fictional figures with such environments is not restricted to black metal, but can be observed in a broader pop culture tradition. Movies such as *Conan the Barbarian* (1981) and *Batman Begins* (2005) similarly place their heroes in wintery landscapes to illustrate their physical and mental strength. In the case of Immortal, the warrior does not merely endure the cold, but rather draws his power from the forces represented by the wintery landscape, showing himself as a superhuman in league with the supernatural.

The motif of a terrifying and supernatural North returns in cryptic and declamatory lyrics. The following verses from Darkthrone's "Where Cold Winds Blow" demonstrate the signature fusion of Nordic, dark, satanic, and martial aspects of black metal in a few words, and the narrator turns out to be the voice of one long dead:

Where cold winds blow I was laid to rest
I cannot reach my rusty weapons;
The blood and sword that guided my path
For they drowned in the sands of wisdom

I was, indeed, a king of the flesh
My blackened edges; still they were sharp
Honoured by the carnal herds
But asketh thou: Closed are the gates? ...

I entered the soul of the snake
And slept with the Armageddish whore
But without my throne and my weapons;
Where cold winds blow became my grave.

While the snake is obviously Satan, and the king and whore refer to Revelations 17–18, the song title and respective lines localize the speaker in a northern environment typical of black metal aesthetics. Although this album does not explicitly include topics from Norse mythology, the speaking dead are known, for example, from medieval Icelandic texts such as *Völuspá* ("The Prophecy of the Seeress") and from *Brennu-Njáls saga*. They appear again in nineteenth-century poetry, for example in William Morris's "Gunnar's Howe Above the House at Lithend" and Henry Wadsworth Longfellow's "The Skeleton in Armor."[6] Likewise, ideas of supernatural forces linked to the cold, the night, and a downward movement emphasize the perilous and Nordic character of the scene in this example from Immortal: "Winds have come for me / Descending now / Towards the frostmoon eclipse // A spectral spirit kingdom rise."[7] Such lyrics do not contain a particular ideological message, but are meant to create a certain atmosphere. Images of the supernatural and the Nordic winter support black metal aesthetics that generally focus on obscurity, irrationalism, and menace.

Furthermore, such typical features of black metal are frequently linked to martial themes and imagery. Album covers display military gear such as swords and helmet masks, and in their album booklets several bands depict themselves carrying weapons including axes, halberds, and swords, or wearing ammunition belts and other armaments (see Figure 15.1).[8] These images are marked as Nordic, for example, by references to Viking culture. For example, Thor's hammer Mjölnir, a pagan symbol well known from archeological findings (see Lindow), is common in album artwork and merchandise. In the booklet of their album *Nemesis Divina*, Norway's Satyricon depicted the Mjölnir pendant of Skåne with the word *krig* ("war") written across it, next to their band photos. In cases such as these, black metal bands imagine Nordic characteristics as intrinsically martial.

Lyrics dealing with martial topics associated with images of Viking history and religion can easily be found in "pagan" or "Viking" metal, an offshoot of black metal.[9] In the song "Dragons of the North" by the Norwegian pagan metal band Einherjer, the lyrics envision war as a lifestyle of the Vikings, who are affirmatively pictured as virtually amoral conquerors: "Villages burn, burn cities to dust / And for fun they torture the rest // Cold, blue steel through a nice lady's breast / An avalanche of heathens set sail / To show to the world of which men is best / To conquer where others would fail." Moreover, such violence is linked to paganism in the

FIGURE 15.1 *Satyricon as seen in the booklet for their album* Nemesis Divina.
Band members are shown holding halberds and wearing ammunition belts.
[Courtesy of Per Heimly]

song: "Odin is working to eagerly form / A great heathen fist from the
north." The narrator invokes the chief Norse god as the "great warlord"
whose help is needed against Christianization, before the lyrics take a
comical turn in the last line: "This new god is weaker of class / Grant me
thy powers, your secrets unveil / And I'll kick this Christ right in the
ass."[10] Of course the literal content should not be mistaken as the message,

but as an expression of varying interests such as entertainment, the rejection of Christian ideas, or perhaps both. Although this more or less obvious humour is not very common in black/pagan metal, a certain irony occasionally occurs in the handling of such topics. Evil is taken in good humour (see Wagenknecht). At the same time, these issues can be treated with irony because of the very fact that there is a basic seriousness to their production and reception. This imagining of pagan barbarians shows how metal bands take up semiotics of popular media and put them into a new context. These violent northmen resemble those in movies such as *The Vikings* (1958) and *Pathfinder* (2007), but the metal musician shows them affirmatively as his ancestors resisting Christianization.

Some of these groups also express their idea of Northernness through references to mythological tales from Old Norse literature. Bands are frequently named after mythological places or entities mentioned in the Eddas,[11] such as *Nåstrond* (from the Old Norse *Nåströnd*, "Corpse-strand"), a place of torture for perjurers and murderers in the underworld; Naglfar, the ship of the dead on which they will set out to their final battle with the gods; and Einherjer, the fallen warriors chosen by the Valkyries to gather in Valhalla (see Lindow). The martial character of an album can also be underlined by titles like *Fist of the Northern Destroyer* and *Rage of the Northmen*.[12] Choosing such names or titles does not necessarily imply that Norse mythology plays an important role in the band's work, but some do focus strongly on Viking-related topics, to the extent that their music is labeled "Viking" or "pagan metal." Musically, these bands often build upon a black metal base, integrating other metal styles as well as folk, rock, or ambient influences, which make their music more melodic and accessible than "true" black metal. The folk influences can appear in the use of certain keys, phrasings, melodies, and traditional instruments such as the Hardanger fiddle.

Finally, pagan metal employs theatrical elements, for example band members dress up in archaic-looking garb or as mythological figures for promotional photos and concerts. Einherjer have posed as their eponyms, the slain warriors brought to Valhalla, and Enslaved, on one album cover, are pictured as Vikings on a shore with a dragon boat in the background.[13]

Thus, it is clear that band names and presentation, music, and lyrics connect to and comment on each other. For example, the harshness of the music signals that a rather dreamy scene pictured on an attendant album cover should be perceived as ghostly, brooding, and perilous. In turn, a cover may add new meaning to the music, so that the latter is not perceived as solely aggressive, but as romanticizing in a broader sense.[14]

LOST IN THE MOUNTAINS: FAIRY TALES, SAGAS, AND NORDIC NATURE

With the inception of black metal in the early 1990s, bands emerged that shared a Romantic emphasis on inwardness, archaic or folk beliefs, and the presence of the natural world. Bands such as Ulver, In the Woods..., and Borknagar (all hailing from Norway) wrote and performed black metal that retained the genre's musical characteristics, but largely dismissed the martial and satanic imagery. Instead, they strengthened black and pagan metal's partial romanticizing approaches that take an interest in folk-lore and nature. Musically, this approach allowed for the combination of black metal's harshness with folk elements. These aesthetics are supported by album covers that might seem quite atypical in other metal genres. In some examples, modified photos of rural sites are used as album covers. These almost peaceful pictures are, for example, saturated with blue or violet tones, or combined with Viking-styled ornaments.[15] This makes clear that the artists do not aim at realism, but at creating an atmosphere suited to mythical and fairy-tale topics.

Although such landscapes are set within a mythical framework rather than concrete history, black/pagan metal bands reference histor-ical events as well. On the inner back cover of their album *Dragons of the North*, Einherjer uses a photo of the monumental swords of the Norwegian "Sverd i fjell" memorial, which was built in 1983 to commemorate the Battle of Hafrsfjord in the ninth century. Other bands also refer to this event, in which Harald Fairhair united the whole of Norway under him. In those cases, songs about historical events stand next to lyrics derived from the Eddas, so that historical and mythological topics are melded together to present an archaic utopia.[16] However, some bands attempt to

FIGURE 15.2 *The cover of Borknagar's self-titled debut album. The logo incorporates a stylized Thor's hammer in the centre, beneath the "N."*

[*Courtesy of Hammerheart Records*]

reference early Icelandic literature while avoiding fantasy-style clichés of Vikings. The German/Icelandic band Árstíðir Lífsins released the concept albums *Jötunheima Dolgferð* (2010) and *Vápna lækjar eldr* (2012) about tenth-century Icelanders, their struggles with nature, and the effects of social customs such as blood feud. The stories are imbued with references to Norse mythology, but because they are told from the perspective of farmers, they do not foreground popular ideas about Viking warriors. While the metal songs are not particularly folk-influenced, the album *Jötunheima Dolgferð* does include a traditional Icelandic poem known as *ríma* as lyrics for a non-metal composition.

However, folklore, mythology and the natural world remain greater influences for these metal bands than historical events. Depictions of nature are often placed in a supernatural context by combining them with allusions to myths and fairy tales. For example, the title of Enslaved's album *Frost* is written in runes on the cover, which depicts a cloudy fjord from a bird's-eye view. Amon Amarth (Sweden) and Týr (Faroe Islands) regularly employ mythological or archaicizing motifs on their album covers: the fire giant Surtur wields his sword against the gods on the former's *Surtur Rising*, and a Viking warrior is cutting down a wooden cross on the latter's *By the Light of the Northern Star*.[17] Several band logos, such as that of Borknagar (see Figure 15.2), incorporate Thor's hammer, which instantly connects an album with ideas of Norse paganism. Such logos can also reflect motifs of nature and the supernatural, since they can be drawn in the style of antlers, twigs and roots, or Norse interlace patterns. The letters of the old logo of Ulver, used on their first four albums, end in cow tails, which points to the world of Scandinavian fairy tales: The cow tail is a feature of the women of the *huldrefolk*, a kind of forest spirit (see Bringsværd 11). Ulver's debut album *Bergtatt* ("taken into the mountain") tells a tale of trolls thirsting for Christian blood and abducting humans, a common theme in ballads and folklore. The lyrics of this album are written in an archaicizing Norwegian, so that its folklore content is reflected in its linguistic form. Likewise, several lyrics by Amorphis are taken from or inspired by the Finnish national epic *Kalevala* and the songs of the *Kanteletar*.[18] The supernatural is visually represented by, for example, the hammer of the deity Ukko in the cover painting of their album *Tales from the Thousand Lakes*. For other bands, this interest in folklore appears visually in the use of drawings by Theodor Kittelsen, the late Romantic Norwegian artist known especially for his illustrations in books of fairy tales. His pictures chosen by metal and neofolk bands are usually those of supernatural creatures and landscapes that convey a strong sense of mystery and inwardness, but also fear and danger.[19] Kittelsen is certainly the most influential artist when it comes to fairy tale illustrations in metal and neofolk artwork, but drawings and paintings by John Bauer[20] and Albert Engström,[21] for example, also appear as album covers in those music genres.

In some cases, references to folklore are linked more definitely to the eeriness and imagination of violence in black metal. The Norwegian black metal band Troll used the slogan *drep de kristne* ("kill the Christians") as an album title, and in its lyrics, trolls are celebrated for this habit. As indicated in the previous section, the militancy inherent in the use of some archaizing and anti-Christian motifs should of course be taken with a grain of salt. It appears now and then as a part of a subcultural backdrop and should not be interpreted as an instruction for action. First of all it seems to serve as a rejection of mainstream culture, a gesture of rebellion typical of rock music. Having said that, there have been a few incidents in which artistic images of violence became linked to real violence among some black metal bands and fans, mainly in Norway during the mid-1990s.[22]

The subcultural use of mythology and folklore is in fact quite versatile. Since the end of the 1990s, when Finntroll and later Ensiferum began to combine extreme metal and *humppa* (a Finnish foxtrot style) with lyrics based on supernatural-themed folklore, the fun factor in extreme metal gained more importance. Today there is a whole scene of such folk metal bands, and the German label Trollzorn ("Troll Wrath") is widely dedicated to a style of pagan/folk metal that relies on drinking songs rather than eerie atmosphere and musical radicalism.

WHEN THE TREES WERE SILENCED: MOTIFS OF MAGIC AND NEO-PAGANISM

Images of natural and supernatural worlds sometimes correlate with neo-pagan ideas and environmental concerns. Veneration of nature is a common topic in neo-pagan inspired music of Nordic and non-Nordic groups. As Irish pagan metallers Primordial put it: "This is my church / It stands so tall and proud / It has done for all time // It has no walls / Yet its vast halls / Reach from shore to shore."[23] So it comes as no surprise that some bands that endorse neo-paganism also promote environmental protection. An example of this is the Finnish pagan/folk metal band Korpiklaani ("forest clan"). Their video for the song "Keep on Galloping" (2008) tells in a humorous tone the story of a magical revenge on an overzealous lumberjack who, in the end, seems to have developed a new ecological consciousness. This stands in the tradition of Skyclad, the British pioneers of folk metal, who in numerous songs connected neo-paganism to ecological and social criticism.[24] Outside the context of specific music styles, this connection was set with certain notions of nature and irrationality in neo-paganism. In his poetic, rather than scholarly, book, *The White Goddess* (1948), which has been highly influential in neo-paganism, the writer and poet Robert Graves claims that poetry is linked to a mythical thinking manifested in several pagan traditions, and that such thinking has its own rules that cannot be translated into terms that are commonly considered to be logical and rational. As an early example of what he takes to be a halved ratio, he relates Socrates' dictum that one could only learn from other people, not from the fields and trees outside the city (Graves 11). In contrast, Graves defends the wisdom that, as he sees it, can be gleaned from nature and its cycles. This is a telling description of a neo-pagan belief that is also expressed in music subcultures.

The religious connection of allegedly primordial worldviews and contemporary life is explored by neofolk artist Andrea Haugen in both music and writing. Her neo-pagan handbook *The Ancient Fires of Midgard* encompasses a view of the pre-Christian ages as "time[s] where the individual, the community and nature were a unity" (Haugen 144). In the style of a guide to neo-paganism, basic interpretations of the Norse myths are proposed: "The Gods and Goddesses represent the natural forces and are symbols of human qualities with all its aspects. The Pagans saw the value of life in everything, in every tree and in every stone" (Haugen 23). Such harmony and wisdom was partially lost "when the trees were silenced,"[25] that is, when paganism and its natural wisdom (in Robert Graves's sense) were replaced by Christianity and "rationalism." Thus, they have to be regained in a renewed form of paganism.

Despite their symbolic quality, deities and other supernatural beings can be invoked, and magic, rune charms, and trance techniques can play a major role in neo-pagan religious practice. Old Norse reports on *seiðr*[26] and rune magic are interpreted for practical use in occult literature by comparison with forms of shamanism still practiced in various contexts (Fries, *Seidways*; *Helrunar*). Several neofolk and metal artists, such as Wardruna, Waldteufel, and Therion, portray such religious and magical thinking in their works (see Figure 15.3). In their music and self-presentation, these artists explore connections to the divine through the use of runes and meditative, trance-inducing techniques; they also describe pagan cosmology and praise the gods.[27] For this reason, the use of runes in album artwork calls on esoteric meanings that may be important to the artists' intentions. For example, the Othala rune stands for heritage, and Thurisaz symbolizes strength, menace, or defense.[28] In these cases, signatures of the supernatural reflect personal faith or magical beliefs. At the same time, such aesthetics demonstrate the musicians' dissociation from some aspects of mainstream culture—essentially formed by Christianity—that usually deems magical practices irrational.

In some cases, topics of pre-Christian beliefs in Scandinavia and in Central Europe are drawn together in an eclectic manner. Songs about the nine worlds of Norse mythology stand next to others about alpine folklore, while the Christianization of Thuringia is addressed in the same breath as the Norse myth of the *einherjar*.[29] In the latter, Christian imagery is re-encoded in artwork and lyrics. While the image of Boniface cutting down the oak of Donar has traditionally stood for the liberation from superstition and the instalment of true faith, here it becomes a symbol for the tragic destruction of pagan culture.[30] On the one hand, ideas of pagan religious tolerance and affinity with nature are contrasted with Christianity, which is described as intolerant and blind to the sacredness of nature (cf. Haugen 22–3). On the other hand, bands occasionally portray historic pagans as morally superior victims of alleged Christian atrocities, so that fantasies of revenge and just violence are celebrated in pagan metal.[31] Neofolk tends to dismiss fantasies of pagan revenge in favour of portraying mythological motifs and neo-pagan beliefs.[32]

In addition to their interest in Norse religion and magic, the neo-pagan participants of the subcultures in question do not seem to share a

FIGURE 15.3 *Wardruna in concert. The banner shows a combination of several runes, including Othala and Thurisaz. [Courtesy of HeadOvMetal]*

common agenda. While ethno-nationalist ideologies in the nineteenth and twentieth centuries used images of Norse paganism (cf. Goodrick-Clarke), Nordic-influenced ideas of the supernatural can function as parts of magical and/or religious systems without implying racist or other reactionary positions. Although pagan semiotics are connected with extreme right-wing ideologies in some cases, they do not always correlate, and some artists, such as Drautran and Helrunar, argue decidedly against such positions (see Leichsenring; Speit; Dornbusch and Killguss).

Language choice and stylistics function as signs in the total works of subcultural art. While English is the most common language for metal and, to a lesser extent, neofolk lyrics, several of the Scandinavian bands mentioned above use texts written in their native languages. The German band Helrunar combines German, Old Norse, and Norwegian, thereby bowing to classic Scandinavian bands as well as to the literary sources of Norse paganism that originated in medieval Iceland. The band's name is derived from a handbook of rune magic (Fries, *Helrunar*), supposedly meaning "the ones whispering with Hel," the Norse goddess of the underworld. In their lyrics, Helrunar also integrates *kennings*, allusive multi-part metaphors from Old Norse skaldic poetry, into their multilingual lyrics.[33] Like pagan symbols or Viking ornaments, such linguistic features can be implemented as signs in the service of modern pagan self-conceptions without discrediting other religions, similar to the use of Greek and Hebrew signs in Christianity. Such customs do not have to signify that the importance of a subject matter is restricted to some geographic areas or to people of certain origins. Rather, meaning is constructed in recourse to semiotic fields that are important to the articulations of a belief. In this sense the depictions of Nordic nature can be seen as envisioning a magical promised land, potentially for all people; snow, fjords, and lava fields are natural backdrops that support the narratives of neo-pagan faith.

CONCLUSION

The music subcultures discussed in this chapter cover a wide range of depictions and understandings of the supernatural North. Nordic landscapes are depicted as perilous and as loci of ancient magic, gods, and spirits. Tales from the Eddas or the *Kalevala* are employed, as are folkloric figures such as trolls. Representations of the North as supernatural are evident in several common elements, such as ideas of "harmonious nature spirituality," an emphasis on nature, and terrifying divine or ghostly forces. Often, references to a distinctly Nordic supernatural are part of neo-pagan conceptions represented in music. The ways in which black metal, pagan metal, and neofolk partly share, combine, and interpret cultural signs confirm general observations of previous subculture research: Although subcultures are "distinct forms of sociality," they are not necessarily "monocultures," and one should pay attention to "their heterogeneity, their porousness and variability, their transience" (Gelder 11). Indeed the subcultures in question do not form monolithic unities, but share numerous stylistic and thematic elements.

How and why these subcultures' particular elements of meaning adhere to each other may be described in terms of what Wittgenstein calls a family resemblance. His famous example is the notion of games. The activities we describe as games do not share a single element specific to games. Nevertheless, we are able to use the word "game" in many different contexts. The semantics of this word are classified as a group because they constitute a network of overlapping similarities (see Wittgenstein, pars. 66–9.) This is also the case in the subcultural aesthetics discussed here. There is no direct or necessary link between chirring guitar sounds and paganism, between martial imaginations and folk music: nevertheless, the musical aggressiveness of extreme metal suits the non-musical gesture of militancy and anti-Christianism, which connects with paganism as an alternative to Christianity. Folk music is associated with pre-modern societies and their supernatural-themed folklore, thereby meeting black/ pagan metal's interest in the supernatural.

Subcultures can thus overlap: they share elements with other subcultures, and their members can belong to more than one subculture. Apart from associations between metal and neofolk aesthetics, there are also tangible connections between these genres. For example, Kvitrafn and Gaahl of the neofolk band Wardruna were also involved in black metal bands like Gorgoroth and Gaahlskagg. Concerning distribution channels, several mail-order distributors such as Grau (Germany) and Steinklang (Austria) sell both extreme metal and neofolk, indicating crossovers between the audiences of these genres. Several fields of expression and media are interlocked, ranging from music and lyrics to artwork, video clips and theatrics. Combined, these features form semiotic patterns that can be marked as specifically Nordic. The music and artists discussed in this chapter stand for a subcultural production of meaning characterized by the mutual relations of their semiotic elements: the aspects of music, its performance and circulation, refer to and modify each other, thereby forming total works of art and expressing interests that oscillate between entertainment, sensitive romanticism, martial fantasies, nostalgia, and religious practices.

NOTES

1. Suffice it to mention J.R.R. Tolkien's *The Lord of the Rings* as an example of popular books and movies referencing Norse mythology. Video games that employ images of a supernatural North are, for example, *RuneScape* and the *Valkyrie Profile* series, and the card game *Yu-Gi-Oh!* which includes cards such as "Nordic Relic Brisingamen" and "Odin, Father of the Aesir."

2. Cultural tradition may, for example, provide imaginings and stereotypes about "Vikings" as savage and superstitious barbarians. The subcultures in question here take up such attributes and alter and re-evaluate them so that new imaginings of "Vikings" serve as identification models.

3. All metal covers and lyrics mentioned in this chapter can be found at <www.metal-archives.com>. Black and pagan metal belong to the group of extreme metal. An overview of this set of genres and its subcultures is given by Kahn-Harris. Concerning the history of metal in general, see Christie 2004. An extensive analy-sis of the musical language of metal is provided by Elflein.

4. A general overview of neofolk is given by Diesel and Gerten. For a more critical perspective on the role of extreme right-wing ideologies in neofolk see Speit.

5. "Satanic" here means relating to the devil of Christian tradition, particularly in an affirmative way of devil worship, respectively Satanism. Black metal bands usually derive such imagery from Christian traditions and folk beliefs, with signs such as inverted crosses, Satan depicted as a goat, descriptions of occult practices, and so on.

6. Peter Davidson (144–58) provides a short history of the motif of the Nordic, partic-ularly pagan, revenant and speaking ghost.

7. "Cursed Realm of Winterdemons," on *Battles in the North* (Immortal).

8. Cf. *Vikingligr Veldi* (Enslaved), *Panzerfaust* (Darkthrone), *Nemesis Divina* (Satyricon), *Stormblåst* (Dimmu Borgir).

9. The "pagan metal" genre is not restricted to Norse paganism. Bands such as Arkona (Russia), Guahaihoque (Colombia), and Darkestrah (originally from Kyrgyzstan)

deal with what they depict as the pre-Christian culture of their regions. "Viking metal" usually describes pagan metal employing Viking motifs. My use of these genre terms follows music websites and print magazines such as *rateyourmusic. com*, *Decibel*, and *Rock Hard*.

10. Lyrics (including errors) cited after the booklet of *Dragons of the North* (Einherjer). Concerning Viking imaginations, humour, and parody, see also Imke von Helden's analysis of Viking stereotypes in metal, using the examples of the bands Amon Amarth and Vykyng (von Helden).

11. The term "Edda" applies to the thirteenth-century Old Norse texts of the *Prose Edda* and the *Poetic Edda*, the main sources of our knowledge about pre-Christian Scandinavian beliefs (see Gunnel).

12. See *Fist of the Northern Destroyer* (Clandestine Blaze), *Rage of the Northmen* (In Battle).

13. See *Norwegian Native Art* (Einherjer), *Blodhemn* (Enslaved).

14. Examples of this practice include *Bergtatt* (Ulver), *Vittra* (Naglfar), *Filosofem* (Burzum), *Microcosmos* (Drudkh).

15. See *Frost* (Enslaved), *HEart of the Ages* (In the Woods...), *Borknagar* (Borknagar), *The Pagan Prosperity* (Old Man's Child).

16. Cf. *Wrath of the Tyrant/ Hordanes Land* (Emperor/Enslaved), *Eld* (Enslaved), *The Avenger* (Amon Amarth).

17. See *By the Light of the Northern Star* (Týr), *Surtur Rising* (Amon Amarth).

18. See *Tales from the Thousand Lakes* (Amorphis), *Eclipse* (Amorphis), *Silent Waters* (Amorphis). Elias Lönnrot compiled the *Kalevala* and the *Kanteletar* from Finnish folk material and published them between 1835 and 1849 (cf. Branch 1998).

19. See *Fjelltronen* (Wongraven), *Filosofem* (Burzum), *Where at Night the Wood Grouse Plays* (Empyrium), *Vargtimmen Pt. I: The Inmost Night* (Wyrd).

20. See *Buch der Balladen* (Faun); *Wanderer of Grief* (Inflabitan).

21. See *Crown of Winter* (Key).

22. Such crimes attracted media attention to black metal. For example, Burzum's Varg Vikernes was convicted in 1994 of murdering Mayhem's band leader, Øystein "Euronymous" Aarseth, along with three church arsons, one attempted church arson, and possession of weapons and explosives. Later he explained the black-metal–related church arsons as a pagan revenge on Christianity for building churches on pagan sacral sites (Moynihan and Søderlind; Mørk).

23. "Heathen Tribes," on *To the Nameless Dead* (Primordial).

24. See for example "The Cry of the Land," on *Jonah's Ark* (Skyclad).

25. See "When the Trees Were Silenced", on *The Winds That Sang of Midgard's Fate* (Hagalaz' Runedance).

26. Recent research sees *seiðr* as a form of sorcery meant to attract objects or persons and involving ecstatic techniques (cf. Heide).

27. See *Runaljod—Gap Var Ginnunga* (Wardruna), *Secret of the Runes* (Therion), *The Winds That Sang of Midgard's Fate* (Hagalaz' Runedance), *Rûna* (Fire + Ice).

28. See *Kivenkantaja* (Moonsorrow), *Heiðindómr ok Mótgangr* (Helheim), *Thorn* (Enslaved).

29. *Heimliches Deutschland* (Waldteufel), *Thuringia* (Menhir).

30. See *Fatherland* (Ancient Rites), "Bonifatius," on *Thuringia* (Menhir).

31. See "Into the Ardent Awaited Land," on *...en their medh riki fara...* (Falkenbach); "God, His Son and Holy Whore," on *The Avenger* (Amon Amarth).

32. See *Runaljod—Gap Var Ginnunga* (Wardruna), *Heimliches Deutschland* (Waldteufel), *The Winds That Sang of Midgard's Fate* (Hagalaz' Runedance), *Rûna* (Fire + Ice).

33. Cf. *Baldr ok Íss* (Helrunar).

WORKS CITED

Branch, M. "Finnish Oral Poetry, *Kalevala*, and *Kanteletar*." *A History of Finland's Literature*. Eds. G.C. Schoolfield and S.H. Rossel. Lincoln: U of Nebraska P, 1998. 3–33.

Bringsværd, T.Å. *Phantoms and Fairies: From Norwegian Folklore*. Oslo: Tanum, 1970.

Christie, I. *Sound of the Beast: The Complete Headbanging History of Heavy Metal*. New York: HarperCollins, 2004.

Davidson, P. *The Idea of North*. London: Reaktion, 2005.

Diesel, A., and D. Gerten. *Looking for Europe: Néo-Folk & Underground*. Vols. 1 & 2. Rosiers en Have: Camion blanc, 2008–9.

Dornbusch, C., and H.-P. Killguss. *Unheilige Allianzen: Black Metal zwischen Satanismus, Heidentum und Neonazismus*. Münster: Unrast, 2005.

Elflein, D. *Schwermetallanalysen: Die musikalische Sprache des Heavy Metal*. Bielefeld: Transcript, 2010.

Fries, J. *Helrunar: A Manual of Rune Magick*. 3rd ed. Oxford: Mandrake, 2005.

———. *Seidways: Shaking, Swaying and Serpent Mysteries*. Oxford: Mandrake, 1996.

Gelder, K., ed. *The Subcultures Reader*. 2nd ed. Abington: Routledge, 2005.

Goodrick-Clarke, N. *The Occult Roots of Nazism: Secret Aryan Cults and Their Influence on Nazi Ideology*. New York: New York UP, 1994.

Gunnel, T. "Eddic Poetry." *A Companion to Old Norse-Icelandic Literature and Culture.* Ed. R. McTurk. Oxford: Blackwell, 2010. 82–100.

Graves, R. *The White Goddess: A Historical Grammar of Poetic Myth.* 1948. New York: Farrar, 1997.

Haugen, A. *The Ancient Fires of Midgard.* Valkenburg: Well of Urd, 2000.

Heide, E. "Spinning *seiðr.*" *Old Norse Religion in Long-Term Perspectives: Origins, Changes, and Interactions.* Eds. A. Andrén, K. Jennbert, and C. Raudvere. Lund: Nordic Academic P, 2006. 164–70.

Kahn-Harris, K. *Extreme Metal: Music and Culture on the Edge.* Oxford: Berg, 2007.

Leichsenring, J. "'Wir fordern das Unmögliche': Zur Formulierung und Funktion anti-moderner Topoi in einigen Metal-Subgenres." Nohr and Schwaab 291–306.

Lindow, J. *Norse Mythology: A Guide to the Gods, Heroes, Rituals, and Beliefs.* Oxford: Oxford UP, 2002.

Moynihan, M., and D. Søderlind. *Lords of Chaos: The Bloody Rise of the Satanic Metal Underground.* Los Angeles: Feral House, 2003.

Mørk, G. "Why didn't the Churches Begin to Burn a Thousand Years Earlier?" *Religion and Popular Music in Europe: New Expressions of Sacred and Secular Identity.* Eds. T. Bossius, A. Häger, and K. Kahn-Harris. London: Tauris, 2011. 124–44.

Nohr, R.F., and H. Schwaab, eds. *Metal Matters: Heavy Metal als Kultur und Welt.* Münster: Lit, 2011.

Richard, B., and J. Grünwald. "Verführer und Zerstörer—mediale Bilder archaischer Männlichkeit im Black Metal." Nohr and Schwaab 43–53.

Speit, A. *Ästhetische Mobilmachung: Dark Wave, Neofolk und Industrial im Spannungsfeld rechter Ideologien.* 2nd ed. Münster: Unrast, 2006.

von Helden, I. "'...you must be the Vykyngs, the mighty fierce fellas'; Wikinger als Stereotyp im Heavy Metal." *Stereotype des Ostseeraumes: Interdisziplinäre Beiträge aus Geschichte und Gegenwart.* Eds. I. Sooman and S. Donecker. Wien: U Wien, 2012. 15–25.

Wagenknecht, A. "Das Böse mit Humor nehmen: Die Ernsthaftigkeit des Black Metal und deren ironisierende Aneignung am Beispiel von Fanclips auf YouTube." Nohr and Schwaab, 2011. 153–64.

Wittgenstein, L. *Philosophical Investigations.* 4th ed. Chichester: Wiley-Blackwell, 2009.

DISCOGRAPHY

Amon Amarth. *The Avenger.* Metal Blade, 1999.

———. *Surtur Rising.* Metal Blade, 2011.

Amorphis. *Eclipse*. Nuclear Blast, 2006.

———. *Silent Waters*. Nuclear Blast, 2007.

———. *Tales from the Thousand Lakes*. Spinefarm, 1993.

Ancient Rites. *Fatherland*. Mascot, 1998.

Árstíðir Lífsins. Jötunheima Dolgferð. Ván, 2010.

———. Vápna lækjar eldr. Ván, 2012.

Borknagar. *Borknagar*. Malicious, 1996.

Burzum. *Filosofem*. Misanthropy, 1996.

Clandestine Blaze. *Fist of the Northern Destroyer*. Northern Heritage, 2002.

Darkthrone. *A Blaze in the Northern Sky*. Peaceville, 1992.

———. *Panzerfaust*. Moonfog, 1994.

Dimmu Borgir. *Stormblåst*. Cacophonous, 1996.

Drudkh. *Microcosmos*. Season of Mist, 2009.

Einherjer. *Dragons of the North*. Napalm, 1996.

———. *Norwegian Native Art*. Native North, 2000.

Emperor/Enslaved. *Wrath of the Tyrant/Hordanes Land*. Century Black, 1994.

Empyrium. *Where at Night the Wood Grouse Plays*. Prophecy, 1999.

Enslaved. *Blodhemn*. Osmose, 1998.

———. *Eld*. Osmose, 1997.

———. *Frost*. Osmose, 1994.

———. *Thorn*. Indie, 2011.

———. *Vikingligr Veldi*. Deathlike Silence, 1994.

Falkenbach. *...En Their Medh Riki Fara...*. No Colours, 1996.

Faun. *Buch der Balladen*. Banshee, 2009.

Fire + Ice. *Rûna*. Fremdheit, 1996.

Hagalaz' Runedance. *The Winds That Sang of Midgard's Fate*. Elfenblut, 1998.

Helheim. *Heiðindómr ok Mótgangr*. Dark Essence, 2011.

Helrunar. *Baldr ok Íss*. Lupus Lounge, 2007.

Immortal. *Battles in the North*. Osmose, 1995.

Inflabitan. *Wanderer of Grief*. Kyrck Productions, 2010.

In Battle. *Rage of the Northmen*. Napalm, 1999.

In the Woods... *HEart of the Ages*. Misanthropy, 1995.

Key. *Crown of Winter*. Anima Arctica, 2010.

Korpiklaani. *Keep on Galloping*. Nuclear Blast, 2008.

Menhir. *Thuringia*. Ars Metalli, 1999.

Moonsorrow. *Kivenkantaja*. Spinefarm, 2003.

Naglfar. *Vittra*. Wrong Again, 1996.

Nåstrond. *Muspellz Synir*. Debemur Morti, 2008.

Old Man's Child. *The Pagan Prosperity*. Century Media, 1997.

Primordial. *To the Nameless Dead*. Metal Blade, 2007.

Satyricon. *Nemesis Divina*. Moonfog, 1996.

Skyclad. *Jonah's Ark*. Noise, 1993.

Therion. *Secret of the Runes*. Nuclear Blast, 2001.

Troll. *Drep de Kristne*. Damnation, 1996.

Týr. *By the Light of the Northern Star*. Napalm, 2009.

Ulver. *Bergtatt—Et Eeventyr I 5 Capitler*. Head Not Found, 1995.

Waldteufel. *Heimliches Deutschland*. Ultra!, 2000.

Wardruna. *Runaljod—Gap Var Ginnunga*. Indie, 2009.

Wongraven. *Fjelltronen*. Moonfog, 1995.

Wyrd. *Vargtimmen Pt. I: The Inmost Night*. Solistitium, 2003.

16 Men, Women, and Shamans

Daily Ritual Practice in the Supernatural North

ERICA HILL

CHAPTERS IN THIS VOLUME have examined the ways in which the North has been interpreted, conceived of, symbolized, or fetishized. Many address myth or myth-making in some form, suggesting that the North has supplied both scholarly and popular discourse with a rich set of symbols and motifs. In this chapter I discuss the "myth" of shamanism in the North: the implicit assumption that shamanism is coterminous with indigenous religion in Fennoscandia, Siberia, and the American Arctic. Because shamans and their activities were and, in some cases still are, highly salient in native societies, Western observers have tended to focus on them to the exclusion of other forms of ritual practice. As a result, forager belief systems from many world regions have been constructed as essentially shamanic. Using ethnographic evidence, archaeologists have interpreted rock art and other forms of material culture as evidence of shamanism in the past, pointing to transformational imagery and specific motifs as products of hallucinations and trance.

In this chapter, I suggest that the emphasis on shamanism in reconstructions of ritual and belief in foraging societies may be both a simplification and misrepresentation of indigenous cosmologies. Although shamans were critical mediators between the human realm and that of the supernatural, they were not alone in their ability to contact, cajole, and placate spirits and other non-human entities. Exclusive focus on their activities obscures the daily ritual acts and beliefs of ordinary men and women in indigenous societies. I suggest that a more accurate view of nineteenth-century Eskimo[1] belief in Alaska and Siberia privileges the practices of individual hunters and their wives, practices that established and maintained relationships with other-than-human beings on a daily basis. These acts, not those of shamans, constituted the majority of religious activity in many indigenous societies across the circumpolar North. In this discussion, I will provide a brief overview of how shamanism became such a prominent theme in the anthropological and archaeological literature on the North. Then, using examples from Alaskan and Siberian Eskimo, I will offer an alternative view of indigenous ritual and belief that refocuses attention on ordinary men and women.

A BRIEF HISTORIOGRAPHY OF SHAMANISM IN THE NORTH

The historiography of shamanism begins with the expansion of the Russian empire and the increasing frequency and extent of European contact with native Siberians in the 1600s. An Old Believer,[2] exiled to Siberia, is credited with introducing the Evenki (Tungus) word *šaman* into European languages (Pentikäinen 13). Shamanism fascinated European writers and philosophers of the late 1700s and early 1800s, who viewed the shaman through the lens of Romanticism, as primitive man tied directly to Nature and in communion with its forces. Shamans were characterized by one early commentator as "native geniuses": powerful and tragic figures whose "creative talents were...[supposedly] wasted in the barren northern terrain" of Siberia (Znamenski, *Beauty* 21; see also Slezkin 53–4). They embodied a savage nobility that recalled an idyllic time in human cultural evolution. In this view, shamans, and the hunter and gatherer communities that they represented, embodied a past untouched by either rationalism or civilization.

For newcomers to the North, shamans were highly salient figures (Ganley). Russian Orthodox missionaries, like their Moravian counterparts in Alaska, described shamanic behaviour and dress in letters and reports (e.g., Balzer, *Tenacity* 56; Fienup-Riordan, *Real People*; Mikhailovskii; Znamenski, *Shamanism*). Missionaries also collected shamanic exotica for both museum and personal collections (Pentikäinen 8). For nineteenth-century ethnographers, shamans were worthy of written and photographic documentation because, at least in the Boasian tradition of salvage ethnography, their practices were believed to be disappearing (Oosten et al.). Shamans were also viewed as living examples of primitive religion and therefore a source of information on the origins of human belief.

An important watershed in English-language works on shamanism occurred following the Jesup North Pacific Expedition (1897–1902). Ethnographers on the expedition made recordings of shamans from several Siberian Native groups singing, collected their paraphernalia, and photographed them (Freed et al.; Kendall et al.; Znamenski, *Beauty*). Their work (e.g., Bogoras, "Chukchi"; Bogoras, *Chukchee*; Jochelson, "Mythology"; Jochelson, *Koryak*) brought Siberian shamanism to the attention of a broader audience of English-speaking scholars. Shamanism became entrenched in popular imagination about sixty years later, with the publication of the English edition of Mircea Eliade's (1964) classic work. Subtitled *Archaic Techniques of Ecstasy*, Eliade's book continues to influence both popular and academic perceptions of non-Western religions (Sidky; Znamenski, *Beauty* 165), despite the fact that it is "remarkably inaccurate" (Basilov 48) with regard to Siberian shamanism (Bahn; Hutton; see also Balzer, "Introduction"; Kehoe, "Emerging").

In sum, the romantic primitivism of indigenous shamans attracted the interest of Russian, German, and Scandinavian scholars at least as early as the eighteenth century. By the 1900s, shamanism had over two hundred years of documentation and a complex intellectual history. Its prominence in academic literature is such that Graham Harvey (18) suggested that the study of shamanism has produced a "semantic field" in academic discourse. Within this arena, scholars debate whether a certain ritual practitioner has the required roles, behaviours, and material accoutrements to be considered a "real" shaman (Atkinson). While some question to what extent the Tungus term should be applied to practices in other societies (Klein et al.), many anthropologists employ the concept without reference to its Siberian origins.

SHAMANISM IN ARCHAEOLOGY

According to Silvia Tomášková, shamanism first appeared in the archaeological literature over a century ago in interpretations of Paleolithic rock art in France. But it was not until the 1980s that shamanism became the explanation of choice for rock art worldwide. The broad application of shamanic explanations to prehistoric rock art effectively detached the phenomenon from its Siberian roots. As ethnographers had done before them, archaeologists found the suite of shamanic beliefs and practices relevant to the understanding of societies far removed from the Arctic and sub-Arctic. Angus R. Quinlan (92; see also Bahn 108; Klein et al.) credits the work of ethnographer Gerardo Reichel-Dolmatoff with stimulating archaeological interest in shamanism. Reichel-Dolmatoff (e.g., 1968) documented the hallucinogen-induced creation of artwork among Tukano shamans in South America. His work broadly overlapped with that of Eliade and so bolstered a trend that had already begun to engage scholars. In the early 1980s, J. David Lewis-Williams published the first of many works linking African rock art to visions experienced during trance states. He and Thomas Dowson later published an extremely influential article that extended the idea to European Paleolithic rock art (Lewis-Williams and Dowson).

Lewis-Williams' "resurrection of primitivism" (Kehoe, *Shamans* 72) proved attractive to archaeologists working in other world regions and fostered an extensive literature that interpreted rock art—and motifs in other media—as the products or representations of shamanic trances (e.g., Turpin; Cordy-Collins; Reilly; VanPool; Whitley, "Shamanism"; Whitley, *Art*). Much of this rock art has been attributed to hunters and gatherers—people organized in small, mobile bands who hunted, fished, and collected food instead of relying on domesticated plants and animals. Most of the human past—up until about 12,000 years ago—was peopled by such hunters and gatherers. Unfortunately for archaeologists, small bands leave faint archaeological signatures of their rituals and beliefs. Therefore, the possibility that their worldview might be identified as shamanic on the basis of artistic motifs appealed to archaeologists interested in prehistoric belief.

The critical problem with identifying rock art as a product of shamanism is that, as Joakim Goldhahn (22) has observed, "interpretations [of rock art] tend to end where they ought to start" (see also Le Quellec; Sapwell). In other words, shamanic activities may explain the production of rock art images, but such explanations tell us nothing about why rock art was necessary or what it meant to observers. Nor does it explain the role of shamans within communities or help us to understand what people actually believed or experienced. Further, the focus on shamans downplays the potential significance of the supernatural beliefs, experiences, and rituals conducted by ordinary men and women. Prehistories that emphasize rock art and shamans thus implicitly exclude the majority of society from interaction with the supernatural.

By the early 2000s, a burgeoning literature critiquing shamanic interpretations of rock art was being published (e.g., Bahn; Francfort et al.; Kehoe, *Shamans*; McCall; Quinlan; Solomon). One significant point that these critiques have made is that there are many explanations for rock art imagery that have nothing to do with trance, hallucination, or shamans (e.g., Solomon). Finnish and Scandinavian archaeologists, for example, have sought to explain rock art imagery in mythic terms (e.g., Bolin; Helskog). Another set of critiques points out that the shamanic pasts constructed by archaeologists tend to be overwhelmingly male: in interpretations of Paleolithic rock art "hunting, creativity, religion, and masculinity all became one inseparable package" (Tomášková 106; see also Hays-Gilpin). Female shamans are well documented in the ethnohistoric and ethnographic literature (e.g., Burch, *Social* 65; Devlet; Jordan, "Materiality"; Serov), so masculinist reconstructions may be both sexist *and* inaccurate.

Timothy Insoll (64, 143) sums up the problem with what he calls "shamanic archaeology" in this way: "the 'shaman' might be the interpretively fashionable religious label of the moment, but it too would seem to be, in the majority of its applications, a miscategorisation, a reduction of something infinitely more complex to a label which is, even in its relatively recent creation, little understood." Not only does the archaeological focus on shamanism blur cross-cultural differences (Pharo 6), it also implicitly devalues the religious experiences, acts, and beliefs of everyone else in society.

In a thoughtful review of his own work on shamanism, Thomas Dowson ("Debating" 58; see also Eastwood) noted that "supernatural potency is not the exclusive preserve of the shaman." Ethnographic research in Africa and elsewhere supports this assertion. Peter Jordan's work among the Siberian Khanty is an excellent example. He notes that "every human action, journey, or movement involves some form of encounter or connection with another presence. This web of relationships cuts across social and species lines and grounds each human person into a wider set of obligations [with] divine forces" (Jordan, "Northern" 236; see also Jordan, "Materiality" 88). Hunting, gathering, travelling, *being* are not mundane tasks; rather, they are activities that implicate every person—including non-human persons such as prey animals and charismatic predators (e.g., bears, jaguars) who possess a human-like subjectivity (Hill, "Archaeology")— in the wellbeing of the world (Dowson, "Debating"). In other words, the abilities often associated with shamans, that is, the capacity to communicate with the supernatural, to mediate between worlds, and to harness the power of the numinous, were possessed by many—perhaps all—members of hunter-gatherer societies. Shamanism simply represents one, "albeit celebrated, dimension to a much wider dialogue between human and spiritual domains" (Jordan, "Materiality" 88).

In this discussion, I will describe how contact-period Eskimo of Alaska and Siberia engaged with the supernatural. Nineteenth-century Eskimo constructed the landscape and its inhabitants in dynamic, relational terms. Ordinary people—not just shamans—communicated with spirits, especially those of animals, through ritual acts, speech, and song, and materialized their beliefs about the world and their places within it. They used amulets and clothing to negotiate relationships with other-than-human beings and adhered to a complex set of taboos that ensured their welfare and the survival and regeneration of the animal spirits they depended on. "Humans and non-human animals, shamans, hunters and gatherers, mothers and fathers, and their children, were all sentient beings" who were intimately involved with constituting and reproducing the world in which they lived (Dowson, "Re-animating" 385). Shamanic activities represented only one form of interaction in a cosmological system that valued proper behaviour, respectful speech, and conscious-ness of the fact that every thought and action had implications for human relations with other-than-human beings (Fienup-Riordan, "Compassion").

OTHER-THAN-HUMAN PERSONS IN THE SUPERNATURAL NORTH

Alaskan Eskimo recognized a diverse set of supernatural entities, which I will gloss here as "other-than-human" (*sensu* Hallowell). Land- and seascapes were replete with "nonempirical" creatures that a traveller or hunter might encounter (Burch, "Nonempirical"; Fienup-Riordan, *Boundaries*; Hill, "Animals"; Hill, "Reconstructing"; see Grønnow for an example from Greenland). Blaisel et al. (373) observe that "any Inuk [Inuit person] could and would have his own experiences with game and spirits." Hunting, in particular, was a cosmologically charged activity that brought the hunter into direct contact with the *inuat* of marine mammals (Crowell; Fitzhugh and Kaplan; Ray). *Inuat* (pl.; Yup'ik *yuit*) were spirit-like "persons" who animated animals and many objects, such as boats or driftwood. They constituted an entire class of supernatural beings and were capable of regeneration. In this discussion, I focus on the beliefs and ritual acts concerning *inuat* and hunting-related activities, as it is in the domain of hunting that Eskimo cosmology is most clearly expressed. Hunting involved much more than the harvesting of game: for Eskimo, it entailed the complementary ritual acts of husband and wife throughout the year. As I suggest, hunting beliefs and ritual, rather than shamanism, constituted the essence of Alaskan and Siberian Eskimo cosmology.

Shamans concerned themselves primarily with "spiritual emergencies" (Jordan, "Materiality" 102); regular men, women, and children, although not equipped to determine the cause of a supernatural crisis or defuse it, were responsible for maintaining good relations with the *inuat* of animals and objects on a daily basis. Ideally, these relations were founded on mutual respect and the principles of reciprocity (Fienup-Riordan, "Eye"; Fienup-Riordan, *Boundaries* 58–9; Fienup-Riordan, "Compassion"; Ingold "Totemism"; Jordan, "Northern" 236–9). Humans and animals had obligations to each other and failure to honour those obligations endangered families and potentially the entire community. Prey animals, such as seals, walrus, and whales, were obliged to allow themselves to be taken by human hunters, but only when those hunters and their family members behaved properly. Proper behaviour included speaking respectfully, treating animal bones in specific ways, and observing taboos. A hunter was especially enjoined to avoid boasting, which animals found offensive (Fienup-Riordan, "Eye" 258). In return for the animal's gift of itself, the hunter and his wife were responsible for treating animal remains in a way that facilitated the rebirth of the *inua* (sing.; Yup'ik, *yuit*) in a new form. Bones, especially, were subject to ritual injunctions (Hill, "Archaeology"). Some were to be deposited in the sea so that the animals' *inuat* could reclaim them and return the next hunting season to give themselves again. In this way, relations between men, women, and animal spirits served as the foundation for Eskimo existence, implicating each of them in a regenerative cycle of mutual obligations.

Animals and objects with *inuat* possessed a latent sentience that enabled them to observe and experience for hours or days after they had been taken by hunters. The *inua* of an animal therefore knew whether its body was being treated properly and spoken about respectfully (Brewster 143; Turner). For example, seals and whales were believed to be thirsty after they were taken and hauled onto the ice; wise hunters or their wives provided the animal with fresh snow or water to drink, a ritual act that the *inua* recognized and appreciated (Fienup-Riordan, *Boundaries* 91; Fienup-Riordan, *Qaluyaarmiuni* 285; Lantis, "Alaskan" 445; Ostermann and Holtved 122).

The thoughts and behaviours of women, particularly the wives of hunters, were just as essential to the success of the hunt as those of men. Women had their own sets of taboos to observe before, during, and after the hunt. Their thoughts and chants could attract animals, just as self-ishness or sexual misbehaviour could drive them away (Fienup-Riordan, *Boundaries* 163–8). Women danced on the beach to honour whales that had just been taken (Lantis, "Alaskan"; Søby) and were responsible for the generous distribution of meat. To Alaskan Eskimo, women's thoughts and actions had as much effect on the availability of prey animals as those of the hunter himself. Their knowledge and observance of taboos and proper behaviour were as essential to hunting success as their husbands' skill (Bodenhorn; Brewster). Women, men, and animals were there-fore connected by a complex set of ritual obligations that underpinned every aspect of daily life. While shamans were certainly critical in cases of famine or illness, most adults interacted routinely with the super-natural in the form of animal *inuat*. Reconstructions of Eskimo religion or cosmology must appreciate the extent to which such ritual obliga-tions were the purview of ordinary men and women. Though thinking good thoughts and chanting are certainly less spectacular than the acts of shamans, Eskimo society was as dependent—perhaps more so—upon the relations of men and women with animal spirits as upon the rites conducted by shamans.

MATERIALIZING THE SUPERNATURAL

Men and women materialized their interactions with the supernatural in at least three ways: the use of amulets, the sewing of skin clothing, and the treatment of animal bones. Several ethnographers have remarked on the importance of amulets or "charms" in the lives of Alaskan Eskimo. Significantly for the argument advanced here, amulets could be made and used at the discretion of the individual, "not under the direction of a shaman" (Burch, *Social* 369). Men, women, children, and whaling boats (VanStone) had amulets, which were generally of animal origin and attached to clothing (Fienup-Riordan, *Boundaries* 201–2; Jolles 154–5; Lantis, "Alaskan"; Søby; Tein). The purpose of amulets was to protect the wearer; prevent misfortune; secure a particular outcome, such as hunting success; or harness the attributes of the animal represented. The power of an object, which was vested in the spirit of the amulet (Ostermann and Holtved 129), could be recognized and appropriated by anyone (Lantis, "Social" 201). In other words, supernatural potency was the province of ordinary men and women, as well as shamans. As Margaret Lantis ("Social" 205) observed: "[The shaman's] real strength (apart from the impressive but unessential tricks) was based...on those same compulsive influences over the supernatural which every man and woman possessed to some degree because he or she knew the right songs and had the right amulets."

In addition to amulets, women interacted with animal spirits through skin sewing, which Valérie Chaussonnet (209) has referred to as "women's magic": "seamstresses expressed through clothing the magical beliefs and the symbolic values of the group." The process of skin sewing imbued clothing with defensive powers through women's skill, their respectful treatment of the animal skin, and the incorporation of symbolic references (Issenman; Rodrigue and Ouellette). Prey animals were attracted to well-made and beautifully sewn clothing (Bodenhorn 65); poor quality needlework would drive them away (Fienup-Riordan, "Eye" 263). Hunters' clothing thus facilitated the seduction of animal *inuat*. Like hunting itself, clothing represented the conjunction of men's and women's activities with the spirits of animals. Together, they generated a kind of "magic" that ensured their mutual survival. Eskimo families survived through the generosity of animals. Animal *inuat* survived and regenerated through the proper treatment of their remains by the hunter and his wife. Animal remains included not only their hides and skins, which were cared for by women, but also their bones, which required careful curation and disposal.

Proper treatment of animal remains conveyed human respect for prey animals' *inuat*. Several ways of disposing of bone have been documented in the North, including burying, burning, hanging in trees, and caching. Archaeological evidence for ritual treatment of animals appears in the form of piles or caches of certain bones or in the arrangement of bones in a particular configuration (Hill, "Archaeology"). Hundreds of seal skulls, for example, have been found at coastal sites in Alaska (Beechey 355; Giddings and Anderson 130). In the interior, a cache of sheep skulls was maintained by hunters as late as the 1960s as a way of thanking the spirits of the sheep (Binford 413). On Nunivak Island in southwest Alaska, hunters constructed seal "burials" in the rocks along the beach in order for seals to retrieve their bones (Collins 19–20; see also Hill, "Reconstructing"). Finally, across Bering Strait in Chukotka, hunters created "shrines" of walrus and reindeer skulls and whale mandibles (Hill, "Animals"). In each of these cases, the hunter's activity was motivated by a desire to please animal *inuat* and facilitate their return. Like their wives, who sewed clothing according to an aesthetic preferred by seals, hunters sought to determine what treatment would most please the *inuat* of prey and acted accordingly.

CONCLUSION

Each of the examples discussed above—the use of amulets, skin sewing, and the structured deposition of animal bones—illustrates ways in which contact-period Eskimo of Alaska and Siberia interacted with the supernatural. Hunters and their wives were responsible for ensuring good relations with animal *inuat* and communicated this through thought and action. Routine, daily activities, such as skin sewing and hunting, were imbued with cosmological significance and constituted ritual acts. These behaviours, however, are easy to dismiss as mundane; they do not have the spectacular appeal of shamanic dress and behaviour. Yet as long as we focus on shamanism in the North, we obscure the beliefs and practices of a much more representative component of the population—hunters and their wives and children.

Shamans were called upon to deal with a range of illnesses and situations in which an individual hunter's precautions failed, when the hunter or his wife had broken a taboo, or when someone attempted to hide some misdeed and brought misfortune upon others, as well as him- or herself. If hunting was poor, shamans determined what caused offense to the animals and took steps to correct the situation (Jolles; Jordan, "Materiality"). However, the hunter who went out onto the ice each day understood that his thoughts and actions had an impact on his relations with the supernatural. He dealt directly with the animal *inuat* that determined hunting success. Similarly, his wife, in making amulets, attaching them to clothing, and in preparing and sewing animal skins, knew that her work was critical to the success of the hunt because she, too, was responsible for pleasing the *inuat*.

In conclusion, the exoticism of shamanism has "seduced" the anthropological imagination for over a century (Díaz-Andreu). Certainly northern cosmologies had shamanic elements and northern societies had shamans in the past. Yet shamanism represents only one way of communicating with the supernatural and ought not to be "privileged over those of other humans and non-human animals" (Dowson, "Debating" 59). The beliefs and practices of ordinary men and women among Alaskan and Siberian Eskimo are just as essential to our understanding of the supernatural North.

AUTHOR'S NOTE

The research presented here was conducted with the generous financial support of the Arctic Sciences Division of the National Science Foundation (NSF award #ARC-1022523), Alaska EPSCoR (NSF award #EPS-0701898), and the state of Alaska. I am most grateful to the editors of this volume for making suggestions that have greatly improved this chapter.

NOTES

1. The term "Eskimo" is used here to refer to speakers of both Inuit and Yupik languages and dialects in Alaska, Chukotka, and the Bering Sea region. The term is more inclusive than "Inuit." Inuit are the Arctic-adapted descendants of the Thule culture living in northern Alaska (Inupiat), Canada, and Greenland. Yupik people inhabit southwest Alaska, St. Lawrence Island, and parts of Chukotka. In Alaska, "Eskimo" is not considered a pejorative term, although more specific ethnonyms are preferred when appropriate.

2. The term "Old Believer" designates a member of a persecuted religious minority group who separated from the Russian Orthodox Church in the late 1600s in protest of liturgical reforms.

WORKS CITED

Atkinson, J.M. "Shamanisms Today." *Annual Review of Anthropology* 21 (1992): 307–30.

Bahn, P.G. *Prehistoric Rock Art: Polemics and Progress.* New York: Cambridge UP, 2010.

Balzer, M.M. *The Tenacity of Ethnicity: A Siberian Saga in Global Perspective.* Princeton: Princeton UP, 1999.

———, ed. Introduction. *Shamanic Worlds: Ritual and Lore of Siberia and Central Asia.* Armonk: M.E. Sharpe, 1997, xiii–xxxii.

Basilov, V.N. "Chosen by the Spirits." Balzer, *Shamanic Worlds*, 3–48.

Beechey, F. W. *Narrative of a Voyage to the Pacific and Beering's Strait.* London: Henry Colburn, 1831.

Binford, L.R. *Nunamiut Ethnoarchaeology.* New York: Academic, 1978.

Blaisel, X., F. Laugrand, and J. Oosten, "Shamans and Leaders: Parousial Movements among the Inuit of Northeast Canada." *Numen* 46 (1999): 370–411.

Bodenhorn, B. "'I'm Not the Great Hunter, My Wife Is': Iñupiat and Anthropological Models of Gender." *Études/Inuit/Studies* 14 (1990): 55–74.

Bogoras, W. *The Chukchee.* Leiden: E.J. Brill, 1904–09. Memoirs of the American Museum of Natural History 11.

———. "The Chukchi of Northeastern Asia." *American Anthropologist* 3 (1901): 80–108.

Bolin, H. "Animal Magic: The Mythological Significance of Elks, Boats and Humans in North Swedish Rock Art." *Journal of Material Culture* 5 (2000): 153–76.

Brewster, K., ed. *The Whales, They Give Themselves: Conversations with Harry Brower, Sr.* Fairbanks: U of Alaska P, 2004.

Burch, E.S. "The Nonempirical Environment of the Arctic Alaskan Eskimos." *Southwestern Journal of Anthropology* 27 (1971): 148–65.

————. *Social Life in Northwest Alaska: The Structure of Inupiaq Eskimo Nations.* Fairbanks: U of Alaska P, 2006.

Chaussonnet, V. "Needles and Animals: Women's Magic." Fitzhugh and Crowell 209–26.

Collins, H.B. Field Notes, 1927. Box 53, file "Archeological Expeditions—Nunivak Island and Bering Sea Region," Henry B. Collins Collection, National Anthropological Archives, Smithsonian Institution, Washington, D.C.

Cordy-Collins, A. "The Jaguar of the Backward Glance." *Icons of Power: Feline Symbolism in the Americas.* Ed. N.J. Saunders. London: Routledge, 1998. 155–70.

Crowell, A.L. "Sea Mammals in Art, Ceremony, and Belief: Knowledge Shared by Yupik and Iñupiaq Elders." *Gifts from the Ancestors: Ancient Ivories of Bering Strait.* Eds. W.W. Fitzhugh, J.J. Hollowell and A. Crowell. Princeton: Princeton U Art Museum, 2009. 43–55.

Devlet, E. "Rock Art and the Material Culture of Siberian and Central Asian Shamanism." Price 43–55.

Díaz-Andreu, M. "An All-Embracing Universal Hunter-Gatherer Religion? Discussing Shamanism and Spanish Levantine Rock-Art." Francfort, Hamayon, and Bahn 117–33.

Dowson, T.A. "Debating Shamanism in South African Rock Art: Time to Move on." *The South African Archaeological Bulletin* 62 (2007): 49–61.

————. "Re-animating Hunter-Gatherer Rock-art Research." *Cambridge Archaeological Journal* 19 (2009): 378–87.

Eastwood, E.B. "Animals Behaving like People: San Rock Paintings of Kudu in the Central Limpopo Basin, Southern Africa." *The South African Archaeological Bulletin* 61 (2006): 26–39.

Eliade, M. *Shamanism: Archaic Techniques of Ecstasy.* Princeton: Princeton UP, 1964.

Fienup-Riordan, A. *Boundaries and Passages: Rule and Ritual in Yup'ik Eskimo Oral Tradition.* Norman: U of Oklahoma P, 1994.

————. "Compassion and Restraint: The Moral Foundations of Yup'ik Eskimo Hunting Tradition." Laugrand and Oosten 239–53.

————. "Eye of the Dance: Spiritual Life of the Bering Sea Eskimo." Fitzhugh and Crowell 256–70.

————, ed. *Qaluyaarmiuni Nunamtenek Qanemciput / Our Nelson Island Stories: Meanings of Place on the Bering Sea Coast.* Seattle: U of Washington P, 2011.

————, ed. *The Real People and the Children of Thunder: The Yup'ik Eskimo Encounter with Moravian Missionaries John and Edith Kilbuck.* Norman: U of Oklahoma P, 1991.

Fitzhugh, W.W., and A.L. Crowell, eds. *Crossroads of Continents: Cultures of Siberia and Alaska.* Washington, DC: Smithsonian Institution P, 1988.

Fitzhugh, W.W., and S.A. Kaplan. *Inua: Spirit World of the Bering Sea Eskimo.* Washington, DC: Smithsonian Institution P, 1982.

Francfort, H.-P., R.N. Hamayon, and P. Bahn, eds. *The Concept of Shamanism: Uses and Abuses.* Budapest: Akadémiai Kiadó, 2001. Bibliotheca Shamanistica 10.

Freed, S.A., R.S. Freed, and L. Williamson. "Capitalist Philanthropy and Russian Revolutionaries: The Jesup North Pacific Expedition (1897–1902)." *American Anthropologist* 90 (1988): 7–24.

Ganley, M.L. "The Role of Anatguk in Northwest Alaska: Historic Transformation." *Naos: Notes and Materials for the Linguistic Study of the Sacred* 12 (1996): 5–19.

Giddings, J.L., and D.D. Anderson. *Beach Ridge Archeology of Cape Krusenstern: Eskimo and Pre-Eskimo Settlements around Kotzebue Sound, Alaska.* Washington, DC: National Park Service, 1986. Publications in Archeology 20.

Goldhahn, J. "Rock Art Studies in Northernmost Europe, 2000–2004." *Rock Art Studies: News of the World.* Vol. 3. Eds. P. Bahn, N. Franklin, and M. Strecker. Oxford: Oxbow, 2008. 16–36.

Grønnow, B. "Blessings and Horrors of the Interior: Ethno-Historical Studies of Inuit Perceptions Concerning the Inland Region of West Greenland." *Arctic Anthropology* 46. 1–2 (2009): 191–201.

Hallowell, A.I. "Ojibwa Ontology, Behavior, and World View." *Culture in History: Essays in Honor of Paul Radin.* Ed. S. Diamond. New York: Columbia UP, 1960. 19–52.

Harvey, G., ed. *Shamanism: A Reader.* New York: Routledge, 2003.

Hays-Gilpin, K. *Ambiguous Images: Gender and Rock Art.* Walnut Creek: Altamira, 2004.

Helskog, K. "The Shore Connection: Cognitive Landscape and Communication with Rock Carvings in Northernmost Europe." *Norwegian Archaeological Review* 32 (1999): 73–94.

Hill, E. "Animals as Agents: Hunting Ritual and Relational Ontologies in Prehistoric Alaska and Chukotka." *Cambridge Archaeological Journal* 21 (2011): 407–26.

———. "Archaeology and Animal Persons: Towards a Prehistory of Human–Animal Relations." *Environment and Society: Advances in Research* 4 (2013): 117–36.

———. "Reconstructing the 'Nonempirical Environment': Enculturated Landscapes and Other-than-Human Persons in Southwest Alaska." *Arctic Anthropology* 49.2 (2012): 41–57.

Hutton, R. *Shamans: Siberian Spirituality in the Western Imagination.* London: Hambledon, 2001.

Ingold, T. "Totemism, Animism and the Depiction of Animals." *Perception of the Environment: Essays on Livelihood, Dwelling and Skill.* Ed. T. Ingold. London: Routledge, 2000. 61–76.

Insoll, T. *Archaeology, Ritual, Religion*. London: Routledge, 2004.

Issenman, B.K. *Sinews of Survival: The Living Legacy of Inuit Clothing*. Vancouver: U of British Columbia P, 1997.

Jochelson, W. *The Koryak*. 1908. New York: AMS, 1975. The Jesup North Pacific Expedition 6.

———. "The Mythology of the Koryak." *American Anthropologist* 6 (1904): 413–25.

Jolles, C.Z. *Faith, Food, and Family in a Yupik Whaling Community*. Seattle: U of Washington P, 2002.

Jordan, P. "The Materiality of Shamanism as a 'World-View': Praxis, Artefacts and Landscape." Price 87–104.

———. "Northern Landscapes, Northern Mind: On the Trail of an 'Archaeology of Hunter-Gatherer Belief.'" *Belief in the Past: Theoretical Approaches to the Archaeology of Religion*. Eds. K. Hays-Gilpin and D. S. Whitley. Walnut Creek: Left Coast, 2008. 227–46.

Kehoe, A.B. "Emerging Trends versus the Popular Paradigm in Rock-Art Research." *Antiquity* 76 (2002): 384–5.

———. *Shamans and Religion. An Anthropological Exploration in Critical Thinking*. Prospect Heights: Waveland, 2000.

Kendall, L., B. Mathé, and T.R. Miller. *Drawing Shadows to Stone: The Photography of the Jesup North Pacific Expedition, 1897–1902*. New York: American Museum of Natural History, 1997.

Klein, C.F., et al. "The Role of Shamanism in Mesoamerican Art: A Reassessment." *Current Anthropology* 43 (2002): 383–419.

Lantis, M. "The Alaskan Whale Cult and Its Affinities." *American Anthropologist* 40 (1938): 438–64.

———. "The Social Culture of the Nunivak Eskimo." *Transactions of the American Philosophical Society* 35 (1946): 153–323.

Laugrand F.B., and J.G. Oosten, eds. *La nature des esprits dans les cosmologies autochtones / Nature of Spirits in Aboriginal Cosmologies*. Québec: Les P de l'U Laval, 2007.

Le Quellec, J.-L. "The Sense in Question: Some Saharan Examples." *Rock Art Research* 23 (2006): 165–70.

Lewis-Williams, J.D. *Believing and Seeing: Symbolic Meanings in Southern San Rock Paintings*. London: Academic, 1981.

Lewis-Williams, J.D., and T.A. Dowson. "The Signs of All Times: Entoptic Phenomena in Upper Palaeolithic Art." *Current Anthropology* 29 (1988): 201–45.

McCall, G.S. "Add Shamans and Stir? A Critical Review of the Shamanism Model of Forager Rock Art Production." *Journal of Anthropological Archaeology* 26 (2007): 224–33.

Mikhailovskii, V.M. "Shamanism in Siberia and European Russia, Being the Second Part of 'Shamanstvo.'" *The Journal of the Anthropological Institute of Great Britain and Ireland* 24 (1895): 62–100.

Oosten, J.G., F.B. Laugrand, and C. Remie. "Perceptions of Decline: Inuit Shamanism in the Canadian Arctic." *Ethnohistory* 53 (2006): 445–77.

Ostermann, H., and E. Holtved. *The Alaskan Eskimos as Described in the Posthumous Notes of Dr. Knud Rasmussen.* Copenhagen: Gyldendal, 1952. Report of the Fifth Thule Expedition 1921–24 X/3.

Pentikäinen, J. "Introduction." *Shamanism and Northern Ecology.* Ed. J. Pentikäinen. Berlin: de Gruyter, 1996. 1–27.

Pharo, L.K. "A Methodology for a Deconstruction and Reconsideration of the Concepts 'Shaman' and 'Shamanism.'" *Numen* 58 (2011): 6–70.

Price, N.S., ed. *The Archaeology of Shamanism.* New York: Routledge, 2001.

Quinlan, A.R. "The Ventriloquist's Dummy: A Critical Review of Shamanism and Rock Art in Far Western North America." *Journal of California and Great Basin Archaeology* 22 (2000): 92–108.

Ray, D.J. *Eskimo Masks: Art and Ceremony.* Seattle: U of Washington P, 1967.

Reichel-Dolmatoff, G. "Rock Paintings of the Vaupés: An Essay of Interpretation." *Folklore Americas* 26.2 (1968): 107–13.

Reilly, F.K. "The Shaman in Transformation Pose: A Study of the Theme of Rulership in Olmec Art." *Record of the Art Museum, Princeton University* 48.2 (1989): 5–21.

Rodrigue, J., and N. Ouellette. "Inuit Women as Mediators between Humans and Non-Human Beings in the Contemporary Canadian Eastern Arctic." Laugrand and Oosten 175–91.

Sapwell, M. "The Architect of Decay? Art as Active in Shamanic and Cosmological Interpretations of the Rock Art of Kallsängen, Bohuslän." *Archaeological Review from Cambridge* 25.2 (2010): 77–95.

Serov, S.I. "Guardians and Spirit-Masters of Siberia." Fitzhugh and Crowell 241–55.

Sidky, H. *Haunted by the Archaic Shaman: Himalayan Jhākris and the Discourse on Shamanism.* Lanham: Lexington, 2008.

Slezkin, Y. *Arctic Mirrors: Russia and the Small Peoples of the North.* Ithaca: Cornell UP, 1994.

Søby, R.M. "The Eskimo Animal Cult." *Folk. Dansk Etnografisk Tidsskrift* 11/12 (1969/70): 43–78.

Solomon, A. "The Myth of Ritual Origins? Ethnography, Mythology and Interpretation of San Rock Art." *The South African Archaeological Bulletin* 52 (1997): 3–13.

Tein, T.S. "Shamans of the Siberian Eskimos." *Arctic Anthropology* 31.1 (1994): 117–25.

Tomášková, S. "Yes Virginia, There Is Gender: Shamanism and Archaeology's Many Histories." *The Archaeology of Bruce Trigger: Theoretical Empiricism.* Eds. R.F. Williamson and M.S. Bisson. Montréal: McGill-Queen's UP, 2006. 92–113.

Turner, E. "The Whale Decides: Eskimos' and Ethnographer's Shared Consciousness on the Ice." *Études/Inuit/Studies* 14 (1990): 39–52.

Turpin, S.A., ed. *Shamanism and Rock Art in North America.* San Antonio: Rock Art Foundation, 1994. Rock Art Foundation, Special Publication 1.

VanPool, C.S. "The Signs of the Sacred: Identifying Shamans Using Archaeological Evidence." *Journal of Anthropological Archaeology* 28 (2009): 177–90.

VanStone, J.W. "Eskimo Whaling Charms." *Bulletin of the Field Museum of Natural History* 38.11 (1967): 6–8.

Whitley, D.S. *The Art of the Shaman: Rock Art of California.* Salt Lake City: U of Utah P, 2000.

———. "Shamanism and Rock Art in Far Western North America." *Cambridge Archaeological Journal* 2 (1992): 89–113.

Znamenski, A.A. *The Beauty of the Primitive: Shamanism and Western Imagination.* Oxford: Oxford UP, 2007.

———. *Shamanism and Christianity: Native Encounters with Russian Orthodox Missions in Siberia and Alaska, 1820–1917.* Westport: Greenwood, 1999.

Contributors

ELEANOR ROSAMUND BARRACLOUGH is Lecturer in Medieval Literature at
Durham University. Previously she studied at the University of
Cambridge, before taking up a Leverhulme Early Career Fellowship
at the University of Oxford. Her primary research interests are the
languages, literatures, and cultures of the medieval North, and
human-geographical spaces, both real and imagined. In 2013 she was
selected as a BBC "New Generation Thinker" in a national competition run by BBC Radio 3 and the Arts and Humanities Research
Council. She is the author *Beyond the Northlands: Viking Voyages and
the Old Norse Sagas* (Oxford University Press, 2016).

ANGELA BYRNE is lecturer in History at the University of Greenwich. She is
author of *Geographies of the Romantic North: Science, Antiquarianism,
and Travel, 1790–1830* (Palgrave Macmillan, 2013); *A Scientific,
Antiquarian and Picturesque Tour: John (Fiott) Lee in Ireland, England
and Wales, 1806–07* (Hakluyt Society, in preparation); and (with
Sebastian Sobecki) *Richard Hakluyt, The Principal Navigations of
the English Nation (1598–1600), vol. II* (Oxford University Press,
in preparation).

DANIELLE MARIE CUDMORE has studied comparative literature, classics, and
medieval literature at the University of Massachusetts and Cornell

University. She received her PHD in Medieval Studies from Cornell University in 2015 with a dissertation on landscape in Old English literature. She is currently Vikarierande Universitetslektor in English Literature at Halmstad University. Her research interests include depictions of nature and landscape in the literatures of medieval North Sea Europe and modern Europe and North America, as well as the musical and poetic traditions of Anatolia, the Caucasus, and Iran. She has won several awards for her work as a writing instructor at Cornell University.

STEFAN DONECKER studied history and Scandinavian studies at the universities of Vienna and Umeå (Sweden). In 2010, he received his PHD at the European University Institute in Florence, with a thesis on historiography and scholarly culture in early modern Livonia. He has worked as a junior fellow at the Alfried Krupp Institute for Advanced Study in Greifswald (2010/11) and as a postdoctoral fellow at the Center of Excellence "Cultural Foundations of Integration" at the University of Constance (2011–12). In 2012, he was awarded a Marie Curie Intra-European Fellowship at the Institute for Medieval Research of the Austrian Academy of Sciences in Vienna. Dr. Donecker's research is focused on intellectual history in early modern Scandinavia and the Baltic Sea region, as well as on the cultural construction of Northernness.

BRENDA S. GARDENOUR WALTER holds a PHD in medieval history from Boston University, where she specialized in the history of medieval medicine and hagiography. She has been a Fulbright scholar in Madrid, an Evelyn Nation research fellow at the Huntington Library, and an NEH fellow at the Wellcome Institute for the History of Medicine in London. Her research examines the role of Aristotelian discourse, learned medicine, and scholastic theology in the construction of alterity and the continued influence of medieval otherness on the horror genre, black metal, and beyond. She is Associate Professor of History at the Saint Louis College of Pharmacy.

SILVIJE HABULINEC is a historian and anthropologist from Croatia living in
the United Kingdom. He completed his studies in history and cultural
anthropology at the Univesity of Zagreb and his MRes in social
anthropology at the University of Aberdeen. His research interests
are traditional storytelling in Greenland, the Cold War and military
installations in the Arctic region, and foreign policies and international relations in the period between the world wars.

ERICA HILL is Associate Professor of anthropology at the University of Alaska
Southeast. She studies the archaeology of human-animal relations
and the prehistory of the Bering Sea region. Her work has been
published in *Antiquity, Cambridge Archaeological Journal*, and *Arctic
Anthropology*. She is the editor of *Iñupiaq Ethnohistory* (University of
Alaska Press, 2012) and co-editor, with Jon B. Hageman, of *The
Archaeology of Ancestors* (University Press of Florida, 2016).

JAY JOHNSTON, Associate Professor at the University of Sydney, is an interdisciplinary scholar who investigates ritual and religious belief
and their use in identity formation, healing practice, and cultural
exchange. She is particularly interested in late antiquity, Scottish and
Norse cultures pre-1400, and contemporary spiritual subcultures.
Publications include *Religion and the Subtle Body in Asia and the West*,
edited with G. Samuel (Routledge, 2013). Currently she is finalizing
a new monograph *Stag and Stone: Religion, Archaeology and Esoteric
Aesthetics* (forthcoming Equinox Publishing, 2017).

MARIA KASYANOVA is a senior lecturer of the Faculty of History at the
Lomonosov Moscow State University. She received the Candidate
of Sciences degree in classical studies (Lomonosov Moscow State
University, 2008). Her research focusses on ancient Greek literature and mythology. Besides her academic career, she teaches ancient
languages and culture to primary and secondary school children.

JAN LEICHSENRING studied philosophy, German literature and language,
and history of art at the University of Leipzig (2002–08). He under-
took postgraduate work in philosophy at the Max Weber Center for

Advanced Social and Cultural Studies at the University of Erfurt
(2008–12). His doctoral thesis examines contemporary natural law
ethics. Since 2012 he has conducted postdoctoral research at the Max
Weber Center that focuses on concepts of life in German Idealism.

SHANE MCCORRISTINE is an interdisciplinary historian and geographer with
interests in the "night side" of modern experience—namely social
attitudes to death, dreams, ghosts, and hallucinations. A postdoctoral fellow in the University of Cambridge, Shane has worked as
a researcher at University College Dublin, Maynooth University,
University of Leicester, and the Scott Polar Research Institute,
Cambridge. His publications include *Spectres of the Self: Thinking
about Ghosts and Ghost-seeing in England, 1750–1920* (Cambridge
University Press, 2010).

JENNIFER E. MICHAELS is Samuel R. and Marie-Louise Rosenthal Professor of
Humanities and Professor of German at Grinnell College in Iowa. She
received an MA in German from Edinburgh University and an MA
and PHD in German from McGill University. She has published four
books and numerous articles on German and Austrian literature and
culture with a focus on twentieth– and twenty-first–century literature. She served as president of the German Studies Association and
the Rocky Mountain Modern Language Association.

YA'ACOV SARIG holds a PHD in Hebrew Literature from Hebrew University,
Jerusalem. He conducted research in Scandinavian Studies in the
Department of Folklore at the Universities of Oslo and Copenhagen.
He is adjunct faculty in the Department of History at the Open
University of Israel, Ra'anana, and is author of a book on Scandinavian
mythology, and an annotated translation of Icelandic sagas into
Hebrew (to be published shortly).

RUDOLF SIMEK, PHD Vienna, MTHEOL Vienna, is a professor for Medieval
German and Scandinavian literature in Bonn, and has published
several books on early Germanic religion and culture, as well as a
series of translations of Old Norse sagas into German. His research
interests include early medieval religion, Viking and medieval Norse

studies, as well as late medieval science, especially astronomy and cosmography.

ATHANASIOS VOTSIS is a PHD candidate in the Department of Geography at the University of Helsinki, and is a researcher at the Finnish Meteorological Institute, with a background in urban studies, geography, and spatial analysis. His research work covers urban economics, cultural and architectural semiotics, and quantitative geography. His chapter in this volume relates to his ongoing work on the diachronic relationship between human settlements and their environmental context in quantitative and qualitative spatial terms.

BRIAN WALTER, PHD, is Associate Professor of English and Director of Convocations at St. Louis College of Pharmacy. He is the director, most recently, of the 2015 feature documentary *Farther Along: The World of Donald Harington, Pt. 2*, and his scholarly work has appeared in (among others) *Boulevard*, *The Southern Quarterly*, *Post Script*, *Nabokov Studies*, and *CineAction*.

Index

Britain
  Hereford *mappa mundi*, 66–7
  See also Celts; Gaels; Ireland;
    Scotland
Britain, 19th c.
  clairvoyants and mesmerists, 150–9
  exploration literature, 149–50
  hierarchy of civilization, 135–6, 143
  highest mountain debates, 137
  origins debates, 134–6, 141–3, 243
  renewed interest in the North,
    218–19
  Romantic North, 133–4
  See also Franklin expedition and
    mesmerist clairvoyants
Britain, contemporary
  Gaelic influences on pop culture, 143
  metal bands, 263
  neofolk bands, 252–3
  Otherkin, 238, 243
  See also *The Golden Compass*
    (Pullman); Lewis, C.S.; Tolkien,
    J.R.R.
Brontë, Charlotte, x–xi, xxn3
Brutus (Cicero), 30
Buchanan, George, 117–18, 124n16
Burch, Ernest S., Jr., 199, 200n5
By the Light of the Northern Star (Týr;
    metal band), 261
Byrne, Angela, 131–47, 293

Callimachus, 40, 43
Callisto, 27–8
Campbell, Mary Baine, 123n10
Canada
  Atwood on the North, xi–xii, xxn6
  Gould's *The Idea of North*, 227

Inuit, as term, 287n1
North as process, 228n2
as part of medieval Greenland, 89
Wendigo, xxn6
See also Franklin expedition and
  mesmerist clairvoyants
cannibalism
  Greenlandic tales, 197–8, 200n6
  medieval *Anthropophagi*, 58–9, 61,
    64, 67, 68, 71
  Wendigo, xxn6
cardinal directions. *See* directions,
  cardinal
Carta Gothica and *Carta Marina* (Olaus),
  69–71
cartography. *See* maps
Casius, Mount, 4
Castañega, Martin, 102–3
cats and Otherkin, 242, 248
Celts
  Celtic, as term, 134–6, 144n2
  contemporary mysticism, 143
  Hyperboreans and, 40, 42
  myth and scientific literature, 139–41
  origins debates, 134–6, 141–3
  round towers, 134, 141–3, 144n9
Chaussonnet, Valérie, 280
children. *See* birth and infancy;
  motherhood
China and Otherkin, 241
Chione, 28, 30
Christianity
  about, xv–xvii
  demons, xvii, 98, 102
  medieval treatises on female body,
    xvii, 102

half human and half dog *(eqqillit)*, 196, 199

heroes, 192–3, 195, 197

inland *vs.* coastal dwellers, 186, 194–6, 199–200

magic, 193

Rasmussen's stories, 186–7, 191–4

Rink's stories, 187, 190–4

scientific knowledge, 193–4

similarities to other stories, 196–200

storytelling at night, 191–2

supernatural beings, 194–6

underworld, 197

violence, 193–4, 198, 200n4

Gregory, William, 157

Greimas, Algirdas, 40, 48

griffons, 68

Grimm, Jacob, 179, 183n11

Grœnlendinga þáttr. See sagas and tales about Greenland

Grønnow, Bjarne, 195

Grove, Jonathan, 89–90, 90n3

Gundarsson, Kveldulf, 243–4

Gunnars saga Keldugnúpsfífls, 86

Habulinec, Silvije, 185–201, 295

Haddock, Joseph W., 154–7

Hafrsfjord, Battle of, 259

Harner, Michael, 238

Haugen, Andrea, 263

Hauksbók, 82

heavy metal music, 252

See also black/pagan metal music, contemporary

Hebrew language, 3

See also Judaism

Hedeager, Lotte, 245–6

Hekla, Mount, 116, 118, 124n12, 178–81

See also Iceland

Helike, 26, 35n3

Helrunar (metal band), 265, 266

Henricus Martellus, 69

Hercules, 39, 43, 45, 46, 46t

Herder, Johann Gottfried, 167, 182n4

Hereford *mappa mundi*, 66–7

Herodotus, 32, 40, 42, 43–4

Hibbert, Samuel, 137–8, 140, 141

hierarchy of civilization, 135–6, 143

Hill, Erica, 275–92, 295

Himantopodes, 60, 68

Hippocrates, 99, 104n4, 104n7, 105n8

His Dark Materials (Pullman), 222, 236, 246

See also *The Golden Compass* (Pullman)

Historia de gentibus septentrionalibus (Olaus), 70, 116, 121, 124n14

Historia Norvegiae, 62–6, 71

Histories (Herodotus), 40, 42, 43–4

Holland, Henry, 175, 182n4

Homer, 25, 28, 32–3

Honter, Johannes, 69

horned Finns, xvii, 63, 72n10

"How the Narwhal came" (Rasmussen), 193

Hymn IV (to Delos) (Callimachus), 40

Hyperborea, ancient
    about, xii, xix, 33–4, 39–41, 50–1
    architecture, 40–1, 42–4
    binary oppositions, 40–1, 45–8, 46t, 50–1, 51n2
    comparisons with Greeks and Olympians, 45–51, 46t, 47t, 49t
    etymology of *Hyperborea*, 39

Nabokov, Vladimir, xix, 205–7, 208–10,
213–14

See also *Pale Fire* (Nabokov)

Naglfar (metal band), 258

Narnia series (Lewis), 218, 222–4,
229nn16–18, 230nn21–2, 268n1

national identity

about, xviii

origins debates in 19th c., 134–6,
141–3, 243

Otherkin, 243

Showbread Table and unity of Israel,
17

Nemesis Divina (Satyricon; metal band),
256–7, 257

neofolk bands

about, 252–3, 266–8

distribution channels, 267

folk and black metal, 259–60

musical sounds, 252–3, 258

Nordic cosmology, 263–6, 265

scholarship on, 268n4

See also black/pagan metal music,
contemporary

New Age culture and Otherkin, 237–9,
242, 246–7

Nicolson, Marjorie, 121–2, 123n7

Nider, Johannes, 102

*Nils Holgerssons underbara resa genom
Sverige* (Lagerlöf), x

nonhuman–human identity, 237

See also Otherkin (animal–human
identity)

the North

about, x–xii, xix, 217

Atwood on, xi–xii

aura of wonder, 228n4

cardinal directions, xi, 217

as a dream, 228n4

historical overview, xii–xv

imagined geographies, 133–4, 218

literary visions of, x–xi, xix, 30

location relative to self, xi

more than a direction, xi, 217

as Other, xv, xvi, 244–5

as process, xii, 228n2

Romantic North in 19th c., 133–4

scholarship on, xxn5

sound and Gould's *The Idea of North,*
227

the unconscious, xi

See also environmentalism; literary
visions of the North; science

the North, ancient cultures

about, xv–xvii

See also Boreas; Greeks, ancient;
Hyperborea, ancient; Judaism;
Romans, ancient

the North, medieval and early modern

about, xvii

Aquinas on supernatural, xiv

Aristotle's cosmology, 96–8, 103n11

barbarians from the North, xii

encyclopedists, 59

four elements (earth, air, fire, water),
97, 98–9

location of Far North, 56

See also Greenland, medieval and
early modern; Iceland, medieval
and early modern; medieval
Nordic world; Norway, medieval
and early modern; Scandinavia;
witches, medieval and early
modern; women, ancient period

witches in "The Snow Queen," 223

Sanhedrin, 9–10, 18, 18n1

Sarig, Ya'acov, 3–24, 296

Satan

    metal bands and imagery, 253–9, 268n5

    witches and demonology, 102–3

    witches and storm winds, 95–6, 121

Satyricon, 256–7, 257

Saxe's Kettle, Scotland, 140

Scandinavia

    as Other, 245

    Romantic North, 133

    See also Denmark; Finland and Finns; Iceland; Norway; Sweden

Scandinavia, medieval and late medieval

    Historia Norvegiae, 62–6, 71

    location and description, 56–60

    mappae mundi, 66–71

    monstrous races, 67–8

    witch hunts, 119–20

    See also Gesta Hammaburgensis ecclesiae pontificum (Adam of Bremen); medieval Nordic world

Schiller, Friedrich, 173, 182n4

science

    archaeology and shamanism, 278–81

    clairvoyants and mesmerists, 150–2, 154–5, 159–62

    early modern astronomy, 109

    ethnography and shamanism, 276–8

    Greenland legends, 193

    local vs metropolitan ways of knowing, 138–9

    medical sciences, 151

    naturalist collections, 167–8, 172

Romanticism and sciences, 133–4, 139–43

    volcanoes, 168, 172, 178–81, 182n9

    See also Brahe, Tycho; environmentalism; Kepler, Johannes; maps

Sciopodes, 60, 68

Scot, Reginald, 102–3

Scotland

    Gaels and contemporary pop culture, 143

    Kepler's Somnium, 117–18, 124n16

    long-lived people, 118

    See also Celts; Gaels

Scotland, 19th c.

    about, 133

    Banks' explorations, 131–3

    Gaelic, as term, 144n2

    ghosts and fairies, 139

    hierarchy of civilization, 135–6, 143

    literature, 139–42

    Morvern headlands, 131–3

    myths in scientific texts, 138

    North Berwick witches, 95–6

    origins debates, 134–6, 141–3, 243

    Ossian poems, 131–3

    Romantic North, 133

    round towers, 134, 141–3, 144n9

    sciences, 133–4

    Shetland Islands, 137–8, 140–1, 243

Scott, Sir Walter, 139

Scythians

    ancient texts, xii, 28, 61–2

    locations, 28, 42, 56, 59, 61, 66, 124n18

    Lucumorians in Somnium, 124n18

    mappae mundi, 66–8

    medieval texts, 61–2

Romantic discourses, 172, 181

women travel writers, 165–6, 171–2, 175, 181

See also *Journey to Iceland* (Pfeiffer); maps; Pfeiffer, Ida

Travels in the Island of Iceland (Mackenzie and Holland), 175

Treatise on Witchcraft (Castañega), 102–3

Tristia (Ovid), 28

Troll (metal band), 262

trolls and ogres

    contemporary metal bands, 261, 262

    "East of the Sun and West of the Moon," 225, 231n26

    half-giant half-troll hero, 85–6

    legends in Iceland, 173

    Vínland and Greenland sagas, 80, 83–8, 91n13

"True North" (Atwood), x–xi

Turner, Dawson W., 39–40

"The Two Friends who set off to Travel" (Rasmussen), 193

Týr (metal band), 261

Ulver (metal band), 261

underworld

    Eddas, 258

    Greenland lore, 197

    Mt. Hekla, 116, 118, 124n12, 179–80

    Otherkin, 239

Unipedes, 68, 71

United Kingdom. *See* Britain; Ireland; Scotland

United States

    neofolk bands, 252–3

    See also Eskimo

Ursa Major and Ursa Minor, 26–8, 35n3

Vallancey, Charles, 142

vampires and Otherkin, 240

Vápna lækjar eldr (Árstíðir Lífsins; metal band), 260

"The Very Obstinate Man" (Rasmussen), 193–4

video games and supernatural North, 268n1

A View of the Ancient and Present State of the Zetland Islands (Edmondston), 138

Vikings

    contemporary popular culture, 256, 268n2, 268n9

    mass culture in 19th c., 167

    medieval views on barbarians, xii

    See also medieval Nordic world; sagas and tales about Greenland

The Vikings (film), 258

Vínland, 70

Vínland sagas

    Eiríks saga rauða, 55, 68, 80–5

    Grœnlendinga þáttr, 81–5, 91n13

    See also sagas and tales about Greenland

Virgil and north winds, 29

Virides (Greenlanders), 66

    See also Greenland, medieval and early modern

visionaries. *See* clairvoyants, 19th c.

A Visit to the Holy Land (Pfeiffer), 170

volcanoes, 124n12, 168, 172–6, 178–81, 182n9

von Goethe, Johann, x

von Humboldt, Alexander, 170, 182n4